Glittering stars of the white night,
Moon shining on high,
Piercing the forest with your pale beams,
Stars, friends of white ghosts,
Moon, their protectress!

Pygmy ghosts are released at night to wander by the light of the moon—this song is to placate the spirits of the sky so that they will control the ghosts and keep them from harming the living. Like all primitive song it has a practical purpose; like all poetry it is created with skill, power, and truth.

This fascinating book provides a preface to all subsequent literature. C. M. Bowra examines the contents of primitive song and the part it plays in the social life of modern primitive peoples. He traces its development from meaningless melodic sounds to elaborate constructions that rival the poetry of civilized man. The author shows what living Stone Age men feel about life, death, love, God, in songs that might have been sung millions of years before the recorded word.

MENTOR Books of Special Interest

Folkways *by William Graham Sumner.*

A classic study of how customs originate in basic human drives. This is an incredibly comprehensive research into the cultures of primitive and civilized peoples. (#MT297—75¢)

Bulfinch's Mythology: Vol. I. The Age of Fable.

A retelling of the myths of ancient Greece and Rome, with Introduction by Palmer Bovie.

(#MP449—60¢)

Music and Imagination *by Aaron Copland.*

The world famous composer explains the role of the imagination in composing, performing, and listening to music. (#MP502—60¢)

Modern Music *by John Tasker Howard and James Lyons.*

A handbook explaining the new harmonies and rhythms—including jazz—presenting a history of 20th century developments. (#MP396—60¢)

Primitive Song

by C. M. BOWRA

A MENTOR BOOK
Published by The New American Library

To Joan Rayner

Published as a MENTOR BOOK
by arrangement with The World Publishing Company,
who have authorized this softcover edition.
A hardcover edition is available from
The World Publishing Company.

FIRST PRINTING, MAY, 1963

A hardcover edition of *Primitive Song* is published in England
by George Weidenfeld & Nicolson, Ltd.

MENTOR TRADEMARK REG. U.S. PAT. OFF. AND FOREIGN COUNTRIES
REGISTERED TRADEMARK—MARCA REGISTRADA
HECHO EN CHICAGO. U.S.A.

MENTOR BOOKS are published *in the United States* by
the New American Library of World Literature, Inc.,
501 Madison Avenue, New York 22, New York,
in Canada by the New American Library of Canada Limited,
156 Front Street West, Toronto 1, Ontario,
in the United Kingdom by the New English Library Limited,
Barnard's Inn, Holborn, London, E.C. 1, England

PRINTED IN THE UNITED STATES OF AMERICA

CONTENTS

CONTENTS

ILLUSTRATIONS

PREFACE

THIS BOOK attempts to break into a field which has not, so far as I know, been explored in any history of literature and yet is surely an integral part of any such study. The beginnings of the art of words are hidden in a dateless past, but something about its first processes and developments may be gathered by comparative study from what is known about the poetry of the most primitive peoples still surviving in the world. By examining what is known of their songs and their other attempts to put words into a rhythmical order we may establish some illuminating conclusions about the earliest types of literature. This is what I have tried to do here, and I hope that my results will not seem to be too theoretical or too adventurous. The whole question may be examined externally through the development of poetical technique and internally through the nature of what is said, and both approaches are equally important to the study of primitive man as we now know him and as he may have been for many thousands of years. I have limited my enquiries to a limited group of peoples who live by hunting and gathering because these are the modern counterparts of the lost races of the Palaeolithic Age. I wish that I could have extended the number of such peoples and found more examples of them, but though of course my selection forms only a small part of those still existing, they are the only ones about whose songs I have been able to find reliable and detailed information. For the task which I have undertaken I have no special qualifications, and I am aware that in many respects I lack the right background and specialized knowledge. I am not an anthropologist, and, though I have long been interested in the study of language and languages, I know next to nothing of those with which I deal here. I have relied on translations, and though I realize that this has its dangers, I am convinced that in almost every case my trust in the translators is amply justified. In pursuing my enquiries I have received generous help from scholars who are specialists in fields where I am only an intruder, and I should like to express my warmest gratitude to Professors I. Schapera, M. Gusinde, and P. Schebesta, to Dr. R. M. and Mrs. C. H. Berndt, and Dr. T. G. H. Strehlow. Without their guidance and assistance I could hardly have made any progress at all, and to them and to others like them who have done the first-hand work of collecting the songs and other poems of primitive peoples I am incalculably beholden. It is also a pleasure to thank others who have helped me in hardly less valuable ways, notably Mr. T. K. Penniman, Curator of the Pitt Rivers Museum, Oxford, whose wide learning has been generously put at my disposal, and Miss Sarah Marris, who with great skill and patience has collected the illustrations for me.

I am such obliged to many publishing houses, who have kindly given permission to quote from their publications: to Messrs. Routledge and Kegan Paul for permission to quote from *The Khoisan Peoples of South Africa* by I. Schapera: to The Humanities Press, New York, for permission to quote from *Djanggawul* by R. M. Berndt: to the Cambridge University Press for permission to quote from *The Veddas* by C. G. and B. Z. Seligmann: to Messrs. F. W. Cheshire, Melbourne, for permission to quote from *Kunapipi* by R. M. Berndt: to Messrs. Ure Smith, Sydney, for permission to quote from *The First Australians* by R. M. and C. M. Berndt: and to the Hawthorn Press, Melbourne, for permission to quote from *An Australian Viewpoint* by T. G. H. Strehlow.

CHAPTER *1* *Primitive Man,*
Ancient and Modern

THOUGH man has existed for something like a million years, only the last five thousand provide records of his speech, and for the larger part of this period they are pitifully meagre and uninformative. We are even worse informed on the early history of song, which pre-supposes the existence of speech and is a special, skilled application of it. When words are made to conform to a musical tune, they provide one of the most elemental forms of poetry known to us; for they are reduced to a deliberate order and made to fulfil a function quite different from that of common talk. It is indeed tempting to surmise that in the Late Palaeolithic Age, *c.* 30,000-15,000 B.C., when men delighted in painting and carving and modelling, they delighted also in the melodious arrangement of words, and that the hunters of mammoth, bison, and rhinoceros, who recorded their hopes or their achievements so splendidly on the walls of caves, celebrated them also in song. But just as we know nothing of their speech and can speculate about it only through questionable analogies and *a priori* assumptions, so we know nothing of any specialized purposes to which it may have been put. Certainty of any kind is out of the question, and when we look for the beginnings of song, we are reduced to estimating possibilities for which such evidence as can be found is hard to interpret or to force to any firm conclusions.

Late Palaeolithic man had at least some sort of music. Flutes and pipes made of little marrowbones have often been found in caves, and in the Grotte des Trois Frères at Ariège in southern France there is a drawing of a man dressed as a bison, who plays a kind of flute. Where music exists, dancing is not far away, and scenes of it are not uncommon in the art of the time. There are dancing archers in Spain at La Cueva del Civil, and masked dancers at Marsoulas, Hornos de la Pena, and Altamira. In a deeper cave at Ariège there is a painting of a figure known as "le Sorcier," who has the horns of a stag, the face of an owl, the forelegs of a bear, the tail of a horse, and the ears of a wolf, and is plainly dancing or prancing. Dancing certainly existed and had in many cases a mimetic character, since fifty-five portrayals of human beings dressed in skins, often in a dancing posture, are known from the art of the Ice-Age. Even if some of the pictures are not of human beings or even of magicians, that need not trouble us. Even gods would not be depicted as dancing if men did not dance, and where there is dancing there is rhythm and music, and song may not be unknown, but this is no more than a possibility. These enigmatic dancers provoke many imaginative and alluring speculations, but they cannot be summoned to give substantial evidence.

We are no better off when we turn to the oldest known examples of song, which appear about the middle of the third millennium B.C. in written texts from Sumer and Egypt. The first known fragments of Sumerian song are either long narrative-poems about theological and cosmological matters, or, a little later, full-scale hymns to gods and goddesses. The earliest extant Egyptian song was sung by soldiers of Pepi I about 2350 B.C.[1] Both the Sumerian and the Egyptian texts present a primitive feature in the frequent use of repeated lines, but in other respects they have a mature look. Of course songs existed long before them and may well have been much simpler and more primitive, but they have not survived, largely because they were not recorded in writing, and we have no information about their form or contents. What we have are the unmistakable products of societies far more elaborate than anything possible in Late Palaeolithic or Mesolithic times. They embody the habits and the outlooks of large populations living from agriculture under a centralized government, well acquainted with the use of metals and many consequent techniques, relying to some extent upon writing and helped by it to form and express more or less abstract notions, divided into organized and specialized callings, and enriched by an accumulation of knowledge and speculation which implies centuries of sustained effort in discovery and development. Such peoples are in many ways much closer to our own world than to the small groups of savage men who lived by the chase and changed their habitations to suit its seasonal demands; who were all alike so occupied with the same urgent necessities that specialization hardly existed except sometimes for religious duties; whose slowness to change their ways was due to a lack of accumulated experience and to the difficulty of finding time for anything more than keeping alive. If we wish to know about the songs of the Stone Age, we shall learn next to nothing from our earliest texts, which are already much too modern and too far removed from the social conditions in which primaeval song can have had its beginnings. What concerns us happened long before they began and is lost forever in silence.

It is, then, impossible to discover the beginnings of song, and therefore of poetry, by the strictly historical method of delving into the past in the hope that it will yield the evidence which we seek. The trouble with the art of words, unlike its sister arts of painting and sculpture, is that before the invention of writing it is doomed to perish on the air. A few songs or charms or prayers may be remembered and passed from generation to generation, but these also are fated to vanish, when they are no longer needed, or something more modern takes their place, or language so changes as to make them unintelligible. It is all too clear that if we try to construct the history of early song, we are by the nature of things prevented from finding any materials for it. This means that we must reshape the problem and ask whether there is not some method of enquiry which is not historical in the sense that it explores the past, but may none the less throw some light on song at its most primitive stages. We may look at those songs available to us which are primitive not only in the sense that they are less organized and elaborated than modern songs but are also the products of conditions in many respects close to those of the Late Palaeolithic Age and reflect the outlook of societies which live in a primaeval simplicity. Such songs contain in an undifferentiated and unspecialized form elements which more advanced poetry contains in much more differentiated and more specialized forms. They may not resemble the lost songs, if any, of the historical Stone Age, but they are products of savage societies which still eke out a precarious existence in some parts of the world by the same means and in much the same conditions as Late Palaeolithic man. They reveal what human beings, living in the most elementary conditions, do to make words rhythmical and memorable and different from the parlance of every day. They represent a stage in the evolutionary development of song before it has branched into many later varieties and while it is still closely connected with certain urgent human needs, which call for it as a means of expression but are confined to the lowest level of subsistence known to us. Though we can discover nothing about historical Palaeolithic song, we can examine living primitive song, which is born from what are in most respects Palaeolithic conditions and bears many marks of them.

There still exist in the world, or existed till lately, small, isolated groups of people who maintain the essential habits of the Stone Age, not so much because they use stone weapons and tools, since some of them have not advanced beyond wood, but because their economy is in fundamental respects the same. Song is shaped ultimately by the economic and social conditions in which it is born and by the needs which these create in men. The conditions of these peoples are the simplest known to us, and for this purpose we must choose from among them those about whom we have some information especially concerning their songs. It would be interesting, for instance, to know what songs, if any, were sung by the Kalang of Java, who are said to have been the most apelike of men, but they have perished, and their songs with them. On others, like the extinct Tasmanians, our information is scanty and unreliable. Still others may be suspected of an unwillingness to reveal their songs, which have a holy character, to strangers who might turn their knowledge to evil ends. Of a large number too little is known to justify any conclusions. Yet there remains a small company of savage peoples, about whose songs we have some information, and upon them we may concentrate our attention, provided we remember that they are only a small selection and that others outside them may work in different ways and raise other questions. From Africa we may summon the Pygmies of the equatorial forests of Gabon and Ituri, and the Bushmen and the "hill" Dama (Damara) of the southwest; from Asia, the Semang of the Malayan jungle, the Veddas of Ceylon, and the Andamanese; from Australia, a rich array of aborigines, who form a unity neither in language nor in customs nor in the art of song; from America, the Eskimos of the Arctic north, and the all but extinct Selk'nam (Ona) and Yamana (Yahgans) of the far south in Tierra del Fuego. Though there are many differences between these widely scattered peoples, they all represent a like stage of human development in more than one important respect. They are indubitably primitive, even savage, and much in their way of life recalls that of Late Palaeolithic man, while they have little in common even with his Neolithic successors. They present for our purpose a single body of material, which has indeed marked local variations and idiosyncrasies, but shows on the whole a homogeneous character because of the living conditions which it reflects. This character calls for some notice, since it explains much that is essential in the art of primitive song.

First, all these peoples live by hunting and gathering, if we allow the first to include fishing and the search for grubs, and the second to include a wide range of plants, roots, fruits, honey, and the like. None of them practises agriculture or domesticates animals that it may eat their flesh or drink their milk. They all depend on a food-economy in which pursuit and search are indispensable for survival, and nothing is grown at home. To get food is the first, most insistent, and most absorbing of all needs. Even when animals are plentiful, they are not always easy to kill, and there are times when they are scarce and starvation is imminent. Even roots and fruits are seasonal, as the Yamana recognize when they date the seasons of the year by the kinds of fungi to be found, and may unaccountably die out or appear in short supply. Nor have these peoples, other than the Eskimos, who have their own natural refrigerators and their own methods of drying meat, any means of keeping food for long when they get it. Its pursuit is a daily necessity and may occupy a large part of every day. This was the case with Late Palaeolithic man, whose obsession with hunting is clear from the paintings at Lascaux in which he depicts animals pierced with spears, no doubt in the conviction that by this he is bringing them into his power. Of course the kind and the quantity of food available will vary greatly from place to place according to natural supplies, but the need for it is universal and inexorable, and the means for getting it do not vary in any fundamental respect. When man knows nothing about agriculture or the domestication of animals, he must rely upon what nature provides from her own resources.

Modern primitives use much the same weapons as their Palaeolithic forbears. The spear, normally tipped with a stone point, but sometimes made only of sharpened wood, sometimes fitted with an iron point got by barter, and the spear-thrower are almost universal among them, and if the first has precedents at Lascaux, the second is anticipated by a Magdalenian weapon found at Mas d'Azil. With the exception of the Australians and the Tasmanians, all use the bow and arrow, as it may be seen in full onslaught against deer in the Cueva de los Caballos at Albocacer. It may have come to Spain from the Sahara when this was still parkland, but that would not account for its career in Tierra del Fuego, the Arctic, or the Andaman Islands. Instead of it the Australians use the boomerang, which recalls the throwing sticks of Neolithic times in Jutland, and the Tasmanians, who knew of neither the bow nor the boomerang, made up for it by their skill in throwing stones. A special development of the spear is the harpoon, used by the Eskimos and in a more primitive form by the Yamana, and both have precedents in the barbed harpoon-heads made of reindeer antlers in the Magdalenian age. Other, less common, ways of getting food may be extremely ancient. The Pygmies and the Veddas scale trees and cliffs to find honey, and such activities are nicely displayed on the rock-paintings of Cueva de las Arañas in Valencia and Cueva de la Alpéra in Albacete.

What the land supplies may sometimes be supplemented by the sea, and some almost extinct tribes of western Australia are content to fish from the shore or to gather molluscs at low tide. The Yamana rely for much of their diet upon fish, though the men leave the actual work to the women, who make their catch by swimming in the icy sea. About AD 553 Justinian's general, Nonnosus, found Pygmies on an island in the Red Sea, who wore no clothes except a small loin-cloth and lived upon oysters and fish thrown up by the sea.[2] The middens of Late Palaeolithic man display large heaps of molluscs, but he also fished with harpoons or hooks of bone, and that he knew something about deep-sea fish is clear from the sketch of a tunny on the wall of a cave at Pindal. His successor, Mesolithic man, certainly had means of putting to sea; for the remains of a wooden dug-out canoe have been found at Perth in Scotland, and wooden rudders from Maglemosian sites in Denmark belong to the same pursuit. No doubt practice varied according to the physical situation and the supply of food on land, and this is what we find among living primitives. The Eskimos, Andamanese, Yamana, and certain northern Australians use canoes, while the Tasmanians had flimsy rafts. But the Selk'nam and the Semang, who live near the sea, never venture on it. In most essential respects the food-economy of modern primitives is remarkably like that of Palaeolithic man, and, though it is practised in very different and divergent regions, shows a substantially homogeneous character.

A second characteristic of modern primitives, which follows from their dependence on hunting, is that they tend to have no fixed habitations. This is simply because they must follow their prey wherever it goes, and when it changes its feeding ground, they must change theirs. This means not only that their shelters are of the simplest and most temporary kind, but that sometimes they do not take the trouble to make any but live out in the open if the weather is good or under rocks or trees or in caves if it is bad. They cling to these habits even when they see their more advanced neighbours building more substantial dwellings. The Pygmies make shelters of branches and leaves much flimsier than the kraals of their Bantu neighbours, and the Veddas have not been influnced by Sinhalese or Tamil example to abandon their love of rock-shelters and caves, nor have the Semang been moved by the sight of Malayan huts on wooden props to imitate them. Indeed it is remarkable how the temporary character of a dwelling outweighs even considerations of security, as we see from the Semang, whose forest shelters provide no protection against the tigers and elephants around them. The Eskimos have to abandon their igloos when the snow melts in summer, and put up with movable huts made of skins, while the Fuegians, who suffer from a climate where it rains or snows for 300 days in the year, live in feeble structures of boughs and twigs and leave them whenever the needs of their bellies insist upon it. We cannot doubt that Late Palaeolithic man lived in this way. Though he explored and exploited deep caverns, he used them seasonally or for special purposes. In the Dordogne and the Charente he dwelt in them from November to February, which is the time between the shedding of horns by adult reindeer and the growing of new ones. In the summer, when wild animals ranged far and freely, they had to be followed despite the lack of any solid cover for hunters, and in this period it may have been provided by primitive huts like those thought to be engraved on the walls of Font-de-Gaume.[3] Those who pursue a migratory or half-migratory life travel lightly with the fewest possible appurtenances, not merely that they may not be wearied with burdens, but that they may have their hands free to kill game at any moment. They have indeed their arts, but these tend to be confined either to light and portable objects for ornament or magic or to drawings and paintings in special places, like those of some Australians, the Semang, the Veddas, and the Bushmen, to which they resort at fixed seasons for religious or social ceremonies. Such no doubt were the caves in which Magdalenian man displayed his astonishing artistic talents by putting into visible form his boasts or his ambitions in hunting and his idea of the supernatural powers which decided his success or failure. A life of this kind is not nomadic in the sense that its members range as far as they please. On the contrary, Palaeolithic hunters may well have resembled the Eskimos, the Fuegians, the Pygmies, the Veddas and the Bushmen in limiting themselves to more or less defined areas within which small groups moved as their needs took them, while they left adjacent areas to be exploited by other groups.

Thirdly, these people do not breed or domesticate animals for food. Indeed the only domesticated animal to be found among them is the dog, which is used by the Pygmies, the Veddas, the Australians, the Fuegians, and the Eskimos. The Australians are thought to have taken it with them when they crossed the land-bridge where the Torres Strait now is, and that may explain why it was not known to the Tasmanians, who may have travelled southward considerably earlier. But even the dog is bred and kept entirely for hunting. It may of course keep watch, but that seems to be incidental and not indispensable. Its use is that it can pursue game and help to kill it and bring it in. It is true that some Eskimos drive dogs in sledges, but, after all, that too is part of hunting in a region where it is difficult for a man to go on foot and almost impossible without some extraneous aid to pursue animals who move faster than he does. The dog is not known to have been domesticated in Palaeolithic times, but in Mesolithic times it certainly was. Its unique position emphasizes the paramount importance of hunting. The only animal which has been domesticated is kept not to provide meat or milk but to help in the chase.

Fourthly, all these peoples have a similar social structure. The fundamental unit is the family, but a few families may live and work together in a group. Such a group has not more than a hundred members and may have only about twenty. They have a common hunting-ground, which they exploit together, and they dwell in close proximity to one another. Though a man's weapons are his own possession, and theft of them is rigorously punished, the products of the chase are shared among all the members of the group. The simplicity of this structure leads to more than one significant result. There is no specialization of work, except between men and women, and even that is not absolute. The normal pattern is that, while both have to find food, men hunt animals and women look for roots and fruits and grubs. Even this is not constant. Among the Tasmanians women joined in hunting wild animals in the forest, and among the Yamana, where men do not swim because it is below their dignity, women can, and get food from the sea by doing so. It follows that men use weapons, while women normally do not. The only sign of a professional class is he who claims magical powers in dealing with gods and spirits, whether as a shaman, who is reputed to be able to change his shape, or as a medicine man, who works through a familiar spirit. Yet, though both have sources of information denied to ordinary men, perform special duties, and exert considerable influence, they do not form a class apart but have to fend for themselves like their fellows. Though they are usually men, the rule is not universal, and among the Eskimos some are women. This lack of specialized pursuits means that primitive societies have no social hierarchy or class-structure or anything that we can call government. A member of a family or a group of families who offends against its rules is punished by its members, but there is no chief, judicial, military, or sacerdotal, who has paramount powers over other men and women. Nor does there seem to be any need for one. The groups are so small that decisions are easily taken by adult males in consultation, and the proved skill and experience of individuals may count for much. Something of the same kind may have existed in Late Palaeolithic times, when men were organized in small groups, which would not call for any strict system of discipline, while women, whose chief task was to bear children and find certain classes of food, must have pursued their own tasks. That they did not join in the activities of men is clear enough from the so-called "Venuses" of Lespugue, Sivenil and Lausel in France, whose ample curves and swelling wombs indicate that they cannot have taken any serious part in hunting. If "le Sorcier" of Trois Frères and an animal-headed figure carved on bone at Mas d'Azil are not gods but men disguised in magical garb, shamans or medicine-men existed and must have had duties similar to those of their living counterparts. The structure of primitive society, both ancient and modern, is dictated by the needs of hunting and conforms rigorously to them.

There is, then, good reason to think that in certain fundamental respects the primitive peoples of our selection pass their lives in a common pattern, and that this is not very alien to what we know of Late Palaeolithic man. So far as their essential economy is concerned, hunters and gatherers form a single group, whose homogeneous pattern is not to be explained by any theory of a single racial origin. Of our peoples the Pygmies, the Bushmen, the Andamanese, the Dama, and the Semang resemble one another in their dark colouring and their small stature, but not in all other respects. The Veddas resemble the pre-Dravidian peoples, like the Kadir and the Kurumba, still surviving in the jungles and hills of southern India or in the islands of the Mergui archipelago off south-western Burma, and bear no resemblance to the Pygmoid Negritos or Negrillos. The Australians are like neither of these groups, and the Tasmanians, who had certain Melanesian traits, were not Pygmoid. The Eskimos have Mongolian characteristics, but have questionably been thought to be an indigenous people of Arctic America, while the Fuegians, whose branches differ considerably from one another, may be related to other "Indian" peoples of America, who have come in successive waves over a long period of years from Asia by way of Bering Strait. The similarity of habits between our peoples is not to be explained by any theory of race, nor are their songs, which display equal similarities, to be explained by the notion of a tradition maintained from a remote, common past. The songs of primitive man arise from his economic conditions, and to this degree reflect the mentality of peoples who still in many important respects maintain the habits of the Late Paleolithic Age.

All these primitives live an extremely hard and exacting life. If they have survived at all, it is largely because in their deserts or forests or frozen wastes they have been separated from other human beings, who have, indeed, driven them to their present homes but then left them more or less alone. It is tempting to think that it is this very hardness of life which has kept them to their old ways and so absorbed their energy and their intelligence that they have not been able to look beyond their established economy and its immediate demands. This might seem to be especially true of the Eskimos, who have evolved ways of survival which show an audacious adaptability, and even of the Fuegians, who have learned to endure natural conditions which almost nobody else could. Yet when we look more closely into the matter, it is clear that these hard conditions are largely the result of pressure from recent, more developed peoples, such as the North American Indians, or the Bantu, or the Malays, or the Spaniards, or the English, who have pushed earlier inhabitants into rough places which they themselves do not covet and may even be unable to penetrate. Before the intruders came, a primitive way of life was well established, but it was not always so hard as to forbid any advance. It is true that large areas of Australia are desert, but before the first convicts came to Botany Bay in 1788 the aborigines had a whole continent over which to roam, and not all of it was so poverty-stricken as the regions in which they are now privileged to eke out a forlorn existence. Nor had they to struggle against dangerous animals, as the Semang struggle against bears, tigers, elephants, pythons, and crocodiles. The marsupials and reptiles of Australia are on the whole agreeably harmless, and yet the aborigines made no advance comparable to that in Europe after the end of the glacial epoch and the emergence of Neolithic man. The same is true of the Tasmanians, who lived in quite congenial conditions, but failed to invent any weapon so effective as the bow or the boomerang, or any craft, except fragile rafts, on which to put to sea. Nor can it be argued that the failure of these peoples to develop was simply due to lack of intelligence. Within their own worlds they display plenty of it, and their expert knowledge of nature and their ability to put it to profitable uses are quite beyond the scope of civilized men. Even when they are pitted against enemies armed with weapons infinitely superior to their own, they have shown remarkable ingenuity in avoiding them. The Tasmanians in 1804 succumbed not to the rifles of English colonists but to their broken promises of safety; the Pygmies have for centuries eluded their Negro opponents by hiding in the equatorial forest, and the Bushmen have survived the deadly attacks of the Herero by their skill in movement and concealment. Primitive men may not think on exactly the same lines as we do, but that does not mean that they are congenitally stupid. Indeed when they are faced with new phenomena, which must be incredibly strange to them, they show an unusual ability in understanding at least their practical implications. A characteristic example may be seen in the three young Fuegians, known as Jemmy Button, York Minster, and Fuegia Basket, who were abducted and brought to England in 1830. Even Charles Darwin, who was deeply shocked by the conditions in which they lived at home, was impressed by their brightness, and indeed they needed it if they were to fulfil all that was hoped of them. After being presented to Queen Adelaide and placed under the tuition of a clergyman of the Church of England, the Rev. Joseph Wigram at Walthamstow, they had to adapt themselves to circumstances which must have been inconceivably alien to them. Nor can they be blamed if, after only a year's preparation in England, they failed on their return home to Tierra del Fuego to convert their own peoples to modern, middle-class ways and lapsed into the nakedness in which they had been born and bred.[4] The failure of primitive societies to develop is not to be explained along lines such as these.

Man advances through the acquisition, accumulation and intelligent application of experience. In truly primitive conditions this takes an enormous time, as we can see from the slowness which the Early Palaeolithic Age took to mature into the Late. For such application of experience more than one thing is required. First, men must have sufficient challenge from their surroundings to compel them to make new inventions and solve insistent problems of survival. If they are forced to it, they will do so, as the first hunters of mammoth and rhinoceros knew when they dug pits for them and fashioned weapons which would kill them from a distance. In the second place, they must have neighbours sufficiently close and approachable with whom they can exchange ideas and from whose experience both parties can learn. The vast changes brought by the Neolithic revolution, with the domestication of animals and the establishment of agriculture, were furthered by the freeing of huge areas as the ice receded and gave new openings to exploit unknown regions and meet unknown peoples. Our primitive peoples have on the whole lacked both these incentives. Even before the arrival of destructive intruders they had worked out a scheme of existence which seemed to be sufficient for their needs and was certainly all that they asked for. Nor on the whole had they the stimulus of neighbours sufficiently like themselves to provoke an interchange of ideas. The lack of contacts explains why the Tasmanians never had the bow and arrow, and, even more strangely, why the Andamanese, who knew how to keep fire alight, did not know how to make it, and were in this respect inferior even to so remote a forerunner as Peking man. Even the various tribes of Australia seem to have learned very little from one another, perhaps because in the vast areas open to them each tribe was content to keep itself to itself and to have little to do with other tribes whose languages it could not understand. Conversely, even the most isolated and self-sufficient peoples may occasionally profit from contact with aliens, as the Semang have learned from the Malays how to use blow-pipes in hunting, or Pygmies and Andamanese how to work iron brought by neighbours or visitors. Isolation, whether geographical or cultural, is the enemy of change, and it helps to explain why our primitives have for so long kept to their old ways. When new forces have burst upon them, it has been too late, and they have been unable to resist, still more to absorb or control them.

The explanation of this intense conservatism lies deeper even than this. In conditions where life is reduced to an inexorable struggle for existence, "custom," as the Greeks said, is "king of all." Anything which contradicts or defies it is regarded with harsh suspicion. This is in itself not unreasonable, since custom is the embodiment, in social life, of accumulated experience and has the weight of age and authority behind it. But if it is not exposed to new forces sufficiently powerful to insist on concessions being made to them, custom breeds its own dangers. It lives on its own resources and may elaborate them from within instead of looking beyond or outside them, especially in anything to do with the supernatural and the unseen, but in the essential task of struggling to keep alive it restricts and forbids novelty and invention. The failure to introduce even the most primitive forms of agriculture is a case in point. Primitive peoples may know something about the growth of plants, but they refuse to grow them. One of the reasons for this may be that since the collecting of roots is the task of women, while hunting is the task of men, there is a powerful prejudice against any change which would make women more important by extending their sphere of activity. It might also be argued that when hunters and gatherers take to agriculture, no matter at how primitive a level, it has a depressing effect upon them, as we can see from those Andamanese who have developed their own plots of yams and are rapidly becoming extinct because so tranquil a routine robs them of the zest which inspired them in their old hunting days and they feel that now they have nothing exciting to live for. A similar fate seems to have fallen on the Botocudos and Ge of Brazil, who in their savage days were formidable enemies of the Portuguese colonists, but have now shrunk to a small handful confined to its yam-patches, without adventure and without hope. Yet though this failure to adapt to new conditions is easily understood, it is none the less a sign of the dangers of custom. If it were not so well established, not only in common respect but in primitive psychology, it would cause less havoc when it is broken. It is in the absoluteness of the rule of custom that modern primitives differ most from Late Palaeolithic man. He made experiments and learned from them. In the hunting-field he seems to have had no prejudices but to have pursued most creatures that came his way. Yet custom may interfere even with the pursuit of food. The belief in totems in Australia and Africa forbids a group to eat the animal to whose totem it belongs, and the refusal of the Tasmanians to eat any fish with scales may have been determined by a belief of the same kind. Once a system of life based on hunting has taken a fixed form, it is liable to continue without any changes unless some powerful new influence comes to disturb it. Our peoples have lacked this disturbance, and continued to think that, since life has always been like this, it will and should always remain so.

It is at this point that modern primitives part from their late Palaeolithic forbears. Though their hunting economy is indubitably the same, it has permitted, inside the social frame, certain developments which may in fact be relatively modern. Though not all these may affect the character of primitive song and certainly do not affect the physical conditions in which it arises, they introduce new factors which warn us against thinking that modern primitives resemble the men of Lascaux and Altamira in every way. It is in fact likely that, though there has been very little change in the methods of getting food, there has in other fields been a movement towards an inner complexity which is unlikely to have existed for Palaeolithic man and has grown into great prominence with the passage of centuries. Such developments need not be parallel among all primitive societies, and are not likely to be. But it is natural that a society which is severely restricted in its economic habits may indulge a taste for change in other matters, and it is on such lines that some primitive societies seem to have moved.

First, though primitive social structure is extremely simple and is still based on families and the needs of hunting, it has in some places built elaborate rules inside its unchanging frame. The whole system of totems, which prevails both in Australia and in Africa, may itself be of very ancient origin. The notion that men are somehow connected with the animal or vegetable or mineral world is not in itself absurd, and the appearance of men with the heads of animals in the art of the Magdalenian age suggests that rudiments of it may have existed even in those times. But the enormous elaboration which it has received, indicates that it has followed its own inner line of development, bringing its implications into the open and forcing the formulation of rules to observe them down to the minutest detail. It is in its own way a remarkable achievement, a primitive counterpart to science and philosophy, designed to account for man's place in nature and his undoubted kinship with and dependence on natural things, but it has little to do with his economic structure and, when it has, it may, with its restrictions on certain foods and classes of marriage, be more of a hindrance than a help. So careful and so complex a system implies a long process of elaboration over many centuries and is unlikely to have existed in its present advanced form in Palaeolithic times. It may indeed have its roots in them, but its subsequent development looks like the kind of thing which primitive peoples do when others are busy with technology and applied science.

Secondly, religious cults and beliefs almost always change with time. From a very early date Palaeolithic man had views about gods and life after death, but these changed with the passage of time, even if they were still kept to the same main issues. The development of religious beliefs is usually complex and unexpected, and often they move simultaneously in two directions. While rites get more and more complex, and eventually reach a point where they are hardly understood but performed just because they are ancient and customary, beliefs may at the same time be organized and simplified. Behind the multitude of spirits and other supernatural powers which encompass primitive man on every side, there are sometimes hints of some other, more powerful being who controls them and even manifests his will through them. It is certainly remarkable that the Semang, the Andamanese, the Pygmies, and the Fuegians all believe in some kind of supreme deity. This may, of course, be a heritage from a remote past, but it seems more likely to be a natural movement from multiplicity to unity, and it is unlikely to have come into existence without considerable mental effort. Even when such an idea has not taken a full shape, it is to some degree anticipated by some common notion of what a divine power is, as the Australians assign to mythical ancestors powers which vary in detail but are ultimately of the same kind, since they are thought to be the source of all life in man and nature. Yet these simple and comprehensive beliefs are combined with others which are fundamentally inconsistent with them, even if the inconsistency is not noted and does not matter in practice. These may be variously explained as attempts to explain rites no longer understood, as survivals from a remote past, as ingenious inventions and accretions of later times. But in view of their extraordinary variety and ingenuity, they certainly look as if they had a considerable element of innovation in them. Beliefs are more easy to change than economic habits, and the influence of a powerful shaman or medicine man may cause revolutions in thought which would find no parallel in the hunting-field. Though the religion of modern primitives may have a good deal in common with that of Palaeolithic man, there is no reason to think that it has not undergone a notable movement of its own towards both a central simplification and peripheral complexities.

Thirdly, language presents a special problem. It changes with remarkable rapidity, and analogies from modern times, when writing is a powerful preservative of linguistic usage, may deceive us about the rate at which a language which is only spoken may alter almost beyond recognition. The process is aided and accelerated by the separation and lack of contacts between self-sufficient groups of people. When the first Europeans reached Australia, there were some 500 tribes, none of them at all large, but each speaking its own language.[5] If the first immigrants spoke, as we might assume, a single language, their multiplication and division into an increasing number of units led to a whole host of separate, mutually unintelligible tongues. In Tierra del Fuego the speech

of the Selk'nam has almost nothing in common with that of
the neighbouring Yamana. Of course they may have had different origins, but the bewildering variety of languages in
South America indicates that, whatever the first immigrants
from Asia spoke, it soon split into many branches, between
which we can now distinguish few points of similarity. Even
in Tasmania, where the physical obstacles between tribes were
far less formidable than in Tierra del Fuego or the forests
of South America, the aboriginals spoke five distinct languages. These may indeed be classed into two main groups,
Eastern and Western, and they presuppose a common origin
in such fundamental words as those for "stone," "woman,"
"nose," "arm," "leg," "weep," "speak," and "hit," but even
these vary in form and pronunciation and the speakers of the
different languages may not have been intelligible to one another.[6] Here, and no doubt elsewhere, geographical barriers
must have been less important than the practice by which
each group of people kept to a more or less defined area
and had few relations with other groups outside it. Primitive
language deals much less with ideas than with impressions, and
in a life where every impression counts, it is only natural
that new words should be formed to meet them. Moreover,
each language is likely to be forced to express increasingly
complex relations like those of a totemistic scheme, in which
almost any tie has its own significance and calls for its own
expression in precise words. In language, as in social habits
and religious beliefs, primitive peoples have moved towards
a special kind of complexity within the narrow limits of their
economic organization. In considering their songs we must be
on the look-out for what may seem extremely ancient to us
but is in fact a growth of comparatively recent date.

In dealing with these songs we must make up our minds
how primitive they really are. When we look at what they
say, we find a marked spirit informing them, which arises from
the fundamental needs of their singers in their exacting way
of life. However attractive the subject or the details of a
song may be, it bears the colour of its social setting and
speaks for it, but behind this there is usually discernible an
outlook which is enforced by primitive conditions and to that
degree unchanging. It is not difficult to extract this, if we
compare the treatment of recurrent subjects by different peoples and find what they have in common. This eliminates
purely ephemeral and local features and supplies more solid
conclusions. Such similarities would not occur in so widely
divergent peoples if there were not a good reason for them,
and this may usually be found in the struggle for existence
and primitive methods of dealing with it. If we can establish

the main features in a common outlook, we may be more confident that we are on the right way to understanding primitive man as he reveals himself in his songs, and displays through them a consciousness which belongs peculiarly to men who live in such conditions as his.

In examining such material we must ask how trustworthy it is, and we must admit at the start that in no case are we dealing with a totally uncontaminated source. Our primitives are known to us only because they have suffered from the intrusion of other, more highly organized cultures, which have inevitably affected them in some matters. The Veddas have forgotten their own language and speak that of the Sinhalese, the Dama that of the Hottentots, and we must keep our eyes open for themes in their songs which do not truly belong to their economy but have been appropriated from agricultural neighbours. Though the Bushmen, who once roamed most parts of Africa south of the Zambezi, have imposed their verbal clicks on the Zulus, they have in turn borrowed ideas and habits from them which belong to a different level of organization, while the Pygmies use, at least in the presence of strangers and often among themselves, Bantu languages spoken by their neighbours. The Semang, who still speak a primitive Mon-Khmer language, have also adopted some Malay words, and their use of the blowpipe in hunting is not their own invention. Such cases need not trouble us very much, since these influences from without have not disturbed the essential structure of traditional life or destroyed the local culture. Our knowledge of the Tasmanians is largely derived from information gathered by their English superintendents when they were banished in 1831 to Flinders Island and made to adopt a humble and deadly version of English life. They perished from disease and drink, and still more from depression, and our knowledge of their ideas and beliefs may well be coloured by their state in these last years. We cannot tell how much the Bushmen and the Australian aborigines have lost by being driven from their old pastures to deserts, but it is significant that the former have lost the art of painting scenes on rocks which they once practised from Southern Rhodesia to Cape Colony and Natal. A similar doubt arises with those peoples of whom our first knowledge comes from missionaries, who could hardly fail to introduce novel and surprising elements into the beliefs of those whose souls they sought to save. For instance, a funeral song from the Aëta in the Philippines is indeed remarkable but none the less hybrid:

Call not for your wife, for she is in God.
Make ready the basket for food

And bend the bow for the chase.
Long not for your child, for the Devil has already
called him.
Reach not out to your sister, for the spirit has called her,
Nor to your father, who is in the holy Christ;
Long not for your nephew, for the Devil has already
called him.[7]

The song deals faithfully with the different destinies after death of a family whose members held divergent creeds, but it is a poor guide to what an Aëta would have believed before the arrival of Christianity. We may well question whether such a knowledge of primitive peoples as we can now get is always fully or truly informative about them in their normal state, before they were exposed to disintegrating forces from without.

Conversely, there are some primitive peoples who are now hunters and gatherers, but once lived differently and have evidently come down in the world. A striking case is that of the Kubu of Sumatra, who now just survive by hunting and gathering in the dense forests between the Hari and the Moesi rivers. When they were first discovered by Europeans in 1823, they practised a primitive agriculture, and their present way of life has been forced on them by the Malays, who drove them out of their ancient haunts as they were themselves dispossessed by the Dutch. Again, though it is perhaps dangerous to speculate about the ancient history of the Pygmies, it is worth noticing that when, as Herodotus records, some Nasamonians from Libya travelled southward across desert, parkland, and marshes, they found a race smaller than ordinary men, who lived by a river, full of crocodiles, flowing to the east.[8] Whether the river is the Niger or the Bahr-el-Ghazal, the small men must be Pygmies, but if we press the details, and there is no reason why we should not, the mere fact that they lived in a city indicates that their present method of living in temporary shelters in the heart of huge forests is a reversion to far more primitive conditions. It is at least clear that the Pygmies were more highly organized then than now, and their emergence into the parkland, where they found the Nasamonians, indicates a degree of enterprise in the open which they would not risk in their present circumstances. It is obviously difficult to find a primitive society in its natural, undisturbed state, and even when it looks authentic enough, we may suspect that it suffers from some infiltration of alien ideas or from an enforced, not indigenous, way of life.

The answer to these doubts is that in most matters which now concern us these peoples are as conservative as they are allowed to be. The more they are threatened or oppressed or patronized by strangers, the more strongly they cling to their essential traditions. Of course they welcome with avidity any ornaments or weapons or tools that they can get from their more advanced neighbours or masters, but the more intimate centres of their life continue largely unaffected and unaltered. Even if they accept new religious beliefs, they tend to mix them with old, and when it comes to ancient rites and ceremonies, they forget their new ideas. Even in practical matters their habits are hard to change. A significant example is their refusal to take to agriculture even when they know of it. Some peoples indeed, like the Sakai of Malaya and the Aëta of the Philippines, have recently adopted it to some degree, but others are resolute in their distaste for it. Though the Pygmies live among Bantu peoples who practise it, and are by no means averse from exchanging by "silent barter" the products of the chase, such as elephants' tusks, for the fruit of the garden, such as bananas, which they particularly relish, they make no effort to grow these for themselves. When Captain Fitzroy and his party took back their abducted Fuegians to their original home in 1831 and planted a nice patch of vegetables in the hope that it would lead the Yamana into more god-fearing ways, the natives trod it underfoot, thus earning poor Jemmy Button's protestations and condemnation of them: "My people very bad; great fool; know nothing at all; very great fool."[9] The conservatism which has prevented these peoples from devising adequate means of keeping out foreign exploiters has at least the advantage that it makes them preserve some essential features in their way of life. Because of it we are able to see primitive man very much in his authentic state as he must have been for uncounted centuries. We can interpret his feelings through his songs, and his songs through his feelings, in the knowledge that in certain fundamental matters he is belligerently conservative.

Another powerful force in maintaining a truly primitive outlook is the nature of primitive language. Though the languages of our peoples have very little in common either in structure or in syntax, they tend to show certain common methods of digesting and presenting experience. First, they lack words for general and abstract ideas, and that is why it is often difficult for Europeans to make themselves understood by them. The Australians have not even a general word for "fish," but speak of "food in water." Missionaries have not always found it easy to find equivalents for "God," and more specialized notions require great ingenuity to find a new home; in Labrador Eskimo "forgiveness" has to be translated by "not-being-able-to-think-about-it-any-more." On the other hand these languages are extremely skilful at dealing with all kinds of impressions, whether visible or emotional or audible, and have words which cover a vastly wider range than any civilized language can for such matters as colours or effects of light and shade or the movements of animals and birds and fish or the relations of bodies in space. In some branches of Eskimo a noun can have many forms, each with its own special shade of meaning, and the aboriginal Australians of Arnhem Land have a most apt and rich vocabulary for catching the precise impression of natural things. This means that a very large vocabulary is in daily use, and though Thomas Bridges, who composed a dictionary of the Yamana language, may have treated as different some words which were in fact local, dialectal forms, his estimate that the language contained over thirty thousand words is a tribute to its richness. This means that though such a language is a poor instrument for the expression of ideas, it is admirably suited for emotions and sensations and impressions. Nor does it much matter that in what we might think so important a matter as numerals the Tasmanians, Andamanese, some Australians and some Eskimos count "one, two, many"; for in fact they can enumerate all the members of a class or company present on a given occasion by simply naming them, and their memories are stimulated by the lack of numbers to retain a mental picture of what happens. Secondly, on the whole these languages lack the precision of structure familiar from Indo-European with its different parts of speech and achieved by Chinese through its disciplined word-order. They are by no means lacking in grammar, and in one Australian language there are seven forms of the future, each with a different suggestion of possibility or probability, while even Tasmanian had means to distinguish between past, present, and future. But what counts is that the units of speech are less differentiated and less independent from one another. Each is combined with other units to give a rich, accumulative result, and though such languages may lack the kind of clarity that we demand from speech, they have an immediate and forcible impact for those who know them. Quite a complex picture or effect may be presented very rapidly in a concentrated form, as in a line from a song of the Australian Aranda:

ngkinjaba iturala albutjika

where three fully-charged units are combined: *ngkinjaba* means both "sun" and "afternoon"; *iturala* means both "in the heat of the sun" and "in the brightness of the sun;"

albutjika means "to turn homeward." The whole line thus means "to turn home in the afternoon when the sun is bright and hot."[10] Languages that work on such principles are admirably suited to poetry which aims at conveying a full impression of a state of consciousness in which ideas are far less important than sensory impressions. Such languages reflect the mentality of those who speak them, and have their own refinements and subtleties. They may restrict the development of their speakers in some directions, but in others they open up avenues of expression which are denied to more conceptual languages, and song uses words with a substantial assurance that they are well fitted to its task.

Though our selection of peoples displays a homogeneous group so far as their fundamental economy is concerned, and with it some essential features of their outlook, it might be maintained that they are not all on a like level of development, that culturally we may distinguish various levels of development and complexity. Just as the Eskimos show a remarkable ingenuity in surmounting their physical obstacles, so the abundance and the range of their songs show how well established their art of words is. The same may be said in different ways of the Australians of Arnhem Land and the Gabon Pygmies, both of whom have elaborate and elegant oral literatures. At the other extreme are the Fuegians, who have scarcely an art of words at all, and we can fashion a kind of scale which passes upwards from them at the bottom and takes in turn the Andamanese, the Tasmanians, the Bushmen, the Veddas, the Semang, the Dama, the Australian Aranda from the centre of the continent and other groups from Arnhem Land, to the Gabon Pygmies and the Eskimos. Such a scale is both artificial and inadequate, and must not be taken to prove anything about the historical growth of song, but at least it shows how in societies, which have otherwise much in common, the art of words may vary considerably in skill and scope and develop different facets. Though we cannot hope to write a history of song as it existed in the remote past, we can at least discern some of the ways by which it expands and develops and moves from one level to another. All these are preliminaries and preparations to anything that we mean by civilized poetry, but they are indispensable to its prehistory and without them we should know nothing of its first manifestations and beginnings. If in some cases they are anticipations of modern art, in others they are almost living fossils, which have hardly begun to unfold the possibilities innate and implicit in them.

Though the main object of our study is the nature of primitive song as it is revealed in these modern examples, we shall at the same time learn through it something about the peoples who compose it. Their story is indeed ugly and painful. When the struggle for existence is transferred from beasts to men, it reveals all the unreason of a world in which the stronger wins unless he is prevented by some unforeseen intervention of charity or reason. Of our peoples some have already vanished. The last Tasmanian man died in 1865, and the last woman in 1877; many Australian tribes, especially in Victoria and New South Wales, have also disappeared; the last Fuegians have now followed them. Of others scanty remnants survive, but it cannot be long before the Dama, the Bushmen, and the Andamanese die out in a world which offers them no help and no friendship. Nor are the Veddas and the Semang much better placed, since the replacement of British imperialism by Asian nationalism is not likely to improve their position under governments which have no interest in them. Others may perhaps be more fortunate. Some Australian aborigines are being treated at last with a small share of the care and curiosity which they deserve; it is still possible that the Eskimos, more fortunately placed in their Arctic fastnesses, may escape the worst horrors of American civilization; the Pygmies, enclosed by impenetrable forests, where hardly anyone else wishes to live, may be able to evade their old enemies on their fringes. But already irreparable damage and senseless destruction have been done on a hideous scale. In the first days of discovery these poor savages had no means to protect themselves against greedy, unscrupulous, and self-righteous invaders. When their lands or their women were grabbed from them, they retaliated with what feeble weapons they had, and were mercilessly destroyed. If not every white man resembled the Rumanian Julio Popper, who organized shooting-parties against the naked Selk'nam,[11] or the English settlers of Tasmania, who, after inviting their friends to a picnic, would go out with dogs and rifles in pursuit of natives,[12] yet until very recent years the history of relations between white man and aboriginals has been one of appalling destruction, inspired by accusations which these peoples can never have understood, or by a contempt and disgust for them as lower than the beasts and fit only to perish.

European civilization brought in its train other evils no less deadly than murder. Of these the worst was disease. These peoples, who had adjusted their life very exactly to physical conditions, were immune from most diseases so long as they were left alone. Their bodies, hardened by life in the open air, and sustained by the crude food to which they had been accustomed for centuries, were quite unable to withstand the ailments brought by the whites. A typical example must suffice for illustration. About 1860, when the first English mission was set up among the Yamana, their population was probably about 2,500. They were already subject to such curses as syphilis and smallpox brought by whalers and sailors, but now the destruction began in earnest. Forced by their new pastors to wear clothes and live in smoky huts, they lost their natural powers of resistance, and a series of epidemics worked its savage fury upon them. Between 1863 and 1870 half the population is estimated to have perished from various lung troubles. In 1881 tuberculosis made its no less deadly appearance, in 1884 typhoid from an Argentine ship, in 1890 whooping cough and smallpox. Each epidemic reaped its pitiless harvest of human lives, until by 1925 only a handful of Yamana survived. Though the worthy Thomas Bridges, who devoted his life to converting them to Anglican Christianity and composed a dictionary of their language, could write in 1882: "There can be no doubt that the adoption of clothing and civilized ways is beneficial to the health of the natives," he was disastrously wrong; for it was these civilized ways which rotted their old defences and made them easy victims of death. Clothing unfitted them for facing the rigours of their climate; English food ruined their digestions; alcohol broke their will for action and the daily routine of hunting. The story of the Yamana has been repeated in most countries where white men have exploited primitives; and where white men have been lacking, Bantu, Malays, Sinhalese and other races have pursued a like policy with like results.

The story of these peoples in the last hundred years illustrates Hobbes' famous words that the life of primitive man is "solitary, poor, nasty, brutish, and short." So indeed it seemed even to those who wished to help them; so in their decline, when they had lost the will to live, it seemed to themselves. But such is the power of man to overcome, if only for short intervals, his circumstances, and such his gift for living in the present, that even in their worst times these people clung to their old interests and sang songs about them. Even now the few survivors treasure old songs and even compose new ones when the spirit moves them. In these they celebrate their immemorial pursuits, their pleasures and sorrows, their attachment to the living scene, and their speculations about what happens behind and beyond it. Song is their chief, almost their only, art, and to it they give their concentrated, practised, and critical powers. Through their songs we can see them as they actually are, and not through the distorted vision of murderous enemies or misguided well-wishers. The striking claim of these songs is that, despite all their distance and difference from our own, they have the

power to evoke strong responses and to create a vivid awareness of the present scene or the unknown powers at work in
it. We can easily understand them as records of human life;
we can without much difficulty appreciate their imaginative
and emotional strength; we can even feel something of their
strictly poetical appeal. For these reasons they are worthy of
study. They fill a gap between the living present, with all its
complexity and specialization, and the dateless, irrecoverable
past of our remote ancestors. They speak for a stage in the
development of mankind which is worth knowing as much
from within, through its words, as from without, through its
artifacts and its skeletons, and is after all in some important respects not ultimately alien to our own.

CHAPTER *2* *Composition and Performance*

~~~~~~

IN MOST primitive song words are only a part of a complex unit. In the first place, they are sung, and the singing is done to a recognizable, if simple, tune, and though each people has its own way of composing such tunes, they none the less follow regular rules and qualify to be called musical. Sometimes they are accompanied by instruments, sometimes not. Wind-, string-, and percussion-instruments are used in various degrees by the Pygmies, the Bushmen, the northern Australians, the Dama, the Semang, and the Eskimos, but the absence of anything of the kind from the Fuegians or the Tasmanians means not that their ear for music is less sensitive or their delight in it less vigorous, but simply that they have managed to get on without such extraneous aids and found unaccompanied song perfectly satisfying. Such tunes are short and easy, but that is an advantage when they have to be learned by a number of people who are not professionals, and the limited scope of their repertory does not make them less attractive or less effective in their own setting. Secondly, singing is often accompanied by some kind of action, such as a dance, in which bodily movements are repeated on various patterns, or mimetic gestures, which illustrate what the words say and make their references and implications more forceful, or merely supporting actions, like clapping the hands or stamping the feet to emphasize certain points in the tune or the words. Words, music, and movement present a single unity, and each element can be judged at its full worth only when it is at work with the others. But just as we can derive an unusual pleasure from the words of Greek choral song, or *molpê*, of which both the music and the movements are lost, so we can from primitive song. The pleasure is not so complete as it might be if we enjoyed the whole, proper performance, but in isolation the words give the intellectual content of the composite unity. They take us into the consciousness of primitive man at its most excited or exalted or concentrated moments, and they throw a light, which almost nothing else does, on the movements of his mind. The fact that he has an art of words at all is itself remarkable enough, and though we must not look for too many grandeurs or subtleties in it, we may none the less be surprised and delighted by its accomplishment within its own range. But before we look at his song in its variety, we must try to discover what lies behind it, how it is composed, and in what conditions it is performed.

Song rises from rhythmical action and owes to it some of its most important characteristics. Such action is older and earlier than rhythmical words, which are added to it and give to it a new, clarifying element. It is often found without words or with sounds that have no meaning, and can be perfectly effective in itself, but choral songs are nearly always allied to action, and the dance and other related forms of action are universally popular among primitive peoples. The debt of song to them may be seen in more than one important respect. They are essentially dramatic, the first, faint beginnings of the theatre, and they provide on a small scale that extension of experience through the imagination which the theatre provides on a much more generous scale. In them parts are acted, whether of men or animals or things or spirits, and the actors of these parts feel that they somehow embody them and partake of their personalities. The actor has both his own character and that which he assumes in acting, and for the moment the second is more powerful and more relevant than the first. The performance is accepted at its face value by the onlookers, no less than by the actors, and the former believe that they are really witnessing something which belongs to a different order of being from their ordinary round but is none the less real and significant. The illusion is often helped by the use of masks, by painting the face or the body, by the use of symbolical emblems, and above all by words. All these elements of rhythmical action help song to transcend the limitations of the actual moment and to beguile the imagination into another sphere. This is obviously true of choral song, which normally explains some dramatic action, whether sacred or secular, but it is hardly less true of solo song which a man or a woman sings about personal experience or feelings. The mere act of singing induces a dramatic frame of mind and embodies in an independent form experience which otherwise receives no special notice and is confined to its recipient. Primitive song takes its singers out of themselves by making them act a part, even if this is themselves as they have recently been or hope to be. It gives that distance from the immediate scene which is the foundation of all the arts, and the detachment which enables a man to look at himself or his circumstances from other motives than the need or impulse to perform some action. Song is based on rhythmical movements, which may take the form of dance or pantomine or both, and, when words are added and made to conform rhythmically to them, poetry begins. In the beginning its task is to convey through the ear to the mind impressions which are conveyed by other means to the eye, and the combination of the two functions greatly increases the appeal of both. The words illuminate the action, and the action adds body to the words.

The place of words in this composite art may owe something to the use of rhythmical speech for purposes such as prayer. As such they are not connected with music or necessarily with action, but none the less they have a deliberate distinction which is close to that of verse. Such exist among more than one primitive people and have not only their own impressive, carefully chosen character but a formality which is necessary to their efficacy. Such prayers are not only cast in standard shapes but have conciseness, dignity, and balance. The Yamana, who have not attained to intelligible song, have a number of such prayers, which are more or less formulaic and used, with variations, whenever they are required. For instance, when bad weather threatens, they pray:

Be gracious to me, my Father, save the boat.[1]

When a mother gives thanks for the recovery of her child, she says:

I am content with the Old One, my Father.[2]

When disaster comes, a man may ask his god why he has sent it:

My Father, why has he punished me from on high?[3]

The Ituri Pygmies also have formalized, conventional prayers, which are like those of the Yamana in their simple dignity. When a childless woman goes to fetch water, she prays to the spirit of the forest:

> Give me pregnancy, O Mbali,
> Give me pregnancy that I may bear a child.[4]

When men go out to find termites, which are much prized as food, they pray:

> O Grandfather, may what is mine be in abundance![5]

Before a man goes out hunting, he will offer such a prayer as:

Mbali, tell my Father, that he give me much game to kill.[6]

These simple prayers are not without vestiges of art. They say what has to be said in a very few words and concentrate on an immediate need. They not only have their own structure and balance but sometimes use repetition, which is, as we shall see, fundamental to primitive song. Though they are not sung but spoken, they have their own satisfying effects of sound, and to this degree they anticipate poetry.

Such prayers contribute to song not only by providing it with the kind of matter for which it is well suited, but by having a self-contained unity which is capable of being made to conform to a musical tune. They approach song as they increase in length and formality. So a woman of the Yamana laments the deaths which have befallen her family:

Much water did the old sisters weep for their father to Him
    above, alas!
So too their father wept many tears for the bay that mur-
    dered them.
Against these children He who is above bared his teeth, alas!
May it be given to us to make thy tears flow, alas![7]

In this the repeated "alas," *talauwaia,* and the parallelism in the structure almost qualify it to be called verse, and once such an order is given to words, song is likely to take advantage of it and to treat them in much the same way. Indeed we can almost see how this happens. The Pygmies, who recite prayers before hunting, sometimes sing them as songs to the accompaniment of a dance. A very simple example shows its affinity to spoken prayers:

> Spear, spear, strike home, spear, spear,
> Strike home, *öioö-o, öioö-o,* strike home.[8]

Speech passes into song because it has been conditioned for recitation and made to conform to a certain tone and balance. When it is added to the rhythmical action of the dance, it is absorbed into the complex unity. It looks as if song comes into existence when a rite based on rhythmical movement calls for something more explicit to make its purpose plain, and this need is satisfied by appropriating words from the art of prayer, which in its essential purpose is not very far removed from dramatic actions intended to influence gods and spirits.

Primitive song, which is born from an elemental dramatic rite, is a communal activity. In a world where ceremonies provide a main focus for social life, song is among the chief of them, and is used both to communicate with the supernatural and to express joy or grief or other strong emotions. Choral song is the more popular form in most primitive societies, and though certain songs may be reserved for men or women or children or select initiates, there is in principle nothing which bars any section of the community from taking part in song as such. It is therefore to some degree the voice of a common consciousness, of what a whole society or a representative part of it feels on certain occasions, and we have no reason to doubt that it really does this, or that all its participants share its moods and accept its assumptions. This is of course true of modern singing, especially when it is done for pleasure, but primitive song implies a higher degree of shared assumptions. First, the singers are all disciplined and shaped to the same kind of life and share all its interests and its needs. Distinctions of class or profession or wealth do not exist, and what concerns one will concern all. Secondly, the small numbers which compose a primitive social unit know everything about one another, and, except in certain religious rites, there is nothing that can be called seclusion or privacy, even in the most intimate matters. Thirdly, primitive man seems to be less conscious than civilized man of himself as a separate individual or of his own inner thoughts. Of course he has his own feelings and his own ideas, but he is not acutely aware of his severance from his fellows. Indeed, in most societies he feels that he is inextricably tied to them, whether by common descent or a common totem or some less easily defined relation. It is natural for him to express this feeling through communal song, which enhances and increases it and makes it more real. Though he does not belong to a class of being different from ourselves, he is more aware of his closeness to others, and of this awareness song is an expression. If he feels that something calls for celebration, he assumes that it must be shared with them, if only because it will give pleasure and create confidence all round. There is no question of song being confined to a clique or a class; for such do not exist, and the performers and the audience represent both more and less than themselves—more, because they speak confidently for their social unit; less, because they merge their private, individual feelings into a general mood which they share with others. Such conditions impose their character on song and are responsible for certain features in its creation.

Much primitive song is traditional, passed from generation to generation, even when its first purpose has been forgotten and its words are no longer fully understood. Such songs are held in special esteem and are usually in the keeping of medicine men or shamans or elders who are respected for their powers and their knowledge. It is quite impossible to judge the age of these songs, though a song such as the Australian Laragia sing about the sea must have been composed before they were driven from it by English colonists. Signs of age may be detected in the use of words which are now treated as a special language for song but are in all probability archaic survivals from the past. Such are found in the songs of the Dama, the Gabon Pygmies, the Australians of Arnhem Land, and the Aranda. They enhance the dignity of the singing and convey the air of a special occasion. Yet though such songs may be changed or corrupted with time, they must once have been composed by individuals, whose work they ultimately are. No song, however simple, is the work of a company, still less of some mysterious *Volksgeist* or common consciousness. Among some peoples, notably the Aranda, traditional songs now almost hold the field, and the art of composition has fallen into disuse. But this is a sign of decay and is probably due to the depressing effects of foreign influence, which drives native tribes to treasure their old possessions and to shrink from adding to them. But elsewhere new songs are still composed, and though it is not easy for primitive singers to explain their creative processes, we know enough about them to see what happens.

Primitive songs are of course composed without any help from writing, but this does not mean that they are always improvised on the spur of the moment. Some certainly are, and a few examples are known to have been. They are responses to some unexpected and surprising event which calls for song as a vent for troubling emotions. Since all primitive peoples are trained in song from childhood and practise it constantly, there is nothing astonishing in their ability to burst into it without notice. An Australian of the Wurunjerri tribe composed a song in a boat when he was going to a ritual ceremony, and, on his own admission, the thought of it came to him "not in sleep as to some men but when tossing about on the waves in his boat with the waters jumping round him." The song tells of this situation:

> It capsizes me, it strikes me,
> The wind blows hard over the long stretch of sea,
> It strikes hard, it hits hard, it strikes,
> It dashes me up, it strikes me.[9]

The song is the immediate reflection of an exciting adventure, and it formed itself in the singer's mind not only because he was in danger but because he had been brought up on song and burst naturally into it. Something of the same kind happened to a woman of the Ituri Pygmies, who entered her hut and found that her small child had disappeared. She at once burst into a charming and touching quatrain:

> O Mephimanza, O Mephimanza,
> What have I done to you?
> Come back again and let me
> Rock you in your little swing.[10]

She sings of a trouble which is peculiarly her own, and sets her individual imprint on her song. In these few words she conveys her anguish at an unforeseen loss and her guilty apprehension that it is her own fault. The very force of her anguish makes her sing, and her words have the strength which comes from her anxiety and fear. In singing she not only finds relief for herself but lets her neighbours know what has happened, so that they may help her in her need. In a different spirit, but with much the same immediacy, an Eskimo sings of an accident which has befallen him when out hunting, and he is no less personal:

> I want to laugh because my sledge is broken.
> Because its ribs are broken, I want to laugh.
> Here at Talaviuyaq I struck hummocky ice, I met with
>   an upset,
> I want to laugh. It is not a thing to laugh at.[11]

The singer gives an exact account of his feelings, in which the absurdity of the situation dominates, but he cannot really think the accident funny. Such songs as these are, in Paul Valéry's phrase, *vers donnés*. They make on us an impact as immediate as they must have made on their inventors when they first thought of them, and they show how fully a man feels a situation and how readily he is able to express his feelings.

Not all songs are likely to have been composed in this way. The Andamanese are known to mature songs in their minds until they are ripe for performance at some suitable occasion, and though the songs are always very short, their preparation may take days, while the singer decides what to include and what to exclude from a form which presents a nice challenge by its very exclusiveness. The long songs of the Djanggawul cycle in Arnhem Land must have called for very careful composition, and not all need come from the same singer. Not only are they of an unusual length but they deal with sacred matters which must be treated with caution and precision, and time is needed to make sure that every point is in order. But our best evidence on primitive composition, which in our phraseology calls for both inspiration and art and forces the singer to make the most of what comes unexpectedly to him, may be seen in some words which the Eskimo Orpingalik, well known both as a hunter and a song-maker, said to Knud Rasmussen:

'Songs are thoughts, sung out with the breath when people are moved by great forces and ordinary speech no longer suffices. Man is moved just like the ice-floe sailing here and there out in the current. His thoughts are driven by a flowing force when he feels joy, when he feels fear, when he feels sorrow. Thoughts can wash over him like a flood, making his breath come in gasps and his heart throb. Something like an abatement in the weather will keep him thawed up. And then it will happen that we, who always think we are small, will feel still smaller. And we will fear to use words. But it will happen that the words we need will come of themselves. When the words we want to use shoot up of themselves—we get a new song.'[12]

This is an admirably candid, exact, and percipient account of the creative process by a poet who knows how it works in himself. The unconscious mind matures words until the moment when they rise into the conscious and seem to come ready-made to it. Orpingalik knows his business and can afford to rely on this method of composition. But he is specially fortunate and gifted, and not all Eskimo singers would agree that this is how song comes. Some of them are aware that it is not enough to wait for words to form themselves into a song, that, however forcibly they may come from within himself or even from dreams or spirits, they may still have to be put in order and tidied and made presentable if they are not to be below the proper standard. So Pluvkaq has put his thoughts about composition into an actual song and modestly doubts whether he has done as well as he might have:

> *Avayaja,*
> I know what I want to put into words,
> But it does not become orderly,
> It does not become worth listening to;
> Something that is well arranged,
> *Avayaja,*
> Something well worth hearing,
> Hastily to put that together
> Is often difficult.
> An awkward song, may be, I have put together.
> *Avayaja.*[13]

It is this sense of art and artistic control which gives strength and solidity to primitive song. The varied and often violent emotions which inspire it are subjected to discipline and made to obey an ideal of shapeliness and harmony. No doubt this is often enforced by the need to fit new words to the demands of a tune or a dance or a ceremony, but it is equally present when such a need is absent, and the singer is guided only by an idea of what will please his fellows and make them wish to hear his song. He must sing of something which they can take to their hearts and absorb and share. If he does this, his song will be passed from mouth to mouth and may, as sometimes happens in Australia, be adopted even by people who speak a different language and do not know what his words mean. Primitive song is an authentic form of art because of the trouble and respect given to its making, and these are given by the individual song-maker, who has indeed his audience or his colleagues in his mind but none the less speaks from his own experience as he himself understands it. In doing this he enriches the resources of his society and is honoured for it.

Pluvkaq, who matched his keen insight into the creative process with an ability to express himself in effective words, understood the difficulties of composition and retails with illuminating clarity his efforts to make a song and the obstacles which hinder him:

> I wonder why
> My song-to-be that I wish to use,
> My song-to-be that I wish to put together,
> I wonder why it will not come to me.

At Sioraq it was at a fishing hole in the ice,
I could feel a little trout on the line,
And then it was gone.
I stood jigging.
But why is it so difficult, I wonder?
When summer came and the waters opened,
It was then that catching became so hard:
I am not good at hunting![14]

Composition is here not so much illustrated by fishing as identified with it, on the assumption that both are examples of a single kind of activity which calls for practised skill and often ends in disappointment. Pluvkaq seeks for a song just as he plays a trout, and when he thinks he has caught one, it eludes him. Such a task is tricky enough when he has already something to play, but it is much more elusive when he has the whole open sea, or the whole range of possible subjects, at his disposal. In another song he uses the same method to stress how, in making a song, he is unable to do what he wishes:

It is lovely to put together
A bit of a song,
Avaya,
But I often do it badly, *avaya*!
It is lovely to hunt,
But I seldom shine like a burning wick
On the ice, *avaya*!
It is lovely to have wishes fulfilled,
But they all slip past me!
It is all so difficult, *avayaya*![15]

Pluvkaq has no abstract vocabulary to describe the creative process, but his identification of it with hunting is flawlessly apt and conveys just the mixture of ambition and frustration which he has in mind. No man would speak in this way if he had not a firm conviction that the composition of a song is a demanding task which calls alike for luck and skill.

These examples show that the Eskimos are perfectly able to think about even so mysterious a process as poetical composition and have their own entirely acceptable ideas on it. Other primitive peoples provide no information so enlightening as this, and we may well feel that among the Eskimos the art of song has received more special attention than elsewhere. Indeed, though some other primitives take credit to themselves for composing songs, they tend to attribute more power than Orpingalik or Pluvkaq to external influences. Australians often attribute their songs to ancestors who have appeared to them in dreams, and though this still leaves much to be done, it implies a greater trust in unseen sources than the Eskimos allow. At the opposite extreme from them is a remarkable case from the Selk'nam. A medicine man, or *xon,* called Tenenesk, would summon his spirit to his aid, and this might take a long time, during which he would sing to a tune, thought to be of his own composition, sequences of meaningless sounds such as *lolololo . . . hoiyoiyoiyoi . . . yeiyeiyeiyei.* After a time he would announce that he had done his own task and his spirit would take over from him. He then sang a series of sentences which make perfectly clear sense but, in the one example known to us, have no very clear connection with one another, except as a brief conspectus of certain important figures in the mythical history of the Selk'nam. In turn Tenenesk mentions Kran, who is the child of the sun and embodies some of its powers; the Howenh, ancestors who went to sleep and thereby brought death into the world; Kwanyip, the father of the race; the Caskels, who were monstrous cannibals and the deadly enemies of the Selk'nam; and Canem, which is not quite on a level with the other figures, since it is the power of medicine men to harm others and is here personified as a supernatural being:

> All our forefathers were very mighty,
> One of them was a great magician.
> Kran is the strongest.
> We people in the south know
> How everything happened in the old times.
> The land here is that of the Selk'nam.
> The Howenh lived here before.
> Kwanyip came from the north,
> Ever he drove before him a herd of guanoco.
> He overcame the Caskels.
> Canem was a wicked woman.
> Many wrong things our magicians do
> When they take service with a Canem.
> Through the magicians were many Selk'nam killed.[16]

This looks very much like automatic utterance, coming from a man who has hypnotized himself into a trance, and in its certain themes, which are very much the concern of a medicine man, rise to the surface and break into bald, brief sentences. What he sings is hardly a poem and certainly not a work of art, but it illustrates what may happen when the conscious control on composition is relaxed. Tenenesk believed that his spirit spoke through him, and that in his state of trance he would not be able to improve on its words, even if he thought it right to do so. Their strength is that they come from his inner being and illustrate the melancholy with which he, like other Selk'nam, looks on his vanishing world. Yet though we might expect this kind of thing to happen quite often, it is very much of an exception. The unconscious mind plays a large part in primitive song, especially through images which come from dreams, but the song-maker seldom surrenders himself completely to it. He is usually an artist who believes that words must be shaped and ordered by choice and judgment.

The task of composition, which is treated with such care and seriousness, is helped, as in all oral poetry, by the existence of formulas, of ready-made phrases, which a man is entitled and even expected to use when he makes a song. They are respected because they have been tested by time and have proved their worth, and though they may not meet every possible need or challenge, they are undeniably useful in handling recurrent themes. So, when the Bushmen address the new moon, they tend to begin in the same way:

> Ho, moon lying there!

When the Dama lament their dead, they stress their sense of loss by singing:

> When will you arise?

An Eskimo will address his familiar spirit as:

> Little child like a Tuneq,

Or, in speaking magic words over a child or a dog, use a phrase which stresses its tender age:

> See, its heart
> Tastes of luscious lubber,
> Really tastes of luscious lubber.

Of course such formulas may do no more than state a familiar theme which can be expanded as the singer chooses, but even in this they help him in so far as they strike the note which he is to maintain and indicate what kind of song he is about to sing. They are used extensively in the Djang-gawul cycle of songs from Arnhem Land. There the words are connected with a long and complex rite and gain a special solemnity from it, and no doubt their repetition also serves a ritual purpose. But they none the less help the composer in his difficult task of constructing one scene after another in which events of the same kind take place. With very slight verbal alterations themes are often repeated. The mythical ancestors move their buttocks and their hips as they paddle their canoe; the red feathers of the parakeet are caught by the rays of the setting sun; the sun sets behind Milingimbi; water rises from the ground splashing and bubbling; flying foxes cry out from trees; the heat of the sun beats on various sacred emblems. With such aids at his disposal the singer is guided and sustained in his task. He knows what is expected of him, and with support of this kind he can proceed to make his own variations on traditional themes.

Once a song has been composed, it has to be communicated and taught to others. On religious occasions the main part is usually taken by elders who are the repositories of tradition and able to instruct others what to do, but secular songs cannot claim such an importance and yet are brought into circulation. One influential way of doing this may be illustrated by the practice of the Andamanese. A man composes a short song, from three to five lines in length, and when he thinks that it is ready, he sings it to his fellows, and at the end of it repeats the last line, which they pick up and repeat after him as often as their fancy wills. The whole song may then be repeated in the same way on this or any other occasion. A very simple example tells of hunting turtle and fixes on the exact moment when the hunter and his companion, who poles his canoe for him, reach the reef where the turtle come to feed. This is the thrilling crisis of their search, and the song-maker concentrates his words on it:

> This is the right place, there are his breakers,
>   therefore I stop.
> This is the right place, there are his breakers.
> He poled for me slowly,
> *He poled for me slowly.*[17]

This is illuminating in more than one respect. The song-maker is also the song-leader and takes the chief part in the performance. He says the most important words, while his last line is repeated after him as a refrain by the rest of the company. Primitive song is commonly performed in this way. The leader is responsible for most or all of the words, while the others accompany him with rhythmical actions. Sometimes the leader dances, sometimes he does not. In Eskimo dance-songs the singing is done by one or two people, while the rest confine themselves to the dance. In laments of the Euahlayi of New South Wales the main work of singing is done by a man, while women mourners wail at intervals during his song. The part played by the leader is settled by the need to have someone who knows the right words, but it may be derived from the way in which the song-maker makes his song known to others and enables them to join in it. Because he teaches it in this way, this is the way in which it is subsequently performed. Even if the leader has not actually composed the song but merely learned it, he still maintains the part which properly belongs to the song-maker.

This manner of composition also explains a feature of primitive song which is by no means confined to it and has a very long history in quite other settings—the refrain. In origin the refrain is that part of a song which the singer composes for the company to sing. It must have its own attraction and may to some extent contain the kernel of his theme. In the Andamanese example it draws attention to an essential point in hunting turtle—the moment when the hunter reaches the reefs and care must be taken not to frighten the prey; so the boatman poles slowly. The words sung only by the song-man anticipate the refrain and are closely connected with it, but their main task is to create interest and prepare the way for it. The refrain need not be kept to the end of a stanza; it may equally come at the beginning and give some hint of what the song is about, and then be repeated after it. Such refrains are to be found in most parts of the world and have their accepted place in almost all poetry, even if few remember that their original function was to bring others into a song which an individual has composed and in which he takes a chief part. They assert the communal character of poetry and belong to its choral performance. That is why they are common even in forms so relatively advanced as the Provençal *balada* and the English ballad, both of which are ultimately dance-songs in which the performers claim a share more substantial than mere dancing but less than the whole burden of recitation.

The elementary refrain found in Andamanese songs has its parallel in other countries, even in Tasmania, but it easily grows into something longer and more elaborate. Instead of a single stanza with a repeated refrain, a song may consist of several stanzas, each of which is followed by a constant refrain. A simple example is an Eskimo dance-song from the Coppermine River, and in it the main stanzas are sung by the leader, while all the dancers sing the refrain:

> He constantly bends it, he constantly sends it
> straight,
> The big bow, he constantly sends it straight.

He constantly bends it,
He constantly bends it.

Just as he seeks well for words in a song,
The big bow, he constantly sends it straight.

He constantly bends it,
He constantly bends it.

He constantly bends it as he walks along,
In summer as he walks along.

He constantly bends it,
He constantly bends it.

It is clearly easy to shoot big birds,
As he carries his pack walking along.

He constantly bends it,
He constantly bends it.[18]

The main theme is the hunter's bow, and while the stanzas speak of this from slightly different angles, the refrain sticks to a single point upon which the stanzas also touch. The leader, who illustrates the use of the bow by various gestures, sets the theme for his companions who dance as he does so. There is one main theme, and the whole poem makes small variations on it.

This art can be greatly extended and elaborated, and the natural tendency is for the refrain to become less important as the stanzas extend their scope. The more important an occasion is, the more the leader himself will have to sing, while his companions may do little more than give mild support. Among the Gabon Pygmies hunting the elephant is a primary activity, which is extremely dangerous and calls for extensive preparations, both practical and spiritual, beforehand. The gods of the forest must be appeased, and the elephant itself must be subjected to magical incantations to bring it into the hunters' power. So before setting out on such a hunt the Pygmies sing a song remarkable for its sense of a brave occasion and its expert knowledge of what lies ahead:

On the weeping forest, under the wing of the evening,
The night, all black, has gone to rest happy;
In the sky the stars have fled trembling,
Fireflies which shine vaguely and put out their lights;
On high the moon is dark, its white light is put out.
The spirits are wandering.
Elephant-hunter, take your bow!

Elephant-hunter, take your bow!

In the frightened forest the tree sleeps, the leaves are
    dead,
The monkeys have closed their eyes, hanging from branch-
    es on high.
The antelopes slip past with silent steps,
Eat the fresh grass, prick their ears attentively,
Lift their heads and listen frightened.
The cicada is silent and stops his grinding song.
Elephant-hunter, take your bow!
Elephant-hunter take your bow!

In the forest lashed by the great rain,
Father elephant walks heavily, *baou, baou,*
Careless, without fear, sure of his strength,
Father elephant, whom no one can vanquish;
Among the trees which he breaks he stops and starts
    again.
He eats, roars, overturns trees and seeks his mate.
Father elephant, you have been heard from afar.
Elephant-hunter, take your bow!
Elephant-hunter, take your bow!

In the forest where no one passes but you,
Hunter, lift up your heart, leap, and walk.
Meat is in front of you, the huge piece of meat,
The meat which walks like a hill,
The meat which makes glad the heart,
The meat that will roast on the hearth,
The meat into which the teeth sink,
The fine red meat and the blood that is drunk smoking.
Elephant-hunter, take your bow!
Elephant-hunter, take your bow![19]

The main text is sung by the leader, and the refrain by his
companions in the chase. Yet though the performance is
closely connected with the actual hunt and the song is not
sung simply for pleasure like the Eskimo dance-song, its
technique is essentially the same on a much ampler scale.
The greater elaboration is a matter not of principle but of
emphasis. The central theme is the hunting of the elephant
and all that this means; to this the refrain gives practical
support by telling the hunters to get ready.

Songs with refrains arise from the desire to combine individual performance with communal interest, and that no
doubt is why they are popular. They allow full play to the
creative song-maker and to the company whose feelings he

shares and expresses. But their existence does not exclude that of truly choral songs which are sung without any aid from a leader by a company engaged on a common task. Among the scanty remains of Tasmanian song is one of which the first editor gives a translation, which may indeed be questionable in places but probably gives the right sense on the whole. It is a song sung by women about hunting, and it is rigidly factual and precise:

> The married women hunt the kangaroo and the
>   wallaby,
> The emu runs in the forest,
> The boomer runs in the forest,
> The young emu, the little kangaroo,
> The suckling kangaroo, the bandicoot,
> The little kangaroo-rat, the white kangaroo-rat,
> The little opossum, the ring-tailed opossum,
> The big opossum, the tiger-cat,
> The dog-faced opossum, the black cat.[20]

This represents an entirely communal state of mind. Before going out to hunt, the women name the animals which they hope to find and kill in the forest. In this they are all equal, and there is no need for anyone to direct either the song or the hunt. A similar common consciousness, based on a common purpose, appears in a Dama prayer for rain:

> Father, bless us still!
> Father, reward us still!
> May the land have onions!
> May it have *ou*-berries!
> May it have ground-nuts!
> May the clouds still rain![21]

On such occasions there is no call for an individual to have a special part, since the words are easy enough for a company to learn and everyone is equally interested in obtaining a successful result. Yet on the whole such songs are not common. A song-leader is usually necessary if only because his part is not easy to play and calls for some skill in remembering words and performing the right actions with them. Without someone like him to control the activities the performance might go wrong, with dire results for all concerned.

Choral song develops its own characteristics just because it is sung by a company and has to be adapted to suit its members' capacities and requirements. The same is not true of solo-song, which is hardly less common among primitive peoples. Such songs come into existence when someone, moved by a sudden inspiration, bursts into song, or when an occasion, which is essentially personal, calls for an individual interpretation. They cover a wide range and include almost any subject which excites the emotions and calls for an outlet in musical words. They deal with the more intimate matters of family life, with affections and hatreds, with casting spells and breaking them, with instructions to children and cautionary tales, with all the accidents and incidents which primitive man and primitive woman meet in their daily struggle. They too have their full share of formulaic phrases, but unlike choral songs, they have much less formality. They are usually confined to a few lines, like a Dama lament for a dead girl:

> My husband's daughter is dead.
> Arise that I may suckle you.
> The milk will now be spoiled.
> Daughter of Daoseb, my daughter,
> Arise that I may kiss you.[22]

Or a Semang love-charm that accompanies a magical rite of pouring oil:

> Look, look Comrade!
> As this oil drips,
> Alone by yourself
> Approach towards me
> And yearn towards me
> As this oil spreads upwards.[23]

Nor have solo songs any very obvious structure. Even when they have a certain elaboration, they tend to lack the division into marked stanzas which we find in choral songs. Their interest is much less in their form than in their contents, and on this something will be said later.

Primitive song may, without straining the words, be divided with sacred and secular. The first deals with gods and spirits and aims at achieving something beyond its own performance; the second deals with human matters and aims at no more than being itself. Of course the two classes overlap, and it is not always easy to decide to which a song belongs, as, for instance, some songs, which look as if they were composed simply for the pleasure of description, turn out to be charms aimed at securing power over what they describe, while others, which have a fair share of the supernatural, do not in fact aim at influencing it but mention it as a normal background for human routine. Yet the distinction is fundamental; for it explains certain recurring features which might otherwise perplex us. It can of course exist in civilized countries, and might even be said to exist today, if we assume that hymns are instruments for influencing divine powers. But the dinstinction is not so sharp or so relevant for us as for primitive peoples. Hymns may be written for their own sake as exercises in poetical craft or as personal confessions, and in any case they form only a small part of modern song. In fact we tend to treat all poetry as if it had a single purpose, which is to provide the experience which comes from the use of words in a certain way. This is not the primitive attitude, and we must beware of assuming it when we examine primitive songs.

Sacred songs are, in the first place, intended to establish a relation with supernatural powers and to influence them in a direction desired by the singers. They are composed against a background of accepted beliefs, and use its assumptions to make themselves felt. Primitive man is surrounded by forces which he cannot control or understand, and he hopes that by finding the right words he may gain some hold on them. This applies equally to prospects for hunting and the weather, to birth and death, to puberty and marriage, to the growth of trees and plants, to the supply of animals and of water. Though he has a vast and precise knowledge of the natural world as he studies it in his search for food, he does not begin to understand how it works, and he turns to magic as a means to get what he wishes. Magic, in its essential form, aims at securing a result by means for which no scientific justification can be offered but which is believed to influence the powers who control phenomena. Songs of this kind may be among the most primitive known to us. Though it is natural for a man to sing about his own experience for its own sake and to seek no result from a song but relief or delight, it is clear that this is not indispensable to his existence, since he can display relief and delight in other ways. But if he is to control the unseen, he must have his own methods of doing so, and song is emphatically one of them, more effective perhaps than mere gestures, since it makes its purpose plainer and establishes a relation with gods and spirits by the most trustworthy means, which is through words. Indeed the primaeval character of such a song may be deduced from the extreme simplicity and shortness of some of its examples, which stand at the very beginning of poetry and are not yet fully emancipated from merely imitative action unaccompanied by words.

The different requirements of sacred song determine the manner of its performance. It may be attached to almost daily occasions, such as hunting, or to less regular occasions, such as marriage, birth, and death. It may equally be performed in mysterious circumstances at special seasons in connection with sacred emblems and rites, such as are common in Australia. On the whole the degree of its elaboration seems to vary with the rarity of its performance. Common occasions are treated with relatively simple words; choice occasions call for something more complicated, and the ritual songs of the Aranda and other Australians, fashioned for very special rites, are the most advanced primitive songs known to us. The difference of degree in the complexity of the words corresponds to a similar difference in the rites which they accompany and illustrate. Though there is nearly always a dramatic element in sacred songs, it can be greatly expanded and add almost a new dimension to them. Such songs differ from charms and prayers and are so closely tied to complex actions that they may be unintelligible without them and are in fact intended to explain them. More than this, while in charms and prayers the singers speak for themselves, whether individually or collectively, in ritual songs they act a part and present dramatic versions of their totems or mythical ancestors or other supernatural beings. This is to be seen in the totemic songs of the Aranda, in which there are many parts from totemic animals to divine beings, in the long cycles of ritual songs from Arnhem Land, in which the progress of mythical ancestors is acted and accompanied by explanatory songs, and in some songs of the Semang, in which men appear as divine or half-divine beings and identify themselves imaginatively with them. In all these, acting has an important place, and words are used not merely to express a personal or even a communal experience but to bring the singers into another order of being by making them perform actions which belong to it. In other words, the element of drama, which is implicit in primitive dancing and miming, reaches a new importance in a fuller, more truly dramatic poetry, in which the acting is essential for reasons of religion, and the words because they explain it. Such songs are much more objective than many primitive songs, and for this reason they stand rather apart. They are intended to secure a result, which is usually no less than the continued maintenance of life in man and nature, but this is not pursued from a personal angle or for an immediate, particular purpose. For this reason they are the ancient forerunners of both narrative and dramatic poetry, and we may see how both types emerge from them.

In north-eastern Arnhem Land the aborigines have a cycle of ritual songs concerned with mythical ancestors called the

Djanggawul. Since they are regarded as the source of every kind of life, and the ritual presents this as it is believed to have been in the beginning of things, the cycle is long and contains 188 songs. Each is more or less complete in itself and deals with only one theme at a time, though it may give as many as forty lines to it. The separate songs follow the order of the ritual and mark different stages in the journey, actions, and experience of the Djanggawul. The songs are accompanied by gestures of much variety and complexity. The participants, led by elders well acquainted with their task, paint their faces and bodies with patterns to indicate what parts they are playing, make much ado with ritual objects symbolizing procreation and fertility, and perform vigorous, illustrative actions. In this the beginnings of both narrative and drama are combined. But the cycle is not independent narrative, because it relies on acting to make itself clear, nor is it drama, since it describes as many scenes as it enacts, and the only dramatic parts are those of the Djanggawul themselves unaided by other actors. The setting is provided partly by ritual objects, partly by abundant and picturesque words, and the imagination is kept continuously at work in an effort to envisage the behaviour of the Djanggawul as the actors portray it. An art like this is closer to drama than to narrative, but out of it either or both forms could easily emerge.

Drama, as such, emerges when there is no element of narrative and the whole story or sequence of events is enacted by persons embodying certain characters, without any introduction from the poet or any help from him beyond the provision of words to be learned. Such a song moves in its own quarter of the imagination, and to primitive onlookers it suggests something outside their own circuits and personalities. Such is the art of dramatic song among the Semang. It is closely tied to religion and sung by actors who take the parts of minor deities called Chenoi, a higher god called Chemen, a shaman or *bidog,* who is present in a hut and is thought to be a tiger acting as an intermediary between gods and men, and a lesser Chenoi, who appears as a pheasant. The lines may be varied, and the form is not constant, but though there is room for a certain amount of improvisation and adaptation, the main character is kept, and we can see how religious drama sets to work in its most elementary stage:

Female Chenoi.
     Peak, navel of the world, greeting! I cling fast!

> Forthwith I spring up! I cling fast to the breast
> of the peak.
> We go upward to the sky-god through the abyss
> of the rambutans.

Male Chenoi.

> Greeting, head of my father! I rise at once
> upward.
> Father, come forth from inside the earth!

Bidog.

> I am the tiger Liwon, coming forth! Make way
> for my own!

Female Chenoi.

> What is the song? Where is the garland? Spin!
> I rise on high.
> To the peak's crest, high level of the sun's
> road, I rise on high.

Chemen.

> Clap your hands and rise up! Greeting! Father,
> I rise on high.

Bidog.

> Spin, spin colours of the smock, on the shore
> of the Sengo river.

Chemen.

> Father, father, the sun rises on its path,
> It goes through the folding doors, there! there!

Bidog.

> Surely I spin, spin, spin, surely I spin, spin, spin.

Female Chenoi.

> What says the teacher?
> The maiden Chenoi pant up the hill.

Pheasant Chenoi.

> We, maidens of the moon, fly straightway
> upward.[24]

This little play has its own setting, by the mountain Batu
Rib'm, which mean "pillar of heaven" and stands on the up-
per waters of the river Tadoh on the borders of Perak and
Kelantan. It is regarded as the road by which gods and
spirits ascend to heaven to the high god who dwells there.
The play brings men into contact with this divine activity.
Though the action tells more than the words, the words express its inner significance, as each actor takes a part and
the ascent of the Chenoi to heaven is indicated by spinning
imaginary threads in the air. The actors feel themselves introduced into the central mysteries of being, and it is not surprising that the whole occasion is of high rejoicing. Such a rite
is intended to set divine beings to work, but, in so far as it

gives delight and stirs the imagination to take part in it, it is drama. In it men move for a few moments in a celestial order and share something of its exhilaration and felicity.

In primitive song sacred themes play a large part, no doubt because primitive man is encompassed by so many mysteries which he wishes to master that he evolves his own technique of dealing with them, and among the best, in his judgment, is song. It is an enhanced art of words, and words are his chief instrument in forming a relation with the unknown. This means that shamans and medicine men have a large role in both the composition and the performance of songs. Since they claim to have a special knowledge of the supernatural and to receive information and even actual words in dreams, they have in sacred matters an advantage over their lay brethren. But this does not mean that singing is confined to them, as it certainly is not, or that sacred song is necessarily older than secular. It seems likely that once men began to sing words to music, they would use them for anything that concerned them, and there is no need to give historical priority to themes of the supernatural. Indeed the two kinds seem to exist happily side by side. It is true that our known examples of Andamanese songs are all secular, but this does not mean that sacred songs have never existed in the Andaman Islands. Though we may distinguish between sacred and secular songs by their difference of intention, to primitive peoples they seem very much alike, since the supernatural is so accepted a part of their existence that it demands the same attention as what is immediately present and practical. Indeed, the difference between them calls only for a slight adjustment of the mind from asking for something to happen to celebrating or lamenting it when it does. Each is closely related to the dance and uses words to illustrate rhythmical action. Song comes into existence whenever a need for it is felt, and this need is as likely to be connected with the commemoration of some ordinary action as with the desire to get something done through divine assistance.

Unlike sacred songs, secular songs do not fall into any very obvious classes. We can of course divide them into choral and solo, and sometimes it is helpful to do so. We can also divide them according to their subjects, and this may illustrate their range. But for our present enquiry we may perhaps note their more important points of difference from sacred songs. Though they are composed and sung in much the same way, they differ in their contents and their handling of them. Though sacred songs often have a personal note which reflects the outlook of the song-man, secular songs have this in a more emphatic degree and are often remarkably individual, the reflection of a marked personality. Nor is it hard to explain this. Unlike the sacred singer, who has to conform to belief and ritual, and to maintain a tone suitable to dealing with the supernatural, the secular singer is free to sing about anything which catches his fancy or stirs his emotions or is likely to interest his fellows. Though his experience is bound to be narrow by our standards, that does not prevent him from noticing keenly all manner of things in it, and though he may have to limit himself to a few lines, that does not mean that he will fail to hit the mark. On the contrary, it compels him to take care with what he says and make it as effective as possible in its own compass. That is why secular songs are rich in surprises. They often say something quite unexpected because it is just this which has excited the singer and made him feel that he must perpetuate it in words. He is not hampered by considerations that song must fall into certain categories, and though nearly all his work is lyrical in the sense that it tells something about himself, it can hardly be defined more closely. It is not so much a question of its differing from one people to another, as of wide differences in tone and temper which are permitted inside a single people. Secular song is an instructive ancillary to sacred because it shows that primitive man is capable of many moods and observations which would normally be stimulated by the need for charms or prayers or commentaries on ritual actions.

Though narrative poetry in any full sense seems to be lacking from primitive peoples and its place is taken by primitive drama, we can perhaps discern its first beginnings. Nearly all these peoples tell stories in prose about all manner of subjects, and sometimes these contain snippets of verse. The Eskimos have a variety of tales from religious myths to animal fables; the Bushmen tell stories to illustrate the behaviour of animals and men; the Gabon Pygmies illustrate nice points of conduct with pieces of verse in a setting of prose. When verse appears in a prose setting, there is no need to think that it is a late, corrupt survival from what was once entirely in verse. Rather the snatches of song are used to emphasize a particular point or to draw attention to something out of the ordinary. So in a Bushman tale, the quagga's children sing a song about their mother when she has been given poison, and pray that at least she may drink before she dies:

O poison,
O poison,
O poison,
O poison,

> O poison,
> Let the poison hold up
> Our mother's heart,
> That our mother may go to drink
> At the Neck-vulture pool.[25]

They sing it again when she goes to the pool, and then she drinks and dies. The song is a central point in a story which ends in the vengeance which the young quaggas take on the dogs who have poisoned their mother. It is not difficult to advance from this very primitive example to something more elaborate, as when the Gabon Pygmies with lively perception tell of characters and careers. So in a tale of a girl and three young men, each suitor is characterized in song. The first, whose name means "chimpanzee," is large and strong:

> He was called Se-khu,
> And all the women ran after him,
> He knew very well how to beat them.

The second, whose name means "arrow of the forest," is small and neat and gay:

> He was called Bébébili.
> He ran after all the girls.
> He knew well how to talk to them.

The third, whose name means some kind of poisonous toadstool, is renowned for his meanness:

> Okhuata was the third,
> He made the girls afraid.
> The girls guarded themselves when he came.[26]

The three young men raise the general question of what a suitor ought to be, and that is the purpose of the story, but it gets a special point from the emphasis given to the three different types by putting them into song.

This kind of art is a remote progenitor of objective, independent narrative in verse. If it is sometimes intentionally didactic, so is much early narrative; if it combines prose and verse, so does much other narrative in the maturer forms of saga and heroic tale. The move to an entirely narrative poetry has not been made by primitive man, but if its roots are to be found in these prose tales, it may have been helped by song to tell, if not whole stories, at least relevant episodes about spirits and mythical ancestors, as in the Djang-gawul cycle of Arnhem Land. There the mythical past is told dramatically in the first person by the ancestors, but in their speeches there is much material that would fall easily into narrative. Fully fledged poetical narrative appears among the earliest documents preserved to us, and it is possible that it came into existence when the kind of tale which was told dramatically in ritual songs was told objectively in verse because this was an ancient tradition in some parts of story-telling.

Both sacred songs, which aim at producing results in the known world, and secular songs, which aim at no such result, are authentic branches of poetical art. In both of them words are used with a special purpose, to state with an unusual force what the singer has to say, whether from external or from internal compulsion, and to put into words, which will catch the ears and minds of other men, something that must be said with emphasis and full attention. Indeed we may doubt whether even sacred songs would be composed without some inspiring impulse; for though this need not be purely artistic, it must conform to artistic demands and standards. In them we can detect the same kind of selection and energy which goes to the composition of secular songs, and we can hardly doubt that their makers are moved by a truly creative desire to make the most of something which presses urgently on them and demands to be fixed in memorable words. Though the contents of primitive poetry vary greatly from those of modern, its manner of composition is something which we can understand and recognize as related to what our own poets have told of themselves.

CHAPTER *3* *Technique*

SONG, according to our notions, consists of words sung by the human voice, but we have no right to assume that the first sounds used in songs were necessarily words in the strict sense of intelligible units of communication. Indeed it is unlikely that they were. Song begins with some sort of a tune, and to adapt real words to it is a separate and subsequent task which calls for considerable dexterity. A mere tune, if hummed, can still satisfy its performers, who feel that it expresses something quite adequately, and do not demand words to make it more explicit. In our own world the tune is usually regarded as more important than the words, which need not be remembered correctly and, when forgotten, can be replaced by meaningless sounds. We might expect song to begin with such sounds, and that it did so is confirmed by the practice of more than one primitive people. When Captain Charles Wilkes of HMS *Beagle* visited Tierra del Fuego in March 1838, the first inhabitants whom he met belonged to the Yamana. Two of his company visited them in their huts and received an unexpected greeting:

Their mode of expressing friendship is by jumping up and down. They made Messrs Waldron and Drayton jump with them on the beach, before entering the hut, took hold of their arms facing them, and jumping two or three inches from the ground, making them keep time to the following song:

> *Ha ma la   ha ma la   ha ma la   ha ma la*
> *O la la la la   la la la la la*[1]

These are meaningless sounds and seem to have been intended to convey welcome or surprise or delight. That this is the universal practice of the Yamana is clear from subsequent investigations. They have a number of songs, which have been fully recorded with their tunes, but not one of them is made of real words. They are made of unintelligible, emotive noises, which are repeated with a monotonous regularity to fill the space of a recurring tune. For instance, women and girls dance to such sequences of sounds as

> *ma-las-ta xai-na-sa ma-las-ta xai-na-sa*[2]

or

> *hau-a la-mas ke-te-sa hau-a la-mas ke-te-sa*[3]

This is the only kind of song which exists among the Yamana, and it has some notable characteristics. First, the sounds have no meaning whatsoever. There is no reason to think that they have been taken from a foreign language, since they seem to bear no resemblance in structure or phonology to any known language of South America. Nor are they likely to be an inheritance from the past, a relic of an old speech which has passed out of use. It is true that a number of South American tribes claim such an origin for their own meaningless verses and may be justified in so far as the verses are traditional and ancient, but there is no reason to think that this is the right explanation of them. The syllables used by the Yamana are emotive noises, which certainly have some sort of significance for those who sing them but not any intelligible meaning. They express a vague mood, which accords with the tune, but nothing more. Secondly, each set of such sounds is constant and tied not only to its own occasion or ceremony but to a fixed tune. There is no question of transferring them from one tune or occasion to another. They are established by custom and regarded as obligatory. Thirdly, a song of this sort, which is always extremely short and never longer than these examples, may be sung over and over again, whether it is tied to dances and games or to feasting by day and sitting up at night. Yet these are undeniably songs. They display in musical composition and singing a skill which they do not display in words. They play an integral part in the lives of those who sing them and whose relaxations are few, and they partake of the nature of ceremonial. This is a very primitive kind of song, and it represents a whole class of songs which have not attained to the dignity or the difficulty of real words.

We might of course regard the practice of the Yamana as an eccentricity, due to their long isolation in a very remote land. But this is not the case. Such meaningless sounds really look as if they were the earliest kind of song practised by man. There is in this an *a priori* probability. Such sounds are easier to fit to music than intelligible words are, and to a people conscious of musical effects they may even seem more appropriate in so far as they interpret a general temper but do not make it too particular. Once they have been fitted to tunes and consecrated by custom, they remain in use. There is, moreover, evidence that this is or has been the case elsewhere. The Selk'nam, who are neighbors of the Yamana but are said not to share their taste for singing, have indeed a few songs composed of intelligible words, but these are the monopoly of medicine men and not in common currency. They have also other songs, which are performed communally and in all main respects resemble those of the Yamana. For instance, in the morning they sing:

Ha-ra-xe-u-ka ha-ra-xe-u-ka ha-ra-xe-u[4]

and in the evening,

Hai-ce-rai-ya hai-ce-rai-ya hai-ce-hai-ce-rai-ya.[5]

Since the Selk'nam have little in common with the Yamana, it is significant that they too practise this art of meaningless sound, even if they sometimes use real words in other conditions for a different purpose.

Other primitive peoples also use such emotive sounds, not indeed throughout a song, but at irregular intervals as a kind of padding introduced at certain points. Some of these are obvious enough and play a useful part, as when the Eskimos use *unaya unaya* as a lament or *ayayaiya* to express excitement. More striking is the way in which the Veddas use two formulaic lines:

Tan tandinanan tandinane
Tanan tandina tandinane,[6]

which are unintelligible but used in intelligible contexts, often at the beginning or the end of a song. They resemble the sound-sequences of the Yamana in being fixed and preserved by convention, but differ in being applied to a variety of

subjects and occasions. They look like a survival from an
ancient art in which not words but emotive sounds were used,
and their preservation may be due not only to the innate
conservatism of primitive peoples but to the connection between such sounds and a tune which may be appropriate
for more than one subject.

That such emotive sounds were the first material for song
receives additional testimony from their use by peoples who
live at a higher level of organization than our primitives
but carry into their songs an unintelligible element. This is
particularly true of some American Indians who have a
number of songs composed entirely of such sounds. Their
practice may be illustrated by an Arapaho song connected
with the widely spread Peyote cult:

> ye no wi ci hay
> yo wi hay
> wi ci hay
> yo wi ci no
> wi ci ni
>
> (repeat from start)
>
> wi ni wi ci hay
> yo wi hay
> wi ci hay
> yo wi ci ni hay
> yo wi ci ni hay
> yo wi how
> wi ci hay
> yo wi ci no
> wi ni no wa.[7]

These songs are not related to the ordinary language of the
Arapaho and look like a conscious construction made on
recognizable principles, since each sound consists of a con-
sonant and a vowel, which is not the case with real
Arapaho words. Moreoever, some of these syllabic sequences
are to be found in the songs of other peoples who have different and apparently unrelated languages. This suggests that
such meaningless songs come from an ancient tradition and
have survived because of their connection with a religious
cult which is spread over a number of divergent tribes and
may go back to a time when they were more closely connected than now. This case becomes more probable when we find
that the Arapaho also have intelligible songs composed of
real words without any help from standardized noises. It looks
as if some American Indians once sang in the manner of the
Fuegians, but slowly gave up the practice except in connec-

tion with some ancient rites in which change was not welcomed. We might even go further and assume that such was once the practice in many of the aboriginal tribes of America and that geographical isolation has preserved it in its primaeval form among the Yamana. In any case, senseless sounds seem to be the most primitive kind of song. They anticipate later developments by making the human voice conform to a tune in a regular way, but the first step to poetry came when their place was taken by real words.

The change cannot have been swift or easy, and that is why some primitive song still keeps traces of the old, unintelligible element. But we can discern what happens. Since some of the shortest and simplest songs are charms or prayers, which are closely related to rhythmical, spoken prayers, like those of the Yamana, we may see in them the beginnings of the first truly poetical line. The problem was to bring into music words which have their own full meaning and even distinction, and though at first this may have been thought necessary only for superior occasions, once the idea took root vast possibilities lay ahead. In these songs the unit is the line, the short, single, condensed statement, which may be and often is repeated, but is complete in itself and forms the whole song. The Australian Kurnai, for instance, have several such songs. One, which is believed to drive away pain, was said by its singer to have been given to him by his father in a dream and announces simply:

> Show your belly to the moon,[8]

with a very strong emphasis on the last word. A Kurnai headman, who was credited with the gift of stopping the furious west winds which prevented his people from climbing the tall trees in the forest, did it by singing:

> Carry a bond for the west wind.[9]

This is very much what we find among other peoples. The Bushmen, who hunt the blue crane, ascribe to it songs about itself on the supposition that its head, with its white feathers, looks like a splinter of stone, and when it runs away it sings:

> A splinter of stone which is white,[10]

and this is used as a charm by which the hunter hopes to catch it. It must be repeated three times and may be repeated much more often if it is thought necessary. Much the same kind of thing happens among the Eskimos in weather incantations. If they wish the sun to come out, they sing:

The sun up there, up there,[11]

and if a storm is raging, they try to entice its spirit into themselves:

Man outside, please come in, please enter into me.[12]

Like the charms of the Bushmen, these too are repeated, and they show their closeness to the most primitive kind of song by the addition of such meaningless sequences as *ai yai ye yi yai ai ye*. Nor is this kind of song confined to charms and prayers. Once it has come into existence, there is no reason why it should not be extended to secular topics, and this is just what we find. The Dama sings to his bow:

O the *ha*-tree, O the hard tree![13]

The Bushmen have what they call the jackal's song:

Canter for me, little jackal, O little jackal, little jackal.[14]

In these there is still some lingering element of magic, but they show how the song moves from an immediately useful purpose to an element of art and pleasure. Though these single lines are made more emphatic by repetition, which is the normal rule with them, they show how verse begins. The single line is the first, indispensable beginning of real song. What has hitherto been expressed only in the spoken word is transferred to a tune, and once the transference, with all that it implies in rhythm, has been made, poetry begins its career. The earlier tradition of meaningless sounds may linger on as an adjunct, but it no longer holds pride of place, and a real art of words has started on its career.

If this provides the first step forward in the growth of song, the next step comes when the unit spreads beyond the single line. If the song has no dance-accompaniment, the expansion may be due simply to a desire to give rather more emphasis to a theme than is possible with mere repetition. Such is the case with a song composed by a Bushman, whose tobacco has been stolen by a dog. It consists of a very simple theme expressed three times in the same form but with a tiny addition at the end:

Famine it is,
Famine it is,
Famine it is here.[15]

The variation adds almost nothing to the sense, but shows that the singer feels a need to complete the rhythmical cadence of the song by winding it up with this almost imperceptible climax. In rather the same way an Eskimo weather-incantation repeats its main theme and adds a small variation to it:

> Clouds, clouds,
> Clouds, clouds down below,
> Clouds, clouds,
> Clouds, clouds down below.[16]

Once the right to vary a theme has been established, songs take advantage of it and move towards a greater richness of content, by introducing slightly more elaborate variations. So another Eskimo weather-incantation says:

> Only come, only come,
> Only come, only come,
> I stretch out my hands to them thus,
> Only come, only come,[17]

and a Bushman song from a tale about lion-slayers goes a step farther by giving not only its main point but a background to it:

> O my younger brother, *hn*,
> My younger brother's wind feels like this,
> When he seems to have killed a lion.[18]

Small though these additions and expansions are, they indicate how the single line ceases to be a self-sufficient unit and makes way for a larger unit in which we may discern the first signs of a stanza.

Once this process begins, there is no reason in theory why it should stop, why lines should not be piled up in long sequences to form long poems. So long as words are not attached to a tune or a dance, this is certainly possible, and how it could happen we can see from a prayer of the Yamana, which was not sung but spoken and has a deliberate, formal balance as it unfolds its complaints:

> Why again do you keep watch, O Mighty One, alas,
> So that I cannot enjoy fat food?
> Why up there are you angry with all of us, my Father, alas?
> Now we show you that we also are not content with you, our Father, alas!
> Will He who is above leave my son, alas,
> After He who is above has taken away my daughter, alas?[19]

Though the lines are on the whole independent of one another, the whole effect is of an ordered series in which each point leads without effort to another. The speaker has a feeling for the shape of sentences and says his piece with power and dignity. But though this is easy enough in a spoken prayer, it is not so easy in words composed for song and dance. Here the words are limited and controlled by the scope of the music and the gestures, and though no doubt some adaptation is possible, the natural solution is to confine the words to obvious and necessary limits. What happens is that an idea is presented and then developed in stages, each of which calls for separate expression in a new line. So the Gabon Pygmies, who regard a spider called *rri* as sacred, sing of it:

> *Rri*, your threads are well stretched,
> Clever hunter, your threads are well spun,
> *Rri*, you are sure of abundant food,
> Spirit, be kind to me,
> Grant that, like *rri*, my chase is lucky.[20]

So a woman of the Dama laments her dead husband:

> The father, a tall young man,
> High grown like a tree,
> Lies there and speaks no more.
> No man supports a widow.
> The children of men exist once only.
> The father never smiled on a widow.
> Now that he is dead, whom can I get?
> At him alone people looked.
> To what land shall I now go?[21]

In comparison with the Pygmy song this is complex and heavily loaded. In her grief the widow releases her pressing, crowding thoughts, and her song reveals the tumult in her mind. None the less the sequence of thoughts, each fitted into a single line, is clear enough and proclaims the desolation of her loss. Even for practical purposes the same technique may be useful, as in an Eskimo charm to heal wounds:

> You, who are like a ringed plover,
> You, who are like a wild duck,
> The surface here
> Full of wounds,
> Full of cuts,
> Go and patch it.[22]

In addressing a spirit, the singer first identifies him by the shapes which he takes, and then tells him what to do. It is neat and coherent and does all that is asked of it. In such songs the line is still the fundamental unit, and the singer composes in sequence as many lines as he needs. The length of the line is determined by the tune, which may be an old tune, to which new words have to be fitted, or a new tune, which may form itself in the singer's mind in close relation to the words but still must have its own character and attraction.

This kind of structure extends beyond short songs and can be applied to more substantial pieces than those already quoted. When the song-man is concerned with a single subject and secures variety by approaching it from several angles, it is natural that he should provide his approaches with such a formality as is secured by keeping the lines separate but connecting them by slight repetitions, and so preventing his song from being too discontinuous in shape and contents. So the Semang sing of the *tepus* or wild ginger:

> The stem bends as the leaves shoot up,
> The leaf-stems sway to and fro,
> To and fro they sway in divers ways,
> We rub them and they lose all their stiffness,
> On Mount Inas they are blown about,
> On Mount Inas, which is our home,
> Blown about by the light breeze,
> Blown about is the fog, blown about is the haze,
> Blown about are the young shoots,
> Blown about is the haze of the hills,
> Blown about by the light breeze,
> It nods upon the hills,
> It nods upon the hills of Inas,
> Hills of Beching, hills of Siong,
> Hills of Malau, hills of Kuwi,
> Hills of Mantan, hills of Lumu,
> Upon every mountain is our home.[23]

As the song proceeds and adds new pieces of information about the wild ginger and the places where it grows, each item gets its own mention and a line to contain it, but the whole is held together by the repetition of words and themes from one line to another. The art of this poem is more conscious and more adroit than the lament of the Dama woman. Not only are its separate elements connected in a single subject, but they are firmly presented as so being.

This technique may be extended to subjects which are in their very nature complex in that they deal not with a static situation but with a developing action. A Vedda song, which is said to have been sung by a mother to her children who were frightened at the coming of a thunderstorm, works in its own way to show the confusion and anxiety of the mother's thoughts:

> Darling, darling,
> There you see the wind and the rain coming
> From outside the Seven Seas.
> See the two of them.
> See, brother, thunder and lightning coming from toward
>   the sea.
> It is getting bad.
> My body is losing strength.
> Let us two go to the Rajawala cave.
> No, no my two princes,
> It is not possible to go there; stay.
> O lovely princes, in the forest are spirits and gods.
> Are we not staying in the palace at night?
> The sky is getting dark, the earth is getting dark.
> Are not *kon* fruits falling at Enagal and Malagala?
> Let us go to the Rajawala cave.[24]

This is more excited and more spasmodic than the Semang song, but even in her troubled state the Vedda singer builds up her themes in a regular enough sequence, which is true to her own shifting thoughts, and makes a series of points in more or less separable sentences, each of which gets a line to itself. Though it is not easy to follow the sudden leaps of her thoughts, at least she sets them in order and gives to each enough space to make it effective. Indeed, it is surprising how the woman's tangled emotions are forced into this simple pattern, which certainly gives to each point an emphasis and an interest of its own.

The maintenance of the line as an individual unit seems to be the normal practice of any primitive song which is not accompanied by a dance and tied to its movements. It may be seen even when we might expect a more elaborate subject-matter to call for a more flowing manner. But though the aboriginal Australians of north-eastern Arnhem Land have ritual songs which may contain as many as forty lines, they still keep this same structure. Each line carries a considerable weight of meaning, and because it is accompanied not by the repeated movements of a dance but by an ever-changing series of acts of mimicry, the rhythmical unit remains the single line. A short example from the cycle will illustrate its general manner. The mythical ancestors, called Djanggawul, are still in their canoe at sea and speak of what they mark around them:

> Paddling we hear a sound;

A fish jumped to the water's surface;
A catfish! a sawfish! For us that fish jumps!
A flying fish, making a noise as it jumps, splashing the water . . .
A sawfish beside us; for it hears the sound of our canoe, the canoe of the Djangguwal.
Fish jumping! Sawfish, splashing the water with a sound.[25]

This is a highly developed example of primitive song. It differs from the short elementary pieces in the length of its lines, its marked development and movement from one theme to another, the clarity with which it presents each detail. Yet it is a natural evolution from the most simple forms and shows its affinity with them. In it each line is more or less a self-contained grammatical unit, and a substantial poem is formed from a succession of such lines.

This system of construction reveals its primitive character in more than one respect. The lines, which are more or less independent units, can often be shuffled about and arranged in different orders. The singer who learns them is not bound to present them in the same order if their sense is not seriously disturbed by his presenting them otherwise, and he may add to them or detract from them if he feels like it. Even when such lines have a ritual character, they are not absolutely fixed, and variations of a minor kind are permissible. On the other hand, this lack of order comes much more naturally to primitive peoples than to more advanced because of the nature of their language. Primitive speech has its glimmerings of syntax and is able to express some matters with delicate precision, but it is never so highly organized as an inflected language like Greek or an isolating language like Chinese. It does not need and does not use highly disciplined sentences, and one sentence flows easily into another because the functions of words are not fully differentiated. This means that the loose construction of a song is perfectly natural and a sign not of inferior art but of a less mature language. This is true in different ways of the Australians, the Bushmen, the Andamanese, and the Semang. It is less true of the Veddas, who have adopted Sinhalese, or of the Pygmies when they use a Bantu language. But there are indications that, apart from such radical changes as these, a primitive language may feel its way to a more closely knit unity and turn its paratactic methods to produce a more logical structure, in which the whole meaning is not clear until the end of a paragraph. This is quite common in Eskimo, where the interrelation of words is sufficiently firm to make it possible.

A simple example is a song composed by a boy called Norqaut when he was only ten years old:

> A caribou cow I brought down,
> For I felt that I wanted to kill a caribou cow,
> But my dear song-fellow is like a lazy dog,
> Like a listless hunter,
> But with the white bear
> And the black musk-ox
> On the firm ice one must practise to become their
>   equal.[26]

Here a well-articulated sentence coincides with the song. This is a more advanced technique than that of the line-upon-line method, and perhaps for that reason it is less common. But the use of it by Eskimos looks like another sign that their songs are more accomplished than those of most primitives. The song has its own development through a rather complicated idea, which is presented not through a series of fresh starts but in a single, unfolding movement.

Against these songs which go their own way without having to conform with the requirements of a dance, we may set those which are to some degree shaped by its demands. No dance, however simple, is kept easily within the limits of time taken to sing a single line, or sufficiently monotonous to be satisfied by its repetition. What happens is that the single line is extended not, as in unaccompanied singing, into a series of lines, but into something that is really a stanza. Such a stanza, which is not tied down to any fixed number of lines but usually varies from four to six, may be complete and final in itself, as we can see from an Eskimo women's dance-song from the Mackenzie River:

> My arms, they wave high in the air,
> My hands, they flutter behind my back; they wave
>   above my head like the wings of a bird.
> Let me move my face, let me dance, let me shrug
>   my shoulders, let me shake my body.
> Let me fold my arms, let me crouch down,
> Let me hold my hands under my chin.[27]

Since the subject of this is the actual dance, which can be dealt with in a short space, a single stanza is sufficient, and there is no need to go beyond it. It is perhaps an introductory song, which prepares the way for other songs to follow. This may not be the simplest possible kind of dance-song, but that it is elementary may be seen from like cases elsewhere. The Dama provide examples. One consists of two lines:

You people, who run to the dance, have the women
    gone before me?
Go then to the dance, you women dancers,[28]

and another of four:

> Aarob's lordship has crushed me,
> Manasses' lordship has crushed me.
> Whither should I flee?
> At what water-pool should I stop to drink?[29]

The Gabon Pygmies have a feast of the new moon, at which
women dance and sing to it:

> Moon, O mother moon, O mother moon,
> Mother of living things,
> Hear our voice, O Mother moon!
> O mother moon, O mother moon,
> Keep away the spirits of the dead,
> Hear our voice, O mother moon,
> O mother moon! O mother moon![30]

Such examples come from the dance at its simplest. Once
the form has been established, the desire to repeat its movements soon leads to the creation of more than one stanza
built on the same pattern, and when this happens we find
something parallel to the formation of longer units by the
accumulation of single lines into songs which are not accompanied by a dance.

A natural and convenient way to do this is to make the
couplet the unit of construction, coincident with a single
movement of the dance. This is done by the Australian Aranda,
the Eskimos, and the Dama, and in each much the same result follows. In a bird-dance the Aranda women, who deck
themselves for the part, sing:

> On the rolling stones, the maidens paint themselves with
>   new signs,
> On the small stones they paint themselves with new
>   signs.
>
> They dab signs along the stripes,
> They dab white spots along the stripes.
>
> Twins, who arise from a single group, sing loudly!
> Twins, who come from a single group, sing loudly!
>
> The maidens sing loudly,
> They sing so that the sound echoes from the sky.
>
> Like water-wagtails they wander about,

In the plain they wander about.

On the shore of the salt lake they stand,
Slim, like water-wagtails, there they stand.[31]

Each couplet is complete both in sense and in syntax, and
its extension into a longer poem is secured by accumulating
one couplet on another, rather as unaccompanied songs ac-
cumulate single lines. But the couplet, and not the line, is
used because it allows more scope for the dance and fits
more easily into its performance. What happens with a
couplet can equally happen with a quatrain or with a longer
unit. What matters is that the unit should be rhythmically
constant and suit the tune to which it has to be sung.

The requirements of the dance mean that songs tend to be
restricted in the development of their subjects but acquire
new elegances and subtleties of shape and manner. In general, they are much more static than unaccompanied songs
and turn round a pivotal point with no very great digression
from it. Formally, it is not enough for them to enjoy the
mere repetition of shape in their stanzas, and they introduce
ingenious devices by which this can be made more interesting. The unit may still be the couplet or the quatrain or a
longer stanza, but inside this there may be a break to
mark a change in the movement of the dance. The arrangement may then lead to a structure like that of the following
Eskimo song:

> Let me do nothing.
> The lamp up there flares constantly in spite of
>   everything.
> This too let me tell it:
> In search of meals also, my weapon,
> You get me no game.
>
> Let me do nothing.
> This big bow, this bow is constantly lifted.
> This too let me tell it:
> In search of bull caribou, my weapon,
> You send me home empty-handed.
>
> Let me do nothing.
> This big drum is constantly lifted.
> This too let me tell it:
> For singing dance-songs, my drum,
> You make me weary of lifting you.[32]

Here each stanza resembles the others not merely in its general design but in its interior balances. Each is divided into

two parts, and each part has its own formality. The movement of each stanza is nicely calculated to fit the repeated movements of the dance. In principle this technique can be extended so long as the dance is repeated, and limits are imposed only by the ability or wish of the singer to compose new verses. In practice such songs are never very long, perhaps because the essentially static nature of the main theme does not allow many variations, and there is not after all very much to say.

A dance-song is often accompanied by a refrain, for the reason that the main song is performed by a single singer, while the rest of the company, who perform the dance, cannot manage more than the refrain. This gives an additional variation to the procession of the stanzas, but, unlike the Andamanese refrains, it sometimes comes at the beginning of a song so that all can pick it up at the start. Thus two Eskimo women from Prince Albert Sound sing the main part of a song, while the rest of the company introduce it with a conventional refrain:

> *Let me sing against him, let me sing against him,*
> *Let me sing against him, let me sing against him.*

Though I walked on the ice down there,
Though I walked on the ice down there,
It did not seem like real ice.

Though I walked on the land down there,
Though I walked on the land down there,
It did not seem like real land.

Though I visited the lake down there,
Though I visited the lake down there,
It did not seem like a real lake.

Though I approached the ptarmigan down there,
Though I approached the ptarmigan down there,
It did not seem like a real ptarmigan.

Though I visited the woman down there,
Though I visited the woman down there,
She did not seem like a real woman.[33]

The refrain stands outside the main structure and does not do much for it, but it adds a slightly different theme to the restricted subject and sets it more clearly in its social place. To this degree it extends the use of the stanza as a unit. It still carries out its original function of associating other singers with the leader in the song, but it no longer keeps to the central theme or sets the note for the whole performance.

There is, then, a marked distinction between those songs which are not accompanied by a dance and those which are. The first class uses the line as a unit, the second the stanza. In its fullest forms, like those of Arnhem Land, the first displays a freedom of development not to be found in the second, which is tied to the dance and tends to be static in its handling of a subject. But the two kinds are not kept absolutely distinct, since both tend to be performed by the same singers, who naturally transfer the devices of the one kind to the other. We may, for instance, take a song from a Bushman tale, which is sung by an old woman:

> The old pot must remain,
> The old pot must remain,
> For I lie in the old hut.
>
> The old soupbrush must remain,
> The old soupbrush must remain,
> For I lie in the old hut.
>
> The old kaross must remain,
> The old kaross must remain,
> For I lie in the old hut.
>
> The old bed must remain,
> The old bed must remain,
> For I lie in the old hut.
>
> The old dish must remain,
> The old dish must remain,
> For I lie in the old hut.[34]

This song is undoubtedly intended for solo performance, and the regular refrain is simply a loan from the art of the dance-song. Yet it is entirely suitable here, as it stresses the desolation of the old woman who is unable to get away from her dwelling. Very similar is a lullaby sung by a Vedda mother over her child:

> My beautiful baby,
>
> What do you cry for, my child?
> Child, it is for the *uyila* yam.
> I will give you the whole of it.
>
> What do you cry for, my child?
> Child, it is for the *katawala* yam.
> I will give you the whole of it.

What do you cry for, my child?
Child, it is for the fat of the monitor lizard.
I will give you the whole of it.[35]

The only difference of structure between this and the Bushman song is that this has a small introductory phrase, and
even this would be suitable enough in a dance-song. Once such
forms are established, they naturally extend their uses, and
it is quite understandable that the technique of the dance-song
should invade that of the solo.

Though the main structure of primitive song is provided
by the stanza, if it is accompanied by a dance, and by the
single, self-contained line, if it is not, this does not prevent
the invention of other means to emphasize the shape of a
song or to bind its elements more closely together. Such devices help to give a song a greater elegance as well as to
underline its central theme. Among such devices repetition
has a high place. We have seen how whole lines are constantly
repeated by Eskimos and Bushmen, and no doubt the motive
for this is to draw closer attention to them. A more subtle
device is the repetition of a single word at the beginning or
end of a line throughout a whole song. This may, of
course, be simple and obvious, as when the Bushmen dance
in honour of the new moon and sing to it, since it is thought
to send rain:

> New moon, come out, give water for us,
> New moon, thunder down water for us,
> New moon shake down water for us.[36]

By repeating the same words at the beginning and the end
of each line the prayer gains in dignity and coherence. The
matter in hand is important, and the moon will both know
beyond doubt what is asked for and recognize that it is
asked for with appropriate respect. The Semang use this
device on a more extended scale, and this not only gives to
each line a completeness and independence but also pays a
respectful tribute to the main theme. In one song about a
tangke, or fruit-cluster, we can see how the repeated words
give an opportunity of showing the singer's appreciation of it:

> The fruit-cluster turns in the wind,
> The fruit-cluster at the end of the spray,
> The fruit-cluster turns in the wind,
> The fruit-cluster we climb for,
> The fruit-cluster at the end of the spray,
> The fruit-cluster turns in the wind,
> The fruit-cluster waves to and fro,
> The fruit-cluster, whose fruit is acid,

> The fruit-cluster turns in the wind,
> The fruit-cluster spins round and round.[37]

Though whole lines are here repeated, the additional repetition at the start of the line pulls them together and builds up a unity. The Semang use the device also at the end of a line, as in a song about a creeper called *burin*, and here too this particular repetition is combined with the repetition of whole lines, but it is less static and more dramatic than the song just quoted, and the repetition of the word *burin* emphasizes the action which the song either anticipates or accompanies. It has a magical purpose and is intended to make it easier to gather the berries of the creeper:

> It is long, it hangs down, the *burin*,
> The berries, berries of the *burin*,
> It is long, it hangs down, the creeper *burin*,
> Red *burin*,
> It lies in close clusters, the *burin*,
> Fetch, fetch the *burin*,
> Gone already is the spray of the *burin*,
> Red, red *burin*,
> They are long, they hang down, the berries of the
>   *burin*,
> Fetch, fetch the *burin*,
> They climb high, the berries of the *burin*,
> Climb high, it is very high the *burin*,
> The berries of the *burin*,
> The red, red *burin*.[38]

The repetition of *burin* at the end of each line holds the different statements together and shows that the singer is occupied with a matter which means a lot to him.

The examples already quoted show that repetition, in one form or other, is common to primitive song. Indeed it is more than common; it is fundamental. The theme is thought to be of such importance that it is stressed by repetition in a way that might seem to us unnecessary, and this degree of stress is probably due to magical intentions. If something has to be achieved by magic, it is wise to make clear what it is. The result is that much primitive song, whether composed in lines or in stanzas, consists of a theme which is partly repeated verbally, partly maintained by small variations. For instance, the Bushmen sing communal songs before going out on hunting expeditions, and one is addressed to the constellation Canopus, which is known as the "Bushman rice-star," because its rising is connected with the appearance of termites' larvae, which are known as "Bushman rice":

> O star coming there,
> Let me see a springbok.
>
> O star coming there,
> Let me dig out ants' food
> With this stick.
>
> O star coming there,
> Let me see a springbok to-morrow.
>
> O star coming there,
> I gave you my heart,
> Give me your heart!
>
> O star coming there,
> I may see a proteles to-morrow;
> Let the dog kill it,
> Let me eat it,
> Let me eat and fill my body,
> That I may lie and sleep at night.[39]

The repeated address to the star leaves no doubt what power is most concerned with the coming hunt, and is at once respectful and formal. It keeps the singers in touch with the star and allows them to develop their hopes as the song proceeds. From the need to do its task properly it evolves an artistic shapeliness and balance.

Once reptition and variation have found a place in composition, they can be developed in more than one way to bind various elements together and almost imperceptibly to move from one effect to another. The Aranda, for instance, use both in great abundance, and their method can be seen from a song of the season when the bloodwood trees are in blossom and ring-neck- and shell-parrots circle above them and pick the flowers:

> The ring-neck-parrots, in scattered flocks—
> The ring-neck-parrots are screaming in their upward
>   flight.
>
> The ring-neck-parrots are a cloud of wings:
> The shell-parrots are a cloud of wings.
>
> Let the shell-parrots come down to rest—
> Let them come down to rest on the ground.
>
> Let the caps fly off the scented blossoms!

Let the caps fly off the bloodwood blossoms!

Let the caps fly off the scented blossoms!
Let the blossoms fall to the ground in a shower.

The clustering bloodwood blooms are falling down—
The clustering bloodwood blossoms, nipped by birds.

The clustering bloodwood blooms are falling down—
The clustering bloodwood blossoms, one by one.[40]

The repeated images, and the small variations on them, fix
in the mind what is happening and make it live. Each successive image is introduced firmly and decisively, and kept
going until the next supersedes it. The song-maker avoids
any immediate or abrupt shift from one theme to another,
and this may be because he wishes to convey the complete
effect of a variegated action which none the less remains
single for him. The parrots and the blossoms are inextricably
connected, and he refuses to dissociate them even in a small
degree.

A similar technique, at a more advanced level, appears in
a song which the Dama sing to the harp before going out
to hunt the ostrich. In this the repetitions are fewer and the
variations more adventurous:

> You belly full of rock-flint,
> Great-toed one, who with your feathers say
>   *tsam-tsam,*
> Who eat the heart of melons,
> Give me one of your feathers.
>
> Ostrich, rising and flying,
> Long-necked and big-toed,
> Belly full of rock-flint, great bird,
> Wide-mouthed male ostrich,
> Flying, running, great bird,
> Give me one of your grey feathers.
>
> Ostrich, with dusty flank,
> Running great bird, fluttering feathers here and
>   there,
> Belly that says *khou-khou,*
> Running, walking male ostrich,
> Give me one of your tail-feathers.
>
> Male ostrich, looking up,
> Belly that says *khari, khari,*
> Ostrich, whose bowels alone are not fit to eat,

Give me one of your leg-bones, ostrich!

He who has two bones, which say *hui-hui,*
Male ostrich, who has wonderful marrow,
Who with his face says *gou-gou,*
Might I possess you, my ostrich![41]

The aim of the song is to put a spell on the ostrich so that
the Bushman can kill him, but the purpose is not fully revealed until the last stanza, though it is adumbrated in the
demand first for one of his feathers and then more firmly
in the desire for one of his legs with its rich marrow. The
stanzas develop the theme in a neat and rational way, which
accords with the several stages of hunting the ostrich. The
repeated phrases are few, and the variations on the central
theme have each their own quality of fancy or observation,
so that the whole poem is a lively account of what ostrich-
hunting is.

From repetition comes variation, and from variation comes
that parallelism which plays an impressive part in some
highly developed poetry. In primitive song it has not yet
attained to its later independence and is used more or less
as an alternative to repetition. It does not so much add anything obviously new as give a variant on something already
stated. It is clear enough in the Australian poem on the
parrots and in the Vedda lullaby, but its more advanced
possibilities may be seen in an Eskimo song, which is concerned with the weather and forecasts it indirectly by describing a visible scene:

The great Koonak mountain in the south yonder,
I see it.
The great Koonak mountain in the south yonder,
I behold it.
The gleaming light in the south yonder,
I look at it.
Beyond Koonak it stretches,
The same light that wraps
Koonak towards the sea.
See how in the south the clouds
Swell and change;
See how in the south
They make one another beautiful;
While the peak is wrapped towards the sea
In shifting clouds,
Wrapped towards the sea,
They make one another beautiful.[42]

Here repetition is reinforced by variations which are forecasts of parallelism and pass almost imperceptibly into it. The singer keeps his mind on the central theme and stresses it by familiar means, but he notices new aspects of it and does his duty by them as he introduces variations on his main topic. Repetition leads naturally to parallelism, which is a more advanced application of it and adds something fresh and unexpected instead of hammering away at the same theme. By this means the Eskimo leads to his charming climax, and his song unfolds its implications quietly and impressively. The same art can be seen on a smaller scale in a Vedda song, in which a man declares his high regard for his wife:

> For want of gruel or food, life will not depart;
> Owing to cold or wind, life will not depart;
> Owing to rain or dew, life will not depart.
> If there be no wife, life will depart.[43]

In a sense this is more adventurous than the Eskimo song in that it uses repetition and parallelism to secure a surprise and almost a paradox. The variation in the last words is more than we usually get in primitive songs, and is the more remarkable because it is made on the preceding repeated phrase. It exploits repetition in inducing a certain concentration of mind and then takes advantage of it to say something unexpected.

By the time that it reaches parallelism, primitive song begins to connect with the songs of more highly developed peoples. It is the normal method of making a poetical unit in the ancient literature of the Semitic peoples, and it is combined with repetition in an Egyptian song, sung by the soldiers of a general called Uni, who fought under Pepi I *c.* 2365-2350 BC. On returning from a campaign they sang of their victory:

> This army returned in safety,
> After it had hacked up the land of the Sand-dwellers.
> This army returned in safety,
> After it had crushed the land of the Sand-dwellers.
> This army returned in safety,
> After it had thrown down its enclosures.
> This army returned in safety,
> After it had killed troops in it by many thousands.
> This army returned in safety,
> After it had taken troops in it, a great multitude as
>   living captives.[44]

Here repetition is used in the odd lines and parallelism in the even, and the technique is not very different from that of the

Vedda lullaby. The odd lines speak for the present moment of triumphant pride; the even lines for the different actions which inspire and justify the mood. It is no great step from this technique to unassisted parallelism, in which repetition is omitted or reduced to a minimum and a single main idea is stated in two rather different forms or from two points of view. This art, which is known to us from so early an example as David's lament for Saul and Jonathan, is the direct descendant of the art which is practised among primitive peoples.

Moreover, primitive song has other devices to bind lines together into a recognizable or attractive unity and in this respect resembles much that we know from later literature. First, alliteration, which formed the basis of ancient Germanic verse, is not indeed regular among primitive peoples or exploited very consciously, but it certainly exists and the songmakers must be aware of its attractions. For instance, the Eskimos use more than once the phrase:

> *ata matuma m'mata*
> see its heart

and apply it in charms to the heart of a child or a dog. It surely became familiar and even formulaic because of its soft, purring sound in the repetition of *m*, *t*, and *a*. Effects of a like kind may be noticed in some totemistic songs of the Aranda, which are traditional and have probably been polished and perfected over a long series of years. In a song about the opossum they sing:

> *nutupirkiljirkil nopanama*
> *keratija nuturka nopanama*

> There is the opossum with the swelling belly,
> In the hollow of the plain is he with the swelling belly,[45]

and much of the effect is due to the repetition of *n*, *m*, *t*, and *rk*. So, too, a short ritual song from the Kunapipi cycle of north-east Arnhem Land describes rain-clouds:

| *janindji* | *jalpadu* | *janindji* | *jalpadu* |
| rain, | little cloud, | rain, | little cloud[46] |

where the alliteration of the initial *j* brings the cloud and the rain closer together. Alliteration is not constant in primitive song, but it is quite common, and is evidently thought to be an elegance, though not yet a necessity.

Secondly, rhyme also is used intermittently, as if it were something to be welcomed when available. It can already be seen in the meaningless songs of the Yamana, who have no musical instruments and are therefore free to make sounds as attractive as they can in themselves. A song of men and boys has in its brief passage an obvious rhyme:

> *hai-ye-ka sa-nas-kwa hai-ye-ka sa-nas-kwa*[47]

Similar effects may be found in some perfectly intelligible lines of Australian songs composed in quite different and separate languages. The rhyme may come anywhere, and there is no restriction of it to the end of a line. It comes inside it in a ritual song from the Kunapipi cycle, which gives four names for a bull-roarer:

> *mu: muna maralpindi pundjarlari kindijari*[48]

and the Aranda sometimes use it at the end of a line as an alternative to simple repetition:

> *no:makante: ka:ntanopai*
> *no:matnjenja: lbe:lanopa:i*
>
> The red tjurunga rests on my head,
> Red too is the hollow in which I lie.[49]

Since the end of the line is the emphatic place for a rhyme, it is there that it may often be found. In a Semang song about a coconut ape it is combined with alliteration:

> *o'tign tod'n ca tig'n leg'n*
> *ilel kemo'bateg'n*[50]
>
> He runs up and down, looks on all sides,
> Sees the fruit of the *bateg'n*.

More striking are some short pieces which look like complete rhyming verses. One such comes from the Australian Euahlayi, when a mother beats her child over the shoulders with the wing of a bustard and croons:

> *goobean gillaygoo*
> *oogowahdee goobaygoo,*
> *wahl goonindoo,*
> *ghurranbul daygoo.*[51]
>
> A swimmer be,
> To swim against the flood,
> No water
> Strong enough to stop you.

Something similar may be seen in a Tasmanian song, of which the sense is very uncertain, though it may refer to a water-rat:

> *a re-na-too*
> *ket-a-te-e vepa*
> *mel re-pa-too*
> *a re-na-too.*[52]

So too the Gabon Pygmies sing:

> *Msore i nia n'fare,*
> *Msore i nia n'sare.*[53]

> The Ancient One will tell us,
> The Ancient One will teach us.

These examples, and many others like them, suggest that in primitive song, rhyme, like alliteration, is an incidental, if not quite an accidental, ornament, which the singer enjoys and exploits when he chances on it, but which he is under no obligation to use as part of his technique. It is most frequent in languages where it comes easily because the range of available sounds is limited, and it is natural for anyone who had fallen on a rhyme to keep it for its melody. We do not know how or when rhyme entered into more mature and more highly developed poetry or won an established place in it. It exists from a remote past in China and other Far Eastern countries; it is fully at work in a Lydian inscription of the fourth century BC.[54] But its original roots must be vastly older than any extant examples of this kind, and it is permissible to think that it existed, if only spasmodically, in the very beginnings of verse.

Thirdly, since the words of a song must fit the tune, in this we may discern the beginnings of metre. These lines have at least their own rhythm in that they have to follow the movement of a tune and conform to it, and this usually means that they catch our ear for their own sake by some balance or harmony or equipoise. In their earlier stages they have nothing that can be called metre in the sense of having a regular number of strong beats, determined either by loudness or by the time that it takes to pronounce a syllable. But they move towards metre in more than one way. Sometimes the actual number of syllables in a line is fixed; sometimes there is a fixed number of accented, though not of unaccented, syllables. But some peoples, notably the Australian Aranda, have moved beyond this and construct their lines on recognizably metrical principles. They stress certain syllables, and this gives to the line something like the repetitive element which is the basis of metre. They tend to build a line in two halves, and though in singing they run them closely together, they keep them in action by balancing quick and slow beats. Metre depends ultimately upon music, and the more closely tune and words are united, the more likely it is that some kind of metre will be necessary. The large variety of metrical systems in later literature indicates that in early poetry what really mattered was rhythm, and that metre was evolved from this in different ways to meet the needs of singing.

Once it has developed these techniques, primitive song is in theory capable of almost unlimited growth. But in practice no song is very long. The longest known come from Australia and are concerned either with myths of totemic ancestors or with myths attached to divine powers. Though these sometimes attain fifty or more lines, their real expansion lies not in their own compass but in the arrangement of individual songs or couplets into sequences, which have a certain progression and coherence and contain in themselves the stuff from which long poems, whether narrative or dramatic, are made. If we look at the different phases of primitive song as an evolutionary process, we can distinguish five stages. First comes the single meaningless line, like that of the Yamana. Second comes the single intelligible line, which is often repeated to make its impact felt. Thirdly, lines are accumulated either in a straightforward sequence or to make a single stanza. Fourthly, stanzas are accumulated, as the accompanying dance is repeated, or single lines are expanded into larger units. Fifthly, the accumulation of stanzas or of single lines means that there is no limit in principle to the length of a poem, and the way to the long poem is opened through the arrangement of songs in coherent sections or cycles. We can thus distinguish a process of growth in which the Fuegians are at the beginning and some Australians at the conclusion. It is permissible to assume that this is very much what happened in the historical development of song and that these several stages mark its growth through the centuries from its first, remote, and lost beginnings.

CHAPTER 4 *Manner and Method*

IF THE mental processes of primitive man are hard for us to unravel, this is partly due to his language which secures precision only in dealing with individual objects and sensations, but it is also due to his religious beliefs, which are often derived from his unconscious self and, despite his attempts to put them in order, look confused to us. This might lead us to expect that his songs would be muddled and shapeless, and indeed, if we did not possess examples of them, we should probably guess that one theme would tumble helter-skelter upon another, as befits a singer whose emotions are under no control and who surrenders himself to them without restraint. Yet the opposite is the truth. When he comes to song, primitive man is usually straightforward, even when he deals with religious or ritual matters, which are in their very nature recalcitrant. This is not to say that we can always understand him without effort. We often know too little of the circumstances behind his songs to be able to grasp them in full at a first approach, but it certainly means that he practises his own kind of selection and simplification. This may be partly unconscious, a mood forced upon him by the strength with which he feels something and which compels

89

him to dwell only on what moves him most forcibly. But the process is also conscious; what inspires him to sing calls also for design and discipline. His poetical art consists largely of imposing an order, not merely formally by the devices of verse but internally by the choice and arrangement of themes, on his tumultuous and excited feelings. For him the elaborate as such has no attraction; he wishes to convey to others something as strongly and sharply as he feels it himself, and he knows that, if he approaches his task in the right way, his fellows will understand him and share his experience with him. If his inspiration is unconscious, his art is conscious and he deserves to be called an artist because he reduces his stirring thoughts to order and makes them as effective and attractive as he can. It is this which gives a special quality to his songs and entitles them to be treated as works of art. Nor do the limitations of his technique really prevent him from saying what he has to say. It may start from very humble beginnings, but from these it can advance to richer and more highly wrought effects. While in his natural conservatism he preserves very elementary old songs and even composes new ones like them, he also at other times attempts something more complex, and in the difference between one kind and another we can see a paradigm of evolving song.

Nearly all primitive songs are records of immediate reactions to events or beliefs, of feelings aroused by some unexpected chance or need, and therefore still vivid and powerful in the mind, of a full personality thrown into the task of song with all its strength committed to it, of impressions which may not be analysed or dissected intellectually but are for that reason all the more insistent. Primitive man lacks the inhibitions and obstructions which civilization has imposed upon its creatures, and he responds quickly and readily to any theme which excites or inspires him. Into it he throws his imagination, his emotions, his experience, his delight in words, his first glimmerings of general ideas. Just as in his ordinary behaviour restraint means very little to him and he displays his feelings freely in gesture and facial expression and tone of voice, so in his response to some unusual or disturbing or surprising occurrence he thrills through his whole being. He derives his poetry not from an isolated part of his nature but from the whole of it, and for this reason it gives an impression not only of immediacy and urgency but of a unified outlook, of experience so fully absorbed that it thrives in its own right and has its own unity.

Such a response may come from some very simple impulse and in its simplicity illustrate what primitive man feels at a sudden thrill. An almost elemental case is the song of an Andamanese who makes a canoe. He enjoys the labour so much that he bursts into song about it, even if he says nothing that any onlooker would not know already:

> I am cutting the under part of a canoe's prow,
> I am cutting a canoe,
> *I am cutting a canoe.*[1]

For him nothing matters but his delight in his craftsmanship, and this so absorbs him that, like a child, he has to draw the attention of others to what he is doing and expect them to be as thrilled as he is. For him it has all the fascination of a new discovery. Equally, when something out of the ordinary run happens to him, he feels the same kind of excitement, as another Andamanese song tells of a hunter who hits a turtle:

> Maia Poro saw a big turtle in the water, and hit him
> in the eye.
> Poro laughed when he hit him in the eye,
> *Poro laughed when he hit him in the eye.*[2]

Everyone can understand at once what the hunter feels and enjoy his exuberance with him. In such pieces a single, isolated notion does all the work, but just because the primitive mentality does not analyse a situation into various constituent elements but grasps a complete, unbroken impression, even a very short song may have considerable richness. A theme, which is rightly presented as a unity because that is how the singer sees it, may none the less contain recognizably different elements. For instance, a Bushman song is concerned with a girl who has suddenly been taken ill, and the event is sufficiently dramatic and surprising for someone to describe her symptoms and her situation with lively discernment:

> Poor young Kharis got into a fright,
> She is suffering from gripes,
> And bites the ground like the hyena which ate poison.
> The people run to see the fun!
> They are still all very much frightened,
> And still they say: "Oh, it is nothing!"[3]

This is a single situation, but it has more than one aspect, and the singer is well aware of this and makes the most of it. It is the record of an unusual moment in all its absurdity and paradox, which the singer savours to the full. A similar, unobtrusive richness can be found in almost any kind of theme. It comes from feeling strongly and directly and from putting the whole weight of this feeling into words, without allowing anything to distract the attention from the central, riveting point. So the Gabon Pygmies have a song for initiation-ceremonies, which emphasizes the conviction that a Pygmy is not a Negro but a different and superior being:

> You are not the son of the night,
> Of the deep, treacherous night,
> Black as the soot of your smoky hut.
> You are not the son of the night,
> You are the son of the bright, clear day,
> The son of the rich generous earth,
> The earth, where the sweet fruits grow,
> You are the son of the bright, clear day,
> *Ho, ho mo nga youroü welé,*
> No, you are not the son of the night.[4]

Here the all-important point is that the Pygmy's origin is quite different from the Negro's, and this is presented from more than one angle and with more than one image, but each variation is directed towards a single end, and the theme of the song is indissolubly one.

A similar directness of response may be seen in charms and prayers. Such are composed to meet practical needs, and the urgent sense of these needs gives them their force. Whoever composes them knows so well what is wanted, and how strong the desire for it is, that he gives all his care to it and reduces it to its indispensable elements. There must be no uncertainty about what is asked for, and the tone must be impeccably right. If these needs are to be met, the actual words must have their own little distinction, just because they express something strongly felt and desired, and distil it into its quintessence. So, when the Semang bury a corpse, they hope to avoid all trouble from the departed spirit by singing:

> Go first,
> I afterwards.
> Do not give rain,
> Do not give storms,
> Do not give lightning or thunder.[5]

The prayer is perfectly explicit and makes no attempt to shirk its task. If a suppliant has some private wish and approaches his god about it, he may be as precise as he likes, as when the Bushman hunter prays to the moon for good sport and explains exactly what he has in mind:

> Ho Moon lying there,

Let me see an ostrich early to-morrow;
As the ostrich sits on the eggs,
Let me whisk out the yoke
With the hair-tail of a gemsbok;
It sits together on a little stick,
There the tail of a gemsbok sits.[6]

The exactitude with which the hunter describes the primitive
brush made of a buck's tail on a stick, shows how carefully
he has thought out his requirements and how eager he is
that the moon should understand them. Prayers need not always be so explicit as this, but may have a more evasive
subtlety, especially when they are prompted by some imaginative impulse. For instance, when the Gabon Pygmies dance
in honour of the sun, the leader sings in a low, slow voice:

O Sun, O Sun,
Death comes, the end arrives,
The tree falls and dies.
O Sun, O Sun,
The child is born in his mother's womb.
Death saw, man saw, the Sun saw.
Sun, O Sun, O Sun.[7]

Behind this lies a belief in the life-giving powers of the sun
and of man's dependence on it, but the song scales this down
to a very precise point. It dwells on the contrast between
life and death, and awareness of this contrast forms and fills
it. Because primitive song is an immediate response to some
call or challenge, it is not necessarily thin and obvious. It
can express a complex state of mind in a short space and give
to it a full weight of poetry. All primitive song, however
elementary or utilitarian, betrays this concentration on a given
need and the hold which this has on the singer.

Since primitive song sets to work in this way and rises
from a compelling urgency, it maintains the individual qualities of a single occasion. Like Croce, and unlike Aristotle,
the song-man composes as if poetry were concerned not with
the universal but with the particular. He lacks general ideas
and even generalized experience. His concern is to catch
the unique air of a situation and to show precisely what it
is. This is to be expected in peoples whose attention seldom
reaches beyond the immediate moment or the thought of something just done or about to be done. Though this is forced
upon them by having to live from hand to mouth, it brings
compensation in their songs, which have the freshness of something newly and vividly apprehended. Though their range, if
we view it abstractly, is necessarily very limited, this does

not matter, since what counts is the particular presentation of particular sensations, and for this reason singers display their originality by their unexpected angles of approach or moments of vision. There is little demand for novelties in the sense of new main subjects, but there is a bold and original enterprise in the handling of old. From their narrow and sharply focused outlook primitive singers see in situations which might theoretically be reduced to a single heading highly individual characteristics, and make the most of them.

Primitive song lacks the general character which is imposed on modern poetry by its desire to appeal to a wide audience whose members do not conform to a single system of ideas or beliefs or habits, let alone share their daily activities and interests with one another. The primitive songmaker composes only for his own small group and is free to assume that every detail, however individual, will be understood at his own valuation. This gives him his own kind of depth. Even quite trivial or accidental details have a telling significance for men and women who, in their narrow round of routine, discriminate firmly between matters which might look much the same to us. Each point, however small, has its distinctive character and makes its own impression. Moreover, such sharpness of vision means that many topics which have lost their poetical appeal for modern man keep in primitive song a vivid reality and awake an excited curiosity. This happens largely because even the most common events maintain their individual character and bristle with novel elements which might not appeal to a wide audience but have a considerable lure for a small group whose lives are involved in them. The song-maker does not invent his details; he selects them from the material at his disposal. The particulars which he thinks worthy of mention are taken from a mass of which he omits a large part, and we must therefore respect his decision in making his choice as he does, and not neglect any word that he says. The details are inseparable from the whole effect, and through them and in them the song finds its unique lineaments. If they are repeated, it is because special notice is demanded for them, and if they seem to be unexpected and almost irrelevant, it is almost certainly deliberate. For instance, an Australian woman of north-east Arnhem Land journeyed to Yirkalla with her family, and, when she arrived, her small granddaughter fell sick and died. She bewails this loss in a moving lament, which expresses her grief the more fully because it is confined entirely to her actual, present, personal situation. Though she uses devices which belong to the tradition of song in her people, they are all relevant to her immediate disaster and help her to express her dominating, desolate grief. The central theme of the child's death holds pride of place, as it should, but it gains in actuality and strength from the circumstantial statements which accompany it. Just because it is placed in its real, authentic setting, it keeps its individual pathos and leaves us asking for nothing more:

> The fire is burning at Birginbirgin and Gamwardla and
> Nuga,
> Burning out the wallaby and the kangaroo.
> Ah, my daughter, my brother, my nephew, my grand-
> child, my cousins,
> We came here from our home, my daughter, my
> grandchild.
> We travelled and hither we came,
> We came to this unfriendly place, my daughter, my
> grandchild.
> My baby died here!
> Both of us came with our child, here we found sickness.
> My country is far away, hither we came,
> Travelling from place to place, my brother, my
> brother's child.
> Crying I carried him sick.
> Who is watching and staring while father cries?
> Ah, my daughter, my daughter, my grandchild![8]

The scene is set in the first line, which tells where the tragedy happens. The second line comes from a common stock, and is not intended to be taken literally, but invokes images of desolation and destruction, suitable to the loss of the child. The song begins in this way to show what kind of song it is and where its events take place. The rest is almost pure lament, and the central theme is contained in the words "my daughter, my grandchild," in which the woman sorrows for the bereaved mother and laments the dead child. Round this cluster other closely connected themes—the rest of the family equally broken by the loss, the journey which has come to so melancholy an end, the care shown to the child in it, and the appeal in the penultimate line against anyone who is not moved by what has happened. The situation is presented just as it is, with an exact and loving care, but because it is infused with grief, none of the details is otiose or irrelevant, and the whole piece has a unity in its single, tragic occasion. There are no general thoughts about death or grief, and, more surprisingly, no one is mentioned by name. The various members of the family are introduced through their relationships, including the son-in-law, the father of the dead child, who is called "brother" because of his closeness to the lamenting woman, and this is right because each shares her grief and feels that it is his also. Death has brought her words into action, and fixed them on the loss which obsesses and devours her whole being. Her selection of what matters rises from the very intensity of her grief, and for this very reason her song has its own pattern and completeness.

In such songs it is the particulars which give strength to the poetry. Through them the driving impulse behind the song finds concrete expression and shows what it means to those who are mastered by it. Each point rises from the precarious nature of primitive life and its unabating struggle for survival, and if security is in any way disturbed or threatened, it matters enormously to those who are afflicted. The bare simplicity of existence accounts for the repetition of conventional themes, but this does not dull their relevance or fall below the proper level of song. It means rather that variations on them are always relevant and in some sense new. So the lamentations of the Dama repeat many stock themes, but each has an illuminating relevance in its context, and we must treat them seriously as they appear, and ask what they mean to those who bring them into song. They often exploit the pathetic fancy that the dead person must arise and return to his usual tasks, but even this reflects the essence of loss and is brought into action with a variety of new, individual touches suited to each occasion. So a man laments his dead wife:

> You, full-breasted one, have died,
> Arise and grasp your stick,
> Let us go out together to dig out the field-mouse.
> Your husband—when will he eat onions?
> Are you truly dead? Do you live, and yet lie there?
> Arise, cut a stick and let us look for field-food.
> Unwearying one, digger clothed in a skin!
> Rich in girls and boys, arise!
> Rich in children, arise!
> Mother of boys, arise!
> Who will give them perfume?
> Your companions wish to get perfume ready.
> Arise and help in preparing perfume.
> Short-armed one, arise.
> Tie up your skin, and let us seek field-food.
> While you lie there, the women have already dug up
>   the onions.
> Therefore arise, let us go together and work.
> Let us arise and look for field-mice.

Who is left to your husband to give him field-food?
Arise and say your last words to me.
Without a word of farewell, you die.[9]

The central theme is the death of a man's wife, and the song is composed in direct response to it. If it uses a stock structure, the details are actual and immediate and much to the point; for it is precisely in such activities that the life of a Dama couple is passed. They are the business of all Dama people, and such a song could be sung by any man among them who has lost his wife. To this degree the individuality of the song attains a general character, but it remains individual because the actual choice of details indicates the way in which the man and his wife have lived together and the kinds of food for which they have searched. Behind the conventions and the barren simplicity of life we can see the personal touch, the individual inclination, the ties which have bound man and wife together.

This technique is all the more effective when it is applied to situations or beliefs which are by almost any standard unusual and call for considerable skill to bring out their idiosyncrasies and implications. Then what counts is the strictly human aspect, and the singer's task is to seize on this and make the most of it as he himself sees and feels it. A Bushman song laments the death of a rain-maker, who in his lifetime was believed to make himself known to his friends by sounding a string in the sky. Though to a Bushman there would be nothing incredible in this, he would admit that it is an unusual gift and that a man who possesses it deserves honour and attention. But the remarkable thing about the song is that it concentrates entirely on what the singer feels at the loss of the rain-maker. The string is indeed his theme, but not, as we might expect, as a sign of the dead man's remarkable powers but in a much more human and more poignant temper. The singer concentrates entirely on his own feelings at his loss, and they are quite unexpected, even though they are founded on a keen appreciation of the actual situation:

Those were people
Who broke for me the string.
    Therefore
This place became like this for me,
On account of it.
Because the string broke for me,
    Therefore
The place does not feel to me,
As the place used to feel to me,

On account of it.
The place feels as if it stood open before me,
Because the string has broken for me.
    Therefore
The place does not feel pleasant to me
    Because of it.[10]

What stirs the singer is not the mystery inherent in the very idea of the rain-maker's string, nor even his grief at the rain-maker's death, but the disappearance from his world of something to which he has become accustomed and which he has taken for granted. The loss of it makes him feel that he is no longer at home in his old surroundings, and this uneasy sense of being a stranger disturbs and distresses him. He fixes on this single point because it means most to him, and it is this which gives his song its striking originality. He tells exactly what the loss means to him, and though his presentation is extremely spare and selective, it is surprisingly dramatic and touching.

Once a song-man has decided what is the essential theme for a song and turned his mind to it, he has to give it a fitting emphasis and see that as much as possible is made of it and that its proper implications are not shirked. So the Gabon Pygmies call on the snake whom they regard ambivalently as both their adversary and their protector:

When in the night the foot
Strikes the obstacle which strikes, rises up and bites,
Make, O serpent, you our father, the father of the tribe,
For us thy sons,
Make it to be a branch which rises and strikes us,
And not one of thy children, with its sharp tooth,
O father of the tribe, for us thy sons.[11]

The Pygmy knows far too well how swiftly a snake can bite in the dark to speak of it as being otherwise than it is, and here he describes its menace carefully, so that there is no doubt about his meaning. He asks that what might seem to be a snake may turn out to be only a fallen branch, and this too is closely observed from fact. The emphasis is given to the actual experience with which the song is concerned, and no uncertainty is left about what a snake's bite in the darkness means. In such a prayer the power to whom it is addressed is quite as important as its other contents, and just as here the father-snake is treated as indeed a father, who owes something to his children, so in the rest of the song his threatening character is not shirked but handled with perfect candour. In other songs, when a supernatural power is approached, a like formality is used. The Bushman hunter wishes to establish a personal relation with the moon, and does so by appealing for its attention and help. He knows what he wants, and this impels him to song, but he tempers his words with due modesty. In the result the two themes are inextricably fused, even if the desire for food gets a rather less obvious place than it has in his mind:

> Young moon!
> Hail, young moon,
> Hail, hail!
> Young moon!
> Young moon, speak to me!
> Hail, hail!
> Young moon!
> Tell me of something.
> Hail, hail!
> When the sun rises,.
> You must speak to me,
> That I may eat something..
> You must speak to me about a little
>   thing,
> That I may eat.
> Hail, hail,
> Young moon![12]

The hunter presents his request with tact and skill and pays proper attention to the moon on the assumption that, if he can engage her interest, the rest will be easy for him.

This insistence on a single theme may in certain cases open up exciting prospects. Yet even when they are envisaged, and no one of them has precedence over another, the same structure is maintained. Nor is the unity merely one of mood; it is more one of subject, but the subject is not closely defined, because it lies in the future and does not allow too clear anticipations to be formed. The singer fixes his mind on the possible alternatives and expresses them from a single point of view for a single purpose. So the Dama have a man called the "food-master," and his task is to see that they get their food in the right way at the right time. He has a song which proclaims his importance and his authority and then turns into a prayer for all possible kinds of food, on the assumption that at least some of them will be given to the hunters:

> I, the food-master, am here.
> I have looked after you!
> May the gemsbok come!

> May the springbok come!
> May the wild ox come!
> May the hartebeest fall down and die!
> May the porcupine fall down and die!
> May the badger fall down and die!
> Let us find honey!
> Let us find wild onions!
> May the ostrich draw near!
> May the wild pigeons fall down and die!
> May the antelope come to us![13]

The food-master dwells on a variety of fare but his main purpose is to ask that provision may be made in some form or other. The various possibilities adumbrated are all variations on a single theme, and this holds the song together.

The concentration on one thing at a time and the assumption that a song must have only a single theme make some songs look allusive and cryptic, and this might seem to contradict the notion that they are essentially straightforward. But this enigmatic air is no more than a special effort to stress a particular point and to exclude anything else as irrelevant. Sometimes this happens because the short time at the singer's disposal does not allow him to say as much as he might otherwise, but normally it is a form of stress on what he thinks to be most important. It creates no difficulty for the audience, whose members know the background of the song, whether sacred or secular, and are able to follow him without trouble. This is especially the case when the words are accompanied by illustrative action, and if the action is clear, there is no need for the words to describe it; they are better employed pointing out something of peculiar significance in it. For instance, when the Alawa of Arnhem Land sing of the passage of the ancestress Kadjaru through their territory, they are careful to mention each stage of her long and varied journey, but almost always by indirect allusion, which not only adds something to the picture that already exists in the minds of the audience and is helped by ritual, imitative actions, but also in some sense interprets it or throws a new light on it. It need not therefore be described in its main features. So, when the goddess makes her way up a river in a rainstorm, all that is said is:

> *galan'bulga i'madali' i'madali galan'bulga*[14]

which means literally "rain-clouds . . . raining . . . raining . . . rain-clouds." Again, when spirits come out of the jungle in the morning and hear a pigeon, the song says:

> *manaitja'manaitja djigaija'djigaija*[15]

which means "jungle-tree . . . cry of the morning pigeon." The intervening steps, which we might think necessary, are left out, and what matters is a strong emphasis on a single point. This isolates the central theme and draws everyone's attention to it. The apparently impressionistic art of the words is largely a linguistic matter, due to the way in which these Australians build up their sentences, but it helps to make the chosen moment more vivid.

A similar allusiveness appears in some magical songs of the Gabon Pygmies, which are sung when a medicine man throws bones for divination before hunting. Here the difficulty comes partly from concentration and therefore omission, partly from the desire to compress a lot into a very few words. The songs are concerned with the prospects of hunting. They are three in number, of which the second balances the first. The first is

> Man goes, runs, and falls,
> The arrow starts, flies, whistles,
> Spirits, spirits,
> Seed, hero and plant,

and the second

> The man has fallen.
> *Vué, vué!*
> Day succeeds to night, night to day.
> The man has fallen.

These are forecasts not of what will happen but of what may happen, and are preventive charms which hope to anticipate and stop failure by imagining what it means if a hunter becomes the victim instead of the victor. Everyone who sings or hears the words knows that this is their purpose, and then all is clear. They are followed by a third spell:

> The arrow has flown, has whistled, *vué, vué!*
> The earth has opened,
> The spirit is roaming, the guilty one is far away.
> Father, father, your children! Storm-wind, thunder,
> Turn away your blows.[16]

This is not a forecast but a prayer, and in a concise, elliptic manner it explains what success in hunting means. The arrow will fly, an animal will fall, and the shock of its falling will be as if the earth were to open. The animal's spirit will wander, and a storm will come, which the god of the forest is asked to turn away. It is all there, the action and its consequences, but as a prayer it is entirely coherent and rational. Each part makes its point—the general character of hunting, the immediate effect of the kill, the possible results in nature and the supernatural. While the songs are sung, each is accompanied by an elaborate ritual, and there is no impenetrable obscurity in them.

In these cases the obscurity is lessened or removed by the actions which accompany and illustrate them. But the same kind of oblique reference is also found in secular songs which are not illuminated by any such accompaniment. What matters is the single main point which the songman has in mind. In the short Andamanese songs this is nearly always the practice and comes from the intense vision of a brief moment, which has to be set in a short conventional frame. A striking example is a song composed by a man whose son has been killed and who proposes to take vengeance on the killer, and addresses himself to the father:

> Bringing up the boat to the beach, I shall see your fine
>   grown-up son,
> The grown-up son, who threw the youth into the sea,
> The fine grown-up son—
> My adze is rusty, I will stain my lips with his blood.[17]

There is no need to say who "the grown-up son" and "the youth" are or to speak more overtly of the coming vengeance. What counts is the mood which inspires the song, and the prospect which fills the singer's mind. The few words go straight to the point and leave no doubt what they mean. There is no need to explain the background or to fill in the outlines, since the slayer's father will understand them well enough, as will anyone else who hears them. So another Andamanese, who had been sent to prison for killing a sailor who took liberties with his wife, made a song:

> Thou art sad at heart,
> Gazing there at the sky's surface,
> Gazing at the ripples on the sky's surface,
> Leaning on the bamboo spear.[18]

He addresses himself as he was just before he killed the sailor and revives his state of mind at the time, in its grief at what has happened and his decision to kill as he leans on his spear. He sings to unburden himself, and his song tells everything that needs to be told.

Immediacy of reaction, concentration on a single theme, and a tendency to stress it by isolating it are characteristics of primitive song. If they reveal the singer's desire to make

the most of what occupies his mind and to present it as
pertinently as he can, they are the fruit of a conscious art, of
a clear conception of what a song ought to be. But such a
conception rises from a special habit of mind. Primitive song
works in this fashion because the singers, accustomed to
keep their eyes and ears alert all the time, make a strong
effort to discipline their feelings in a song since the occasions which it celebrates have a commanding immediacy
and impose their will on those who take part in them. Primitive man may not be capable of prolonged stretches of
abstract thought, but he is capable of seeing and feeling
something very sharply and vividly for a short time. The
very intensity of the moment brings it home to him in
its essential peculiarity and stamps it on his consciousness.
He recalls it not in tranquillity but in passion and excitement, and when he turns it into song, he lives through it
again, just because it has never left him. This means that
on the whole primitive song keeps to one theme because it
needs no more, that it presents a crowded moment and
nothing else, and this moment is itself slimmed to its essence. It may be looked at from more than one angle, but
it is hardly developed or expanded or made to prepare the
way to something else. So even when it deals with action,
whether real or mythical, it reduces it to a moment and puts
all its strength into it. Naturally this hampers its scope and
its range, and partly accounts for its failure to expand on
any large scale. Yet though it is tied in this way, it can
turn its position to advantage and make more of it than we
might think possible. It keeps its original nature and the rules
which it has evolved to suit it, but from these it advances to
a variety of other effects. In particular it sometimes expands
by making more of its theme than actual conventions demand. Though this is hardly to be found among the Veddas,
the Andamanese, or the Semang, it is common enough among
the Gabon Pygmies, the Dama, the Eskimos, and certain Australians. It represents a stage in the growth of song, which
starts from a simple, single impulse, and then comes to see
that the unity which it demands can still be maintained and
even strengthened by adding a certain elaboration.

A first type of this is when a theme presents alternatives.
This is already present in an undeveloped form in the song of
the Dama food-master, but it contains more possibilities
than he exploits. It means that some elementary need or
activity or relaxation can be displayed in more than one
example, and that each receives full attention. When this
happens, the song, in some degree, transcends the moment
and looks at a common experience from a more general

point of view. This is in itself an important step forward,
since it liberates song from its subservience to the present
and makes it take notice also of the past and the future.
So the Gabon Pygmies celebrate with gaiety and humour
the pleasures of eating fish, and a song tells of three kinds,
the *won*, the *ngol*, and the *mpoi*, giving to each its appropriate praise:

> If you wish to walk for long in the forest
> And to feel your heart strong,
> Your breasts swell sturdily,
> And your legs run quickly,
> Friend, grill on the charcoal,
> On the red coals of a burning fire,
> The *won* with the cruel teeth,
> The carp with a thousand colours
> And the delicate firm flesh.
>
> If you wish for calm sleep
> To come softly and close your eyelids,
> For joyful dreams, messengers from the dead,
> To run and hunt at happy hunting,
> The friendly place, where in the dark forest
> The quick boar crouches near the stream,
> And in the clearing among the peppermints
> The fast antelope pricks up his ears,
> Friend, in the leaves with which you are surrounded,
> Friend, bake the *ngol*.
>
> But if you wish for your heart
> To be glad without regret,
> For your belly, sated and full,
> To say: "Oh! Oh! that's enough!
> Oh! Oh! I have eaten well!"
> If you wish that your swollen belly
> Should resist the finger that gladly presses it,
> And sound under your hand like a stretched tom-tom,
> A tom-tom of skin stretched to the utmost,
> If you wish that your belly should sing a glad song,
> Friend, take a *mpoi*, friend, eat a *mpoi*.[19]

The three stanzas and stages of this poem are closely parallel
to one another, and each deals with a separate satisfaction—
energy, or happy dreams, or physical repletion. Each satisfaction is depicted with a keen appreciation of its worth.
Though the song consists of a theme with variations, the theme
is general—the eating of fish—and the variations are particular, alike in the search and in the results obtained, and
there is some art in the climax when the *mpoi* is presented

as being in the last resort more desirable than the *won* or the *ngol*, though these have their ample claims. The song is not quite an encomium of eating fish as such, but it is more than a celebration of three individual occasions.

Fishing is so habitual among the Gabon Pygmies that they are able to generalize about it and to compare and contrast one outing with another. A similar process may be seen in songs from elsewhere which deal with hunting, and are concerned not with what has happened but with the various possibilities which lie before the hunter when he sets out. The unity lies in the anticipation of the hunt, and the variations in the inevitably different prospects which, in its very uncertainty, it offers. So an Eskimo dance-song deals with a range of chances and choices:

> How am I to strike this one with a missile?
> As it walks, let me strike it.
> Since I cannot do it with a winged arrow,
> With a stone let me strike it.
>
> How am I to strike this one?
> The king-eider—let me strike it.
> Since I cannot do it with a winged arrow,
> With a stone let me strike it.
>
> How am I to strike this one?
> The black musk-ox—let me strike it.
> Since I cannot do it with a winged arrow,
> With the horn of my bow let me push it away.
>
> How am I to strike this one?
> The hare here—let me strike it.
> Since I cannot do it with a winged arrow,
> With a snare let me attack it.[20]

Here the parallelism of the stanzas is both more marked and more mechanical than in the Pygmy song, and there is not even an implicit climax. The similarity of the different targets is marked by the repetitions in the first and third lines, and this leaves no doubt that the hunter has no great confidence in his bow and wonders how he can best secure his prey. None the less this song also passes beyond the present moment into a variety of alternatives, and to this degree it gets away from the limitations of a single occasion. It has a single, uniting theme, which is the hunter's frame of mind before setting out, as he considers his weapons and how best to use them. It is less rich and less accomplished than the Pygmy song, but it too shows how ingeniously a single occasion can be turned to suggest a choice of possibilities.

If this technique is applied not to a choral song but to a solo or to a song in which the individual plays the chief part, it permits a still wider freedom as he displays his tastes and his talents and allows his invention to show its paces. A Gabon Pygmy, whose nickname was Mba Sholé, which means "malicious thief," is reported to have had remarkable gifts for dancing and singing and miming. He would get the company to join in his song but only to the extent of a very short refrain, while he himself sang the rest and illustrated his themes with lively and laughable gestures. One song of his, which is known to us, has no ulterior purpose beyond causing amusement and describes in turn a fish, a bird, and a monkey, each of whom he imitates while he sings about them:

> The fish does . . . *hip!*
> The bird does . . . *viss!*
> The marmot does . . . *gnan!*
>
> I throw myself to the left,
> I turn myself to the right,
> I act the fish,
> Which darts in the water, which darts,
> Which twists about, which leaps—
> All lives, all dances, and all is loud.
>
> The fish does . . . *hip!*
> The bird does . . . *viss!*
> The marmot does . . . *gnan!*
>
> The bird flies away,
> It flies, flies, flies,
> Goes, returns, passes,
> Climbs, soars, and drops.
> I act the bird—
> All lives, all dances, and all is loud.
>
> The fish does . . . *hip!*
> The bird does . . . *viss!*
> The marmot does . . . *gnan!*
>
> The monkey from branch to branch,
> Runs, bounds, and leaps,
> With his wife, with his brat,
> His mouth full, his tail in the air,
> There is the monkey! There is the monkey!—
> All lives, all dances, and all is loud.[21]

Here the external formality is elegantly disposed in the equally balanced structure of the three main stanzas and the repeated line at the end of each. But the central theme is not so obviously displayed. Yet we are surely right to press the significance of the repeated last line and to see in it the singer's conviction that in his antics he somehow embodies the living world of water, air, and land. What inspires him is something which he finds in common between fish, bird, and animal, and this he feels at work in himself as he plays each part in turn. The skill of his technique lies in the sharp discrimination which he makes between the three kinds of living things and the marked personality which he gives to each. His song is a skilful and percipient exhibition of three variations on a partly concealed theme.

A second type of expansion rises from a desire to convey the completeness of a mood which the singer feels to be single but which calls for presentation in disparate details which are not formally brought together, and indeed owe their connection with one another to the unusual strength of a dominating, formative mood. These are often related to an immediate event, which has made a powerful impact on the singer and left him in a highly disturbed condition. Here the fundamental unity lies in the actual mood, and the events mentioned must be closely attached to it. Such may be seen in the lament of an Australian woman who has lost her child:

> Oh, the blowfly is whining there, its maggots are
>   eating the flesh,
> The blowflies buzz, their feet stray over the corpse,
> The buzzing goes on and on.
> Whom is it eating there, whose flesh are they eating?
> Ah, my daughter, come back here to me!
> Ah, our daughter was taken ill—
> You didn't sing for her as a father should!
> You are foolish and silly, you sing only to please the
>   ears of a woman!
> You like to lie close to a young girl, a virgin, and give
>   her a child!
> You will not stay in one place!
> Here and there, all over the place, you go among the
>   camps,
> You go walking hither and thither, looking for
>   sweethearts.
> Ah, before, it was here that you used to stay.
> You should be ashamed to do that before all these
>   strangers,
> Presently I shall take a knife and cut you!
> No, you go to sit down beside some woman,
> You sit close, close beside her . . .
> Ah, my lost child, ah the blowflies![22]

Though the starting point is the mother's grief at the death of her child, and her horror at its decaying body, the central theme of the poem is the careless self-indulgence of her husband, who, instead of looking after his child, pays attention to his new young wives. The common theme of grief at the loss of someone beloved is transformed into something much less common, and though it contains horror, grief, and anger, they are fused into a single effect, a dramatic scene in which the husband's fecklessness is shown up by the tragic circumstances around him. The sudden impact of catastrophe has fastened the woman's mind on points which are by no means simple in themselves but are clarified and brought together into a uniting order by the intensity of her feelings.

A similar art may be observed in other songs which are concerned with a central issue and held together by it but treat it with considerable variety. This happens because the issue itself evokes a number of different emotional responses and may awake more than one imaginative consideration. Yet though there is an appearance of progress and development, the main theme is observed throughout, and there is no real divagation from it. None the less the variety so secured is far richer than anything to be found in the parallel verses of songs which adhere closely to the external identity of a theme. A fine example is the song which the Gabon Pygmies sing to the god of the rainbow, Khwa:

> Khwa! Ye! O! Rainbow, O rainbow!
> You who shine on high, so high,
> Above the great forest,
> Among the black clouds,
> Dividing the black sky.

> Beneath you you have overturned,
> Victor in the struggle,
> The thunder which growled,
> Which growled so strongly in its wrath.
> Was it angry with us?

> Among the black clouds,
> Dividing the dark sky,
> Like the knife which cuts a too ripe fruit,
> Rainbow, rainbow!

> He has taken flight,
> The thunder, the man-killer,
> Like the antelope before the panther,
> He has taken flight,
> Rainbow, rainbow!

Mighty bow of the hunter on high,
Of the hunter who chases the herd of clouds,
Like a herd of frightened elephants,
Rainbow, tell him our thanks.

Tell him: "Do not be angry!"
Tell him: "Do not be provoked!"
Tell him: "Do not kill us!"
For we are very frightened,
Rainbow, tell it to him.[23]

The central theme is the feeling of relief and release at the appearance of the rainbow, which is thought to be a divine power close to the supreme god of the sky. This relief dominates the poem, and is the more impressive because the storm which preceded it was indeed terrifying. Thus, though the song leads up to a climax, which provides a fine, dramatic close, this climax is itself implicit in the mood stated at the start. This is of some complexity, but is clear enough to anyone who knows what fear and the deliverance from fear are and how the second is all the greater because of the strength of the first. The repetitions, introduced with delicate skill and never too assertive, keep the main theme in hand, and the variations on it come with a more striking impact after them, until the climax, which appeals to the religious consciousness and convictions of everyone present, emerges powerfully at the end and brings the several variations together in the main pattern.

It is not always easy to maintain this essential unity when a song celebrates or laments past events, and though such songs are not very common, their occasional emergence shows how difficult it is to abandon the usual discipline and rely upon something less rigid than a central mood or idea or emotion. If the singer wishes to recall a series of events, he must relate them to some centre, even if they look disparate and unconnected. A good example of how this can be done successfully may be seen in a Dama song which is concerned with bad luck:

While I cut an arrow for my quiver,
My son burned himself.

While I cut a poisoned arrow,
My daughter fell into a hole.

While I cut a club of *gom*-wood,
My daughter burned herself.

> While I cut an arrow without poison,
> My son fell into a hole.[24]

Here, of course, a central theme is implied in the association
of bad luck with the cutting of weapons, especially arrows.
But the four events are told from memory and have the
association which it gives to them. The song is saved from
disorder, and indeed brought into an effective order, by the
similarity between the four episodes and the suggestion of an
evil power at work. This is an easy subject, since the singer
sees the connections very clearly, and knows how to set
them in order. The task is less easy when he is obsessed by
the past and feels that he must sing of it, even though its
events have no very obvious connection with one another.
Even so he may be guided and guarded by a mood which
dictates the tone of his song and sets a single impress on
it. Though the songs of the Selk'nam are rare, and usually no
more than meaningless, single lines, there are a few examples
of real song. One such was sung by the old medicine man
Tenenesk, and it is no less than a lament for the doom
which has fallen upon his people and himself. It is indeed
a dirge for a dying world, and though it is not skillfully
fashioned and seems to have been improvised in a moment
of grief so bitter that any artistic refinement is lacking, it
illustrates how a single mood can bring disparate elements
together and present a coherent picture of melancholy and
decay:

> Kausel was a foremost magician,
> And a good man;
> He has long been dead.
> My father was thought to be the best hunter in
>   the whole company.
> Never did he come home without booty.
> When I was still a child,
> O how great then was the number of the Selk'nam.
> Today we are only a few.
> All my brothers and sisters are dead,
> I myself am already an old man.
> My familiar spirit was very strong,
> From afar he brought me news,
> But now he is worn and weary.[25]

In the short series of factual statements, each of which is
briefly, even baldly, stated, there is a persistent mood of
defeat and despair, and it is this which gives unity to the
poem. Just because Tenenesk confines himself to facts and
passes no comments, his impact is all the more powerful,

and his art is to present through a few outstanding instances
the decline of his world, when a civilized man would treat
it, not necessarily with more success, in abstractions and
generalities.

Not wholly unlike this is the song of an old Eskimo
shaman, Italsiaq, who recounts not a general situation but
various, apparently disconnected, events in his own past,
each of which is separate and distinct and presented in an
allusive, almost oracular manner:

> It robbed me, the wind,
> Of my covering the wind robbed me.
>
> Thus much I have saved,
> Of my covering the wind robbed me.
>
> Only that I could not put my hand on;
> I thought of it, but did not put my hand on it.
>
> The singers they take from me,
> They take from me my song.
>
> That song I did not refrain from letting go,
> The drum I held it up again.
>
> It robbed me, the spirit,
> It robbed me of speech.
>
> This much I have spoken,
> The spirit robbed me of speech.
>
> Only at that one—I did not wish to look at him;
> Away to one side I turned my eyes.
>
> It robbed me, the wicked bearded seal,
> Of the harpoon line it robbed me.
>
> Since the sealers too could not catch anything,
> I did not let my harpoon-line go.
>
> Since the sealers too could not catch anything,
> I waited and pulled hard at my harpoon-line.[26]

In this there are four stages or episodes, which are superficially connected by the notion that in each Italsiaq has
been robbed of something. Couplets 1-3 recall a winter journey over the ice on a sledge covered with caribou skins;
the wind blew them away, and in the third couplet Italsiaq
attributes this to the malevolence of enemies, who wished for
his death. He was aware of their activity, but they were beyond his control; none the less he managed to save his

life. In couplets 4-5 he tells how, when a song of his creation
was pirated by others, he defeated them by composing a
new one, not caring what had happened. In couplets 6-8 he
recalls a shamanistic performance when his guardian spirit
took such a hold of him that he was unable to speak, and in
this humiliating situation he turned his eyes away from a
fellow-shaman, who enjoyed his discomfiture, and thereby
prevented his triumph. In couplets 9-11 he nearly lost his
harpoon to a seal, but while other sealers failed to get a
catch, he eventually succeeded. The four episodes are times of
crisis in his life, and in each he has, through his ability and
self-control, been delivered from an ugly or humiliating
situation. In its adroit, oblique way this is a paean of self-
praise. The shaman speaks of himself through carefully contrived boasts. Even these have something in common; for in
each Italsiaq rises to a menacing situation and shows his
worth against his antagonists. What the Selk'nam medicine
man does in lamentation for his country, the Eskimo shaman
does in self-commendation, and though both songs have a
recognizable unity of theme, they show how easily their
method could end in disorder if the singer did not fix his
attention firmly on some central point from which his variations radiate. The primitive mind calls for order in its songs,
and usually secures it even if its means are not immediately
obvious to us.

Primitive man composes songs with an eye to their unity
and shows considerable skill in doing so without losing anything that is essential to them. But there comes a point
when the matter for a song will not allow it to be presented
in this way, notably when it deals with complex matters of
religion or myth, whose different episodes cannot be omitted or neglected. In this case the solution is to compose not
one song but a series of songs, each of which deals with a
self-sufficient stage in a long process, and this is what the Australians of Arnhem Land do with their songs about the
Djanggawul and Kunapipi. Other Australians, especially the
Aranda, have hardly less complex subjects relating to mythical ancestors and heroes, and have developed their own
method of dealing with them. One event succeeds another, and
each song is not a unity of the usual kind but expands
and changes its themes as it proceeds. This is contrary to
the general practice of primitive song, but we can see its
connection with this in more than one respect. First, though
the song moves through various stages, each stage is self-
contained and treats only of a single event, which may indeed be prolonged through several couplets, but remains
complete in itself. Secondly, the transition from one stage to

another is done suddenly and abruptly, perhaps with a pause in the singing, certainly with a change in the accompanying dance or mime. The songman feels no call to provide any machining transition, and there is no need for him to do so, since it is done for him by the actors. Thirdly, the song itself is a commentary on a more complicated rite, which it accompanies and illustrates, but in illustrating omits much that occurs in the rite. This suggests that the composers of such songs feel the need to observe the rule of one thing at a time, even though their task makes this impossible, and that their songs, which are long and variegated, are in effect sequences of separate songs brought together. None the less this kind of composition is certainly more advanced than the normal kind, and in it we can see how, in answer to a special need, the composer passes beyond the usual conventions to something less static and less self-sufficient. In general, it looks as if in manner and method primitive song passes through three stages. First comes the absolute unity of subject; one subject alone is treated, and its nature is perfectly clear. In a second stage a greater variety comes from a wider range of relevant topics, but these are held together by a central mood or idea or purpose. Thirdly, in some Australian songs, this technique passes into something more comprehensive which allows for development in its accounts of varying action, but is still faithful to the tradition of keeping each episode separate in itself.

CHAPTER 5 *Songs of Action*

🙞🙜🙞🙜🙞🙜🙞🙜🙞🙜🙞🙜🙞🙜🙞🙜🙞🙜🙞🙜🙞🙜

THE FORM of action with which primitive man is most occupied is hunting. On this his whole existence depends, and to it he devotes a large part of his time and most of his talents. Such training as he receives from his parents in childhood is expressly designed to make him a good hunter, who knows how to track animals, to make and use weapons, to practise stealth and speed and agility, to have a steady eye and a steady nerve. Hunting is the centre on which his whole life turns, and to it his few handicrafts are ancillary, whether he makes weapons, or canoes, or baskets to carry food, or paints pictures of the animals which he hopes to kill. Occasional activities, like fighting, may be closely related to it and are regarded as an unimportant variation on it, calling with less excuse for similar qualities. No other activity compares with hunting for urgency or variety, and whether the pursuit is of animals or birds or fish or wild honey, it evokes a wide range of responses and becomes a primary theme of song both sacred and secular. More than this, because it imposes a commanding pattern on man's existence, it also shapes his outlook and habits of thought. In his songs about it we can see more clearly than in any other field how he looks at his daily necessities and what they do for him and his understanding of the world and himself. Hunting is not a common subject of civilized poetry. Even in societies where it is a royal or princely sport, it does not inspire much interesting verse. Some pieces in the Chinese *Book of Songs* and the poems carved before 600 BC on stone drums in the Confucian temple at Peking are indeed concerned with it, but mainly as an occasion to show off horses and chariots and to come home with a record bag of deer. This is not the spirit of primitive hunting, which is not a pastime but an imperious need, and just for this reason has not only its unequalled thrills but its paramount dignity. A man may risk his life in it, but without it he will die of starvation. Because hunting is the centre of primitive life, anything that contributes to it has some importance, and no detail is too insignificant to be unworthy of attention.

Hunting sheds an intimate and revealing light on the relation of primitive man to the supernatural world. Believing that he is encompassed on every side by gods and spirits, he assumes that he can undertake no serious action without invoking their good will and help. At the same time he knows that this help is not everything, that he must exert his own powers and skill to the utmost. No doubt his trust in the supernatural enables him to act with fuller confidence and carries him through much that might otherwise be beyond his powers. But in his songs his trust in the supernatural and his trust in himself complement one another and show how, despite his unquestioning belief in gods and spirits, he makes his own efforts almost independently of them. At each stage of hunting he invokes them as necessary to it. It calls for preparations both at the supernatural and at the natural level. A hunt has to be organized with practical foresight, but the spirits who govern the forest or the bush or the desert or the sea have to be cajoled and secured as allies. This may be a simple enough business, but the hunter must give his whole care to it, and his attempts to win his gods reveal how deeply hunting penetrates into his life. Because it takes place every day, it stimulates an expert knowledge and creates a special attitude towards anything that touches it. The hunter thinks about it so continuously that he matures appropriate attitudes towards its preparations and gives to them a care which shows how much they mean to him and how deeply he is absorbed in them. For instance, the Eskimos have magic words which are spoken over dogs trained to pursue the polar bear:

> Little child like a Tuneq,
> Little dog, little dog,

> See its heart
> Tastes of luscious lubber,
> Tastes truly of luscious lubber.
> Your cousin, leap on him,
> Your cousin, fight with him.[1]

The guardian spirit is called to strengthen the dog and make it good at its work; for this the spirit must enter into the dog and inflame its temper by fighting with it. This is eminently practical, but it gains strength from the hunter's intimate companionship with his guardian-spirit and the affection and care which he feels for his dog.

In the same way a Vedda gives all his attention and devotion to his arrow, as he puts a charm on it:

> Go and drop behind the body of the monitor-lizard;
> Pierce it, dear cousin.

> Leave that place, arrow-brother,
> Go and cleave it in the edge of the back.

> Leave that place, arrow-brother,
> Go and cleave it twice in the tail.

> Leave that place, arrow-brother,
> Go and cleave it twice in the neck.

> Leave that place, arrow-brother,
> Go and cleave it twice in the belly.

> Leave that place, arrow-brother,
> Go and fix yourself in the middle of the armpit.[2]

This is noteworthy in more than one respect. First, the hunter really loves his arrow, and that is why he calls it "cousin" and "brother." It is his indispensable and faithful partner in his expeditions, and without it he can do nothing. It is so much part of himself that he ascribes to it his own capacity and purpose and has no doubt that it can do what he wishes. Secondly, as he enumerates the various parts of the lizard which the arrow may hit, he reveals the close and careful thought which he gives to hunting as he turns over its various possibilities and decides which would be most welcome to him. Before setting out he prepares the way to success by applying his whole mind to what lies before him.

In offering prayers, or casting charms for hunting, primitive man is well aware that his own efforts are of paramount importance, but he must first set the scene for them to work in, and this he does by placating the right gods and spirits. Without their co-operation there may be nothing for him to hunt, or accidents may prevent his success; and his prayers and charms are admirably realistic in their demands. When the Bushman hunts the springbok, he sets out at dawn and appeals to the sun to come out and help him:

> Sun, come out,
> That we may see,
> Sun, rise for us,
> Sun, come out,
> That we may see to seek a springbok.[3]

The Eskimo communes with his guardian spirit, who is approached not only with confident affection but also with a practical notion of what is expected from him:

> You, fatherless and motherless,
> You, dear little orphan,
> Give me kamiks of caribou,
> Bring me a gift,
> An animal, one of those
> That provide good blood-soup,
> An animal from the sea-depths,
> And not from the plains of earth,
> You, little orphan,
> Bring me a gift.[4]

He may even ask his guardian spirit to take the form of a seal which he can then catch. This seems to be asking a lot, but the spirit is immortal, and there is no reason to think that it will suffer in so sensible a proceeding:

> Orphan,
> You, little orphan,
> On the other side of the open sea,
> On its beautiful other side,
> Creep there carefully,
> Come out of the water,
> In the shape of a seal,
> Puh![5]

Once he has secured the right help from his spirits, the hunter has confidence that game will be sent to him. It is then up to him to kill it by his own skill and courage. The bargain between man and god is entirely reasonable and arranges a proper partition of labour between them.

This belief in gods and spirits does not mean that the hunter is not to take proper pains to master his craft and to make every possible preparation when he sets out on an expedition. His equipment must be as good as he can make it, and we find an Eskimo from Western Greenland giving full and careful instructions to the young on the uses of a kayak:

> Listen to my words,
> All you children!
> The kayak is very small
> And dangerous;
> Waves and winds have great strength.
> But when your thoughts have become used to them,
> You can travel among them.
>
> Then first, like those who can do everything,
> You will be good hunters of seals,
> Like men when your need afflicts you.
> On the look-out in the kayak you will strike with the
>   harpoon,
> And even in winter, when the cold is strongest,
> You will proudly succeed with it.
>
> Listen to the old,
> The experienced counsellor;
> The orders they give to you
> You must obey.
> Even in winter, when it also happens,
> You will proudly succeed with it.[6]

The first need in primitive education is instruction in hunting, and here an old man gives his wise counsel. He is aware both of the usual dangers and of the ways to overcome them, and his advice is given at a purely human level with no thought at the moment for the spirits who help or hinder the chase. This does not mean that they are unimportant, but his immediate task is to encourage the young, and he does so with the pride of a man who knows his job. Skill in hunting must be treated realistically. If a man fails, he may have good reasons for it, but he may sometimes be to blame for lack of enterprise or skill, and then it is fair to make fun of him, as another Eskimo song does:

> Last year a harpooner, a bungler,
> Kukujuk, Kukujuktek,
> Shot at a whale but his harpoon went past him,
> Kukujuk, Kukujuktek.
> Orders were given to him,
> That he should be a steersman;

> But since he was a booby, they said good-bye
>   to him.
> That was annoying to him.[7]

A man must do his best in his job and may be despised if he
fails too often. He may lose "face" in his society and become almost an outcast, since his world cannot afford to have
people like him who make no contribution to the common
stock of food and are thought to be unworthy of their sex
and kind.

Since hunting is the first activity of primitive man and
shapes the pattern of most of his other activities, it evokes a
wide variety of moods, and there is no conventional standard
for the spirit in which he embarks upon it. We might expect
that he would normally work himself up into a state of heady
confidence in which he feels that he is certain to succeed,
and so he sometimes does. So among the Dama the leader
of a hunting party proclaims his assurance in no hesitant
tones:

> I, the head of the village am here!
> I have caught you!
> Die, elephant!
> Die, giraffe!
> Die, kudu!
> Die, eland!
> Die, wildebeest! [8]

As the actual moment becomes nearer and clearer, this mood
may be tempered, and the hunter may admit what the facts
of the situation are. So the Dama, having expressed their confidence through their leader, turn to more restrained language,
as when in hunting the lion they offer a prayer:

> Give me a poisoned arrow,
> Lion under the *ga*-tree!
> I stand here all alone,
> O poisoned arrow!
> O broad-breasted lion!
> Give me an arrow, whose point is tested,
> Give me an arrow dipped in *gore*-poison!
> O poisoned arrow![9]

As the uncertainties of the chase become more manifest and
more immediate, the first mood of high assurance passes into
a considered estimate of the prospects. The need for success
is an acid test, and though the hunter naturally hopes that
he will get what he wants, he knows the difficulties and
makes little attempt to hide them. So the Eskimos are fully

conscious of the risks of failure, and have their own charms to deal with it. In his own district a man may know how things work, but when he is away from it, he has to face his inexperience and may feel that he is not properly prepared. Then he uses a charm which is delightfully candid and modest:

> I am afraid,
> I feel afraid and perplexed.
> My grandmother
> Sent me out to search.
> I am on an errand
> After the dear foxes.
> But alas! I am in fear and perplexed.
> I am ashamed,
> I am afraid and perplexed.
> My great-grandmother and grandmother
> Sent me out to search.
> I go out on their errand
> After the dear game,
> After the dear caribou,
> But alas! I am ashamed,
> And feel afraid and perplexed.[10]

No doubt the assumption underlying this charm is that the appropriate spirits will be impressed by its modesty and come to the hunter's aid, but it would never have been composed if he did not know how greatly experience and knowledge, especially of local conditions, count in hunting and how little right a man has to assume that all will go well with him when he moves into new hunting-grounds. The realism of the hunter's outlook demonstrates how his knowledge of his craft teaches him also to know himself.

During the chase, and especially at the actual moment of the encounter, song is out of the question, and even afterwards it does not often celebrate them unless something so unusual has happened that it calls for special notice. An Andamanese song is exceptional when it recalls in retrospect the preparations for the kill just before it happens, and conveys an absorbing sense of a thrilling crisis. The hunter sees his prey, in this case wild pig, advances on his belly towards it, and then draws his bow:

> My bow, its lower part, I drew back,
> My bow, its lower part.
> Stooping, softly creeping,
> *Stooping, softly creeping.*[11]

The instant is brilliantly recaptured, and the hunter's pride,

mingled with his thrill at the time, passes into purely factual
statements, but, since on such an occasion it is the action that
counts, he shows his tact in telling of his adventure just as it
happened. So too an Eskimo song deals with a series of
such occasions, and it too catches the breathless tension with
which the hunter watches his prey as it comes into his power:

> Over there I could think of nothing else,
> Beneath me when it breathed loudly through the water.
>
> When the broth-provider was going to rush up to me,
> Beneath me, I could think of nothing else.
>
> While I had to give all my attention to the harpoon of
>   my making,
> It pulled me strongly upwards and downwards.
>
> Over there I could think of nothing else,
> The grub animal—I could think of nothing else.
>
> My fellows went to lay low the caribou.
> The caribou—I could think of nothing else.
>
> Over there I could think of nothing else,
> When the antlered caribou began to come to me.
>
> While I lay thus in my pit and listened intently,
> The antlered caribou began to come to me.[12]

Whether it is the seal ("the broth-provider"), or the musk-ox
("the grub animal"), or the caribou, the Eskimo catches with
faithful accuracy his mood of eager, expectant, anxious concentration when he hopes to make a kill. He is obsessed by
his task and throws himself completely into it. That is why
his song, and others like it, both ring true and have their own
artistic appeal, even though they are little more than statements of fact.

Hunting has its unforeseen surprises and emergencies,
which call for presence of mind in the hunter, but are none
the less thrilling in recollection. An Andamanese song tells of
a man who goes out fishing for dugong. He harpoons one, but
fails to kill it, with the result that it swims away and drags
him after it in his canoe as he holds firmly on to his
harpoon:

> Whew! Out to sea he dragged me! Your belly
>   kept turning!
> Wow! Your belly kept turning!

Ha! Twang! Back he dragged me with a rush O!
Ha! Twang! Back he dragged me with a rush O![13]

As he recalls the perilous moment, the hunter recaptures its
desperate thrill and lives through it again. Indeed, even in
recollection it is so exciting that he is only just articulate
and part of his song consists of purely emotive sounds which
convey the breathless character of his adventure. He sees it
very vividly and immediately and makes it real for his hearers. This is a fine diversion in the usual round of hunting
and calls to be honoured in song.

Many successful kills have this unexpected quality, and
since they make up much of primitive man's daily round
and assume a large part in his repertory of memories, they
tend, as time passes, to assume less breathless shapes and to
gain an enhanced dignity as they recede into the past. A remarkable song, composed by the Eskimo Orpingalik in a time
of sickness, shows how he looks back on his achievements
and examines them separately and finds in each its own
distinction:

> I remember the white bear,
> With its back-body raised high;
> It thought it was the only male here,
> And came towards me at full speed.
> > *Unaya, unaya.*

> Again and again it threw me down,
> But it did not lie over me,
> But quickly went from me again.
> It had not thought
> Of meeting other males here,
> And by the edge of an ice-floe
> It lay down calmly.
> > *Unaya, unaya.*

> I shall never forget the great blubber-beast;
> On the firm ice I had already flayed it,
> When the neighbours with whom I shared the
>   land here
> Had just woken.
> It was as if I had just gone to its breathing-hole
>   out there.
> > *Unaya, unaya.*

> There as I came across it,
> And as I stood over it, it heard me,
> Without scratching at the ice,

At the under edge of the firm ice to which it
    had hooked itself,
Truly it was a cunning beast—
Just as I felt sorry that I had not caught it,
    Unaya, unaya.

I caught it fast with my harpoon-head,
Before it had even drawn breath![14]

Here the reminiscence of struggles in the past is coloured by
pride in their successful outcome. None the less the hunter
remembers them exactly and recalls clearly what he felt and
did at the time. This is the kind of ordeal for which he has
been bred and to which he has given the larger part of his
life. So he marks not only the details of these outstanding occasions but the almost unique character of each. As he lies
in his hut on his sick-bed, he is comforted by the thought
that in his time he has been an adventurous and skilful man
of action and done what anyone would be proud to do.

A successful kill may evoke more than one kind of response for its celebration. The simplest kind embodies unmixed pride and delight and raises no awkward questions
about ghosts or spirits who have to be placated. An example
of this is an Andamanese song, which looks as if it were
composed very close to the event of which it tells. A hunter,
who has killed a wild pig and skewered it, brings it back on
his shoulders:

From the skewer O the blood O on my skin
    dripped down,
On my skin kept dripping down,
From the pig O on my skin kept
Dripping down, from the pig O on my skin kept
Dripping down, from the pig O on my skin kept.[15]

The underlying mood is of triumph, but the hunter expresses
it by drawing attention to its visible emblem, the carcase
which drips blood on him. His mood is not boastfulness but
delight; he feels that he has completed his job and won his
reward in the dead pig, which is there for all to see. At a
greater distance from his successes an Eskimo reveals his
proficiency and expertise by relating a series of them:

I wanted to use my weapon.
There was a big blubbery seal on the ice, even here.
I struck smartly with my harpoon,
And then I just pulled it up, the seal wandering from
    one breathing-hole to another.

I wanted to use my weapon.
There was a big antlered caribou on the land, even
    down there.
I shot my arrow swiftly,
Then I just knocked it down in this place, the caribou
    that wandered about the land.

I wanted to use my weapon.
There was a fish right in the lake, even here.
I struck it smartly with my fish-spear,
Then I just pulled it up, the fish that wandered about
    down here.

I wanted to use my weapon.
There was a big bearded seal, just at the river-mouth,
    even here.
I paddled my kayak hard,
Then I simply towed it ashore, just at the river-mouth.[16]

This is more subtly contrived than the Andamanese song,
and relies more on events which have won a special place in
memory. Each stanza describes not merely a separate occasion but a different way of securing a prey, and there is
a neat climax in the final stanza when a seal is simply
towed to land without being struck by harpoon or arrow
or fish-spear. The Eskimo is more consciously proud of his
performances than is the Andamanese, and his song is meant
to impress his fellows with his resource and skill. Even so,
we can catch his delight as he recalls how he outwitted
and outfought his adversaries on land and sea.

So far these songs of hunting conform to the usual pattern
of human actions and evoke the simplest and most natural
responses. They provide models for many later songs of
action which extend beyond mere hunting, and anticipate
their temper. But for primitive man killing has more tricky
sides than this. In a world governed by gods and spirits,
animals also have their place, and if a man kills them,
he must see that he does not suffer for it. This arises in an
almost embarrassing form for the Pygmies when they kill
an elephant, since it is a sacred animal, the lord of the forest, the embodiment of divine powers, and in some sense
their own father. In their different songs about the slaying
of elephants they show how they try to surmount this perplexity and to put themselves right with the slain beast and
its protectors. In one song the leader of the hunt, supported
by both men and women, dances and sings a song:

Leader I have seen, and we have gone into the forest.

Leader Bow and lance in hand, we have gone into the
          forest.
Women *Tiadele mo, tiadele mo.*
Leader In the black village, the village far away,
          The father was there, the father of past times.
Women Blood, tears, death.
          Tiadele mo, tiadele mo.
All   We made the alliance. We are the masters.
          The sun shines. The moon lightens the night.
          The sun is dead. The moon is above.
          We are masters of the dead, masters of the night,
Men   Masters of the day, masters of the night,
          Death, night shadows, the glow-worms have
          passed.[17]

The leader then takes up his weapons and drenches them
in the blood of the dead beast, and the whole company
follows his example. Then the elephant is cut up for eating.
This is a song of triumph, and it makes no concessions to
the dead beast or its invisible protectors. Its destruction is
seen as a victory in a fight between it, the old master of the
forest, and men, who are the new masters, and this is illustrated by the imagery of night and day. The sun is applied
first to the elephant in his old position of eminence, and
then transferred to the hunters who have taken over his position, and the moon, who is the goddess of hunting, is now
allied with the sun and the men. The dead beast is treated
with considerable deference, but his death raises no uncom-
fortable doubts about his departed spirit or about any need
to appease it.

This need is faced more squarely in another song, which
aims both at glorifying the hunters and placating the spirit
of the dead elephant. The hunter looks upon him as his
father, but advances an ingenious argument against his feeling any anger about his death:

Against your children, father elephant,
Do not be angry!
We have taken you away, we have given you back life.
Against your children, father elephant,
Do not be angry, you begin a better life.
Honour to you, my lance,
My lance of sharpened iron, honour to you! [18]

After doing his best to placate the elephant by assuring it
that it is better off than before, the hunter turns to his weapon and pays his tribute to it. This ambivalent attitude arises
from the relation of primitive man to animals and especially
to an animal so obviously superior as the elephant. On the

one hand, men are connected with animals, often by totems, often by tabus, often by myths of descent from them or beliefs that they were once men. The relation here is not that of a totem, since, though some Pygmies have the elephant for totem, they are in that case not allowed to kill it and eat it, and what counts is some vaguer and more ambiguous kinship, in which the elephant is both honoured as a superior being and yet hunted as man's obvious prey. The elephant is then reasonably imagined to feel some resentment when it is killed. On the other hand, it is a staple source of food, and its killing calls for the highest ingenuity and courage as the Pygmies move under its belly and stab it to death with their spears. It is inconceivable that they should allow considerations of kinship or grandeur to interfere with this. So they contrive an ingenious compromise, by which its death is presented as a right and proper action because it enables the elephant to enter into a new life. None the less, what strikes us most in the midst of these apologies and excuses is the Pygmies' note of triumph over its death. Once its spirit has been placated, song is free to burst out in delight, and the hunter implicitly praises himself while he praises the lance which has brought the huge beast down.

A third Pygmy song deals with a like situation by rather different means. The moment the elephant has been brought to the ground, the hunters raise cries of solemn joy. The leader emasculates it and puts round its neck a garland like that which a woman wears before getting married. The private parts are similarly draped and then buried in the depths of the forest. During this procedure the leader crowns himself with flowers and sings:

> Our spear has gone astray,
>   O father elephant!
> We did not wish to kill you,
> We did not wish to kill you,
>   O father elephant!
> It is not the warrior who has taken away your life,
> Your hour had come.
> Do not return to trample on our huts,
>   O father elephant!

As he puts flowers on the elephant's parts, he sings:

> Do not make us feel your wrath.
> Henceforward your life will be better,
> You go to the country of spirits,
> Our fathers go with you to renew the alliance.

> Henceforward your life will be better,
> You go to the country of spirits.

As he buries the parts, he sings:

> Here you are going to rest for ever;
> Rest henceforward in peace.
> Here are your children,
> Let not your anger fall upon them.[19]

The leader then returns to the corpse and dances a dance of victory. In this song the Pygmies develop their notion that they are doing the elephant a good turn by sending its spirit to join the spirits of their own ancestors, and in this there is a marked contrast with the preceding song. There the final note is of triumph for the hunter; here it is of hope that no evil will befall him. Primitive man lives in too great an uncertainty to enjoy triumph carelessly for long, and wisely looks out for all possible mischances and misadventures. So the cycle of elephant-songs ends on what is essentially a note of modesty, of hope that nothing will come amiss after the thrills and the successes.

These Pygmy songs are devised for success, but of course the hunter may fail and, though then any formal ritual or celebration is out of place, he may have to release his emotions for his own satisfaction or to explain his failure to his fellows. Two Andamanese songs show how this can be done. In the first the hunter does no more than describe his sensations at missing his prey, and they are almost entirely physical:

> By beetles my ears are rasped,
> By cicadas my ears are rasped O!
> My ears are rasped O and buzzing O,
> *My ears are rasped O and buzzing O!*[20]

This lively account of a shocked and horrified state of mind is derived from what the hunter has just seen and heard, the beetles and the cicadas in the jungle where he failed to kill. He still hears them in his ears, and we see just what he means. He is overcome by emotion, but it is not shame, and he does not apologize or explain. Rather he is appalled that he has not brought home anything from the chase. Another Andamanese song does indeed provide an explanation for failure, but it would be accepted at once as entirely adequate and reasonable. It is that the hunter has been put off by dead men's bodies in the forest and has come home without pursuing his prey:

> Dead men's bones, where I am hunting!
> My heart is throbbing, O!
> My heart is throbbing, is pounding away,
> *Throbbing it is, pounding away!*[21]

Like the preceding song, this describes a sensation, and here too the sensation is of shock and dismay. There is no need to think that the hunter intends to explain away his failure. He is so full of it, and so dominated by a horrifying experience, that it drives all other thoughts from his mind.

Hunting is so insistent a necessity, and success in it depends on so many unpredictable and uncontrollable factors, that failure may be the lot of even the most skilful and most courageous, and boasts and lies will do nothing to counter it. So, though primitive man enjoys success in the chase and is proud of it, he is not ashamed to speak of failure. By confessing it freely he may overcome the depression which he feels at having made all his efforts to no purpose. The Eskimos have a number of songs in which they speak not only of bad luck but of their own incompetence. In this there is perhaps an element of good manners, of mock modesty, as if the hunter felt it arrogant to claim too much for himself. Yet we cannot but feel that this masks a real sense of defeat, which it is useless for him to conceal, and the candid admission of it may cheer him by taking it off his mind. So one song runs through the chief victims of Eskimo hunting and announces that all have eluded the hunter:

> Those game animals, those long-haired caribou,
> Though they roam everywhere, I am quite unable to
>   get any.
> I carried this bow of mine in my hand always.
> At last I pondered deeply:
> It is all right, even if
> I am quite unable to get them in the present winter.

> Those game animals, those seals,
> Though they keep visiting their holes, I am quite
>   unable to get any.
> I carried this harpoon of mine in my hand always.
> At last I pondered deeply:
> It is all right, even if
> I begin at last to be greatly afraid in this present
>   summer.

> Those game animals, those fish.
> Though I go out in the middle of the lake, I am
>   quite unable to get any.

At last I pondered deeply:
It is all right, even if
I begin at last to be afraid of the hummocky ice
 within.

Those seals, those fearful brown bears,
Constantly walking about here, I begin to be terrified.
This arrow of mine is fearless, this arrow.
Am I to allow myself to be terrified at last?[22]

This is an acute and revealing piece of self-examination. The hunter knows that he has failed in his tasks, and in the first three stanzas comforts himself with the consolation that it does not matter very much and that in the end all will be well. Then in the last stanza he changes his tone, and begins to see that something fearful may happen to him, and that he ought to do something about it. This change of mood is marked by a change of form, for while the first three stanzas are much on the same model, the fourth is different, and we get the impression that the hunter has suddenly woken up to the realities of his position and begun to think seriously about it without fobbing himself off with false comfort. Yet what moves him in the end is not a sense of honour or even a desire to excel, but simply fear that, if he continues in his present state, something may go seriously wrong. It is reasonable and natural, and it shows how candidly primitive hunters speak of their first and chief activity.

This frank approach to success and failure presents marked contrasts with the heroic outlook which exists in more developed societies and reflects their obsession with vigorous and violent action such as war. Primitive song hardly ever exalts individuals or any class of mythical heroes in the narrow sense. If it tells of ancestors, as it sometimes does, it is not to praise them for their courage or their sacrifices but to present them as examples of human behaviour, as prototypes of subsequent men, and tales of them are meant rather to explain than to exalt. For this absence of heroes there are good reasons. First, a primitive society is essentially communal. The individual nurses his own thoughts and feelings and has to fend for himself, but his existence is so closely interwoven with that of his fellows that he cannot attain any peculiar pre-eminence or be regarded as almost different in kind from them. What he does, he does in their company, and if there is any glory to be gained, he usually shares it with others. Secondly, he is much too concerned with the need to keep alive to make so

abstract a notion as glory the end of life. This is possible only
when the mechanics of survival are so firmly established
that time and trouble can be given to other less immediate
needs. It follows that in our songs there is little boasting of
success even in hunting except at the actual moment of the
kill, and it is certainly not common form to conceal failure
or even to explain it away. It is not in itself thought dis-
graceful, because everyone knows that in so uncertain a matter it is not for men to command success.

This attitude may help to explain the primitive outlook
on war. That these peoples sometimes indulge in it we cannot dispute. In our own time Pygmies, Bushmen and Dana
have resisted invaders by violence. Nor is fighting thought
an unsuitable subject for art. Bushman paintings from
Southern Rhodesia contain scenes of battle, and the Tasmanians are said to have composed songs about their attacks
and depredations on the houses of the white settlers.
Yet war in the sense of an organized campaign, still less as
a pattern of life, is unknown to primitive societies and seems,
like capitalism, slavery, class distinctions, specialized pro-
fessions, and urban civilization to be a development of the
Neolithic revolution. When men value land for what they
can grow on it, they will lust for more, and for this they
are prepared to organize forces on some scale and conse-
quently to develop a *mystique* of honour and heroism to sus-
tain them. Primitive societies lack the organization to make
war on such a scale, and their motives for it are mainly
defensive. They do not fight to gain new lands, but turn to
war when their hunting-grounds are invaded or foreigners
grab their food or their women, and at times they retaliate
by raiding their enemies' cattle. Fighting is a means not to
show individual prowess but to preserve the food-supply,
and becomes in practice very like a branch of hunting.
Primitive peoples sometimes engage in war and even sing
of it, but such emphasis as it receives is only another sign
of the perils which face them when they are threatened
by other peoples more organized and better equipped than
themselves. Their songs of war are incidental to their main
routine, and reflect the frame of mind which we know from
their songs of hunting.

War, like hunting, must be entered upon in a proper spirit.
The gods must be placated, kept informed of what is happening, and asked to give help. So when the Gabon Pygmies
prepare to fight enemies, they first consecrate their arms to
Khmvum, who is lord of the forest and therefore of life
and death, and summon him to their aid much as they would
if they were going to hunt elephants:

Khmvum, O Khmvum, you are the master, the master
  of everything,
Khmvum, O Khmvum, you are master of the forest,
Master of trees, master of things,
Khmvum, you are the master,
And we, the little ones, we are your subjects.
Command, and we shall obey, O Khmvum!
You are the master, the master of everything,
The master of men, O Khmvum![23]

Khmvum is in no sense a god of war as such. His domain is
the forest and all that belongs to it. So in the special emer-
gency of war he is asked for help. War is an undertaking
which calls for the same preparations and the same weapons as hunting, and since it is intermittent, while hunting is
always necessary, it has no special apparatus of song or
ritual. When the Dama go on an expedition to raid the cattle
of their Herero enemies, the food-master pronounces a curse
on them:

        May you be broken like a staff,
        That we alone may have strength!
        May your hearts become afraid![24]

Yet even this is very like a charm put upon fierce animals
before hunting them, and shows how the hunter's mentality
dominates his approach to battle.

This does not mean that, when fighting is a theme of song,
it is not treated with violence. The killing of other men in
battle is a more serious and more bloodthirsty business than
the killing of beasts, if only because both sides possess weapons and intelligence and are in most ways equally matched.
Moreover, since primitive fighting is usually caused by the in-
vasion of hunting grounds which custom and common agree-
ment have allotted to a group of people, this group feels
outraged against the invaders as it never does against animals. So we can understand why a song of the Bambuti Pygmies almost literally breathes fire and slaughter against an
enemy:

        The spear shall pierce him,
        And he shall be stewed
        Over the fire
        In a bag made of leaves.[25]

But despite these angry emotions, songs of victory hardly
exist, and death in battle is not celebrated with any special
honour. War affects primitive peoples in their struggle to live,
and it is this which touches them most deeply. Defeat in it is

like failure in hunting, which may equally bring loss of life, and a Dama song regrets in simple words an expedition which has evidently failed:

> O hillock under the *aro*-tree, you are hard to dig up!
> Of those who set forth, these have come back.
> It is hard to roll away an immovable rock.[26]

When men are killed in war, it is their women who are most affected by their loss and who lament them:

> She, who is not yet ready for a man, is already a widow;
> See the children of sisters fallen into jealousy.[27]

Even mythical ancestors, who might have the making of authentic heroes and be held up as models of behaviour, are treated with less honour than we might expect. The Bushmen have such a hero and tell how in his childhood his mother used to praise his strength:

> Thou son of a great woman,
> Thy body looks like a cow's body,
> Thou big acacia with large branches,
> Thou red bull,
> Thou son of a red she-bull,
> Thou who didst drink my milk,
> Thou to whom I did not give my breast slowly.[28]

This recalls the childhood of heroes in most consciously war-like societies, and this hero comes to a suitably violent end, but after his death his mother has nothing to say about his glory but simply reproaches him for not taking her advice:

> Did I not tell thee, my son,
> Beware of the one who walks quite straight,
> Who has sharp spears and poisoned arrows,
> Whose teeth are like poisonous arrow-heads?
> Thou son of the short-eared one,
> Thou yellow child of the Lion-tail,
> Why didst thou not listen to what thy mother told
>   thee?[28]

In a primitive society courage is important because it helps to get food, but it must be combined with cunning, and if a man loses his life through foolhardiness, his comrades suffer, and he deserves no special glory. The true heroic ideal grows in societies far more complex than any with which we are concerned and in which it has no place and no meaning.

The demands and the discipline of hunting shape the

mentality of primitive men and create a coherent, dominating outlook which informs their songs and passes into their whole lives. Though it is recognized that success is not always possible and that failure is not necessarily dishonourable, the hunter must do his best to kill his prey and above all must not be wanting in comradeship on difficult or dangerous occasions. If through sloth or slackness or cowardice he lags behind in the chase, he fails in his duty to his fellows and must not remain unchidden. So the Eskimo Orpingalik addresses a song to a "song-fellow," with whom he has gone out in the past and who now suggests that they should go out together again. The tone is dignified and on the whole friendly, but it contains a reproof:

> I remember, my dear song-fellow,
> With our songs we were seldom defeated.
> When one with enormous antlers
> Has set out there over its crossing-place,
> And the great lake there
> Covers the kayaks with ice in the cold,
> Let us chase it then.
> Which of us will then fall behind?
> Once long ago at Tigluarfik,
> When you were quite young,
> And the kayaks there
> Seemed to be a pack of wolves,
> The big lake there
> You did not cleave fast enough,
> When you followed behind
> After me there—
> I could not praise you for that.[29]

The words are studiously moderate, and Orpingalik is willing to go out hunting again with his "song-fellow," but because in the past he was once slow in the pursuit, he reminds him of it and implies a hope that this will not happen again. In a small society, where every effort has to be made to keep its members alive, there is no place even for minor slacking like this. The occasion, which Orpingalik recalls, was important in that it offered fine prospects of game and contained elements of danger. To lag behind at such a time is to invite reproof, and the "song-fellow" is perhaps lucky to be let off as lightly as he is. Though primitive song seldom indulges in explicit moral judgments and hardly ever lays down rules of behaviour, here the personal tone of Orpingalik's words is undeniably critical and implies a system of values to which the song-fellow is expected to conform. It is their seriousness which gives dignity to the poem and strengthens its personal touch. Honour exists in primitive societies but it centres not on an individual's pride in his own doings but in what he does for his comrades and his family. The first call on a man is to help them and do all that he can for them, and if he does this, he will win their respect.

The very moderation with which Orpingalik chides his song-fellow reveals how sanely and temperately primitive man treats his sense of honour. It is part of his realism, of his close contact with irresistible, relentless facts. If he applies too exacting a standard to himself or his fellows, he may find that it is more than conditions allow, and may soon prove to be impracticable. He is therefore saved from assuming false airs and encouraged not to treat himself too seriously. Since the rhythm of his life has inevitable ups and downs, and in many places he is at the mercy of unscrupulous and unfriendly neighbours, he must be prepared to take things as they come. Failures, of course, may be lamented, and sometimes are, but it may relieve his feelings if he laughs at them. This laughter may come from surmounting self-pity with irony and humour. So the Pygmy, Nkü, also known as Mba Sholé, sang to some visiting Europeans of his fate, which is no doubt representative of his fellows and consists of being exploited by the peoples who live around them:

> The forest is great, the wind is good,
> Forward the Beku, your bows on your arms!

> This way, that way, this way and that way.
> A pig! Who kills the pig?
> It is Nkü. But who eats it? Poor Nkü!
> Always cut it to pieces! you will feast on . . . the tripe!

> Plomp! an elephant on the ground!
> Who has killed it? It is Nkü.
> Who will have the fine tusks? Poor Nkü!
> Always strike it down! They will leave you . . . the tail!

> Without a house like the monkeys,
> Who gathers honey? It is Nkü!
> Who eats it till his belly aches? Poor Nkü!
> Always get it down! They will leave you . . . the wax!

> The Whites are there, good Whites!
> Who is it who dances? It is Nkü.
> But who will smoke his tobacco? Poor Nkü!

Sit down all the same and reach out your hand.[30]

There is no doubt about the ironical gaiety of this song, nor of its desire to engage the sympathy of the white visitors and extract some tobacco from them. But it is based on prolonged humiliation and privation, and illuminates the conditions in which the Pygmies live. Though they are accomplished hunters, they are liable to be robbed of their prey by more powerful neighbours, and Nkü's reaction to this is to laugh at it and transform his annoyance into comedy. The close contact of primitive man with the natural world and his inescapable dependence on it clear his mind of many illusions which hamper those who live in greater ease and security, and he is not so foolish as to treat himself too solemnly. His privations are serious enough, and he has good reason to complain about them, but laughter is probably a better means than most for surmounting them.

This laughter can of course be turned against others, and then it is not always so good-humoured. The Eskimos often sing songs of derision against one another, and these serve a useful purpose by providing a vent for accumulated grievances. Fortunately they are taken in quite good part by the victims and may even help to repair friendships which have been seriously shaken. They are emphatically *pièces d'occasion*, and it is not always easy for us to reconstruct their background, which is of course perfectly clear to those who hear them. So Pluvkaq derides his nephew, who quarrelled with a man for stealing a dead musk-ox and went to his village, knife in hand, in order to strike him. The song runs:

> Here I am, and I have made ready
> A bit of a song and greatly desire to use it
> In its cutting shape along its wide road . . .
> Down there westwards, down there westwards,
> Here am I, wide awake.
> At night, when people sleep, I hear something that
> comes to my ear
> From the west over there,
> About my little nephew Ahsonenajuk . . .
> Out on the winter ice at Taranjunuaq,
> Over there on the firm winter ice,
> Against dogs and possessions
> You started to howl,
> When there was nothing, when meat was scarce,
> When blubber was scarce.
> What was there, no one should be mean about;
> You should not have thought of it.
> That time, a knife in hand, you called a man out.

I heard you all right, and now I only recall you,
I, who did not then understand what it meant,
I simply forgot it.
It is I who put together
This bit of a song to use it in defence,
Although sometimes it escapes me.[31]

Pluvkaq takes the side of the man and mocks his nephew
for making so violent a to-do about what was after all a
trivial incident. The man, as seen through his interpreter,
has a good case in so far as the meat should be eaten by
someone, and he very prudently took it for himself, no
doubt having some claim to it. The nephew is derided for
his meanness and pettiness in making a murderous fuss in a
matter which should be below the notice of any decent man.
Pluvkaq speaks with some restraint, as indeed many Eskimos seem to do on such occasions, but it is clear where his
sympathies lie and what he thinks about his nephew's behaviour.

The hard calls of primitive life foster a keen insight into
human nature and stimulate the composition of songs which
have a nice touch of worldly wisdom and astute perception.
But this insight depends on the emotions, which are indeed
controlled in the songs, but can in their raw state be for-
midably violent. The uncertainties of primitive life may breed
irony and humour, but there are times when these cannot
be evoked and the naked cruelty of existence has its way
and excites more troubled and more troubling moods. Behind these efforts to master a situation through song we can
often see how unsure primitive man is of himself and of his
ability to dominate his circumstances, how he can take very
little for granted and make no calculation or forecast which
is not likely to be proved false by events. No doubt he surmounts this for a large part of his time by living wholly in
the moment and extracting from it all that it has to give,
but at other times events are so menacing or disastrous that
he feels lost and hardly knows where to turn. Though he
knows his own hunting grounds as well as a man can know
anything, his roots are neither deep nor sure, and sooner or
later he must move from one place to another, not knowing
what lies before him or what it will cost him. He has indeed
his family, and this is the most enduring element in his life,
but he has no lasting dwelling-place in which to keep it.
Though he is often on the move, he faces it with misgiving
and anxiety. He sets out in hopeful enough a mood, as when
a Dama prays that all may be well in his new home:

> May we be fortunate here,
> May we find food,
> May we find flesh![32]

But this is tempered by an acid uncertainty which eats into
his confidence. He knows that he is leaving places which
have many associations and memories for him, as a second
Dama song tells of leaving the grave of a father:

> Father, we shall go away from you,
> That is why we come to you for the last time.
> May you be happy![33]

Once he has set out on his travels, he may find that things
are worse than before and that he is at a loss what to do,
as a third Dama song shows:

> A waterless land is this.
> Women, do you know the land whither I
>   would go?
> A waterless land is this.
> Women, do you know the spring to which I
>   would go?
> I am weary of these words:
> "We have not seen the land."
> I will ask about it.[34]

Though primitive man has his own regions, within them he
is a wanderer, and he never knows what it is to be really at
home for long. Indeed in some peoples this sense of home-
lessness takes a wider and more pathetic scope. The Gabon
Pygmies have a song which recalls freer and better days:

> The night is black, the sky is blotted out,
> We have left the village of our fathers,
> The Creator is angry with us.[35]

They feel that their life on the move is a punishment from
the gods, and they look back with home-sickness to a past
when they had a securer and more lasting habitation. Despite
their belief, or their boast, that they are a finer breed than
their Negro neighbours, they know that these have driven
them out of their old haunts and reduced them to their present precarious state. The uncertainty of primitive life begins
with its dependence on hunting but is greatly increased when
hunting-grounds are restricted or seized or forbidden. In
such conditions men are fated to lack confidence in themselves and their luck, and when things go wrong, they show
how deeply they are affected.

In so unstable a world the most stable element is the

family, and on this every member of it relies as on something fixed in a flux of change. But this means that, though death is always to be expected from disease or starvation or accident or violence, it is none the less an appalling disaster, since it breaks into the one thing which looks firmly established. More than this, the very existence of a family depends largely on the shared or separate activities of its individual members, and the death of one may menace all. Though death may inspire imaginative speculations about what happens to departed spirits, it is more insistent as a destructive force in the familiar scene, and its arrival often means that a man or a woman feels that his whole scheme of existence is annihilated. A touching example is that of a Dama woman, whose husband has been killed at her side when they were out hunting in the country. The song seems to have been composed then and there and is indeed a cry from the heart. Yet for all the immediacy of her grief and the dark prospects which loom before her, she masters her feelings by turning them into song and shows how even at such a moment she grasps the appalling significance of her husband's death:

> Father, guide my poisoned arrow,
> Straight from the bow like a wild ox.
> Husband, my husband, great and slender,
> Whither go you? Far from me!
> Rise up, bring me back
> To the house of our fathers.
> There from my father's hut I left
> A she-goat for you to kill.
> Does it not lure you?—O know it!
> That my father found honey?
> He will surely give you of it!
> Father of my children, come then,
> Kiss these your children.
> Look at the snare for a wild goat,
> See if a wild goat has been caught in it.
> Who else would watch over you
> If you wish me to go?
> The jackals will come
> And eat what is within.
> In spite of everything will you not rise up?
> What else should I now say?
> Nothing can wake you from sleep.
> Perhaps your bow will do it?
> To whom shall I give your bow?
> I am only a woman-creature—
> I cannot use your bow.

Tell me then, whose shall it be?
Who is he to whom I can say:
"Be the heir of the father's possessions!
Be glad in his heritage."
I must burn the bow in the fire.
You can name no heir.[36]

In this a complex theme is nobly developed, but it is held in a firm frame. The lament begins with the woman trying to use her dead husband's bow and ends with her decision that, since it is now useless, it must be burned. She is slow to take in the full finality of death, but, as she does so, she sees that there is no remedy and that death obliterates all that means anything to her. Without her husband she is helpless and does not foresee how she can survive. She makes no appeal for consolation, says not a word about any gods, and asks no sympathy except for the dead man, thinking more of him than of herself. The bow, with which the song begins and ends, is the pathetic emblem of what she has lost in him, and when it is proved to be useless in her hands, she knows how utterly lost she is. In this song the insecurity of primitive life is revealed in a personal, tragic shape, and we see how these people, who can be so happy when all goes well, lose hope when evil fortune strikes them. The very readiness of their response to events makes them easy victims of despair, and the conditions in which they struggle to survive may well appal them when they are robbed of their familiar supports and defences.

Primitive songs show how, when life depends on hunting, it shapes the consciousness of man to a certain pattern and enforces the development of his outlook in certain directions. So far from dulling the sensibilities it makes them more lively just because it limits them in a given field. Any action is liable to take the form of pursuit and to excite the appropriate reactions and emotions. On the one hand this gives a remarkable firmness and clarity to the primitive vision of existence, and on the other it makes it highly sensitive to events and liable to oscillate between exalted excitement and helpless melancholy. Both these extremes find an outlet in song, because song not only relieves the pressure of the emotions but makes explicit many thoughts and considerations which are so closely connected with action that they are almost part of it, and become conscious only when the right words are found for them. These peoples are of course interested in other matters than the calls of action, which is after all no more than a means to keep alive and secure other ends desired by all human beings at all places and in all times, but so far as action is concerned, hunting not only is the chief form of it but imposes its character on a whole outlook and makes men face other forms of action through the experience which hunting provides and the states of mind which it inculcates. This brings advantages to song. Hunting is usually varied, adventurous, and dramatic. It calls for careful preparations, for acute senses, for active intelligence, for delight when it is successful and for a variety of moods when it is not. It sets men to work in a purposeful and concentrated spirit, and it is not surprising that it inspires them to song about its own multifarious possibilities and other activities which are essentially like it.

CHAPTER 6 *The Natural Scene*

~~~~~~~~~~~~~~~~~~~~~~~~~~~~~~~~

PRIMITIVE MAN lives for the most part in the open air and knows the untamed, uncultivated realm of primaeval nature with an intimacy beyond the reach of even the most ardent naturalist, who stands securely apart as a dispassionate observer of plants and animals. Primitive man knows nature because he lives with it and in it and by it. It is his source of life, and he is always in close touch with it. This means that he has a detailed, precise, and practical knowledge of it in all its forms at every season, that at no time can he put the thought of it out of his mind. As a hunter or fisher or gatherer of fruits or roots or insects or grubs, he has a factual, realistic experience, which is more intimate and more expertly first hand than that of any zoologist or botanist. Yet, though he knows when animals breed and when fruits ripen, he does not breed or grow them; though he knows what fungi, tubers, and berries are edible, and what plants will provide poison for his arrows, he knows nothing of the reasons for it. His indispensable asset is precise information on all natural matters which concern him in the search for food, and this is based on the accumulated experiments, the trials and errors, of his forebears, and on his own skilled observation and inference. He is himself an actor on the natural scene, and he knows it from inside as one born and bred to it. But just because nature is so important to him, he is not content to confine himself merely to the possession of useful information. He is also a thinking being, who forms theories on why things happen and creatures behave as they do. So, while nature is both his home and his hunting-ground, it is also the seat of supernatural powers whom he attempts to understand, to assuage, and to control. He knows enough of animals and plants to conclude that they are governed by spirits, and though he may have no very clear notion of their character, he is sure of their existence. His unceasing traffic with nature only convinces him that there is much more in it than meets his eye, and though this in no way diminishes his watchful keenness, it forces him to look on nature with questioning wonder and uneasy awe. So far from having his sensibility blunted by familiarity, he is aware of nature in all its forms and of powers always at work in it, which he cannot explain but which sharpen his notice. That is why, when he sings of it, he often seems to treat it in a practical spirit of common sense without worrying about supernatural forces behind it. He is able to deal with it at two levels, the natural and the supernatural, and for some purposes to keep them apart, or at least not to confuse them. So long as he approaches it as something ordinary and familiar, he creates his own kind of poetry for it, which on the surface seems to be not very closely related to his religious assumptions about it.

Primitive man hardly ever sings of nature simply from delight in it for its own sake. He does not need it as a relief from the strain of urban routine, nor does he find in it a haven for battered nerves. It is always around him, ineluctable and insistent. So, when he sings of it, there is no need for him to make any apology or introduction, and he can go straight to whatever point is his immediate concern. In most of his songs of it he implies an ulterior purpose or assumption, which is so well known to him and his audience that it is waste of breath to state it explicitly, and yet it may provide his central point. He may well find an incidental pleasure in the aspect of nature and pay tributes to it, but these tributes are informed by other considerations which it suggests or illustrates. This gives a striking depth to his songs of it. Superficially they may do no more than portray a visible scene, but we must always suspect that in fact they do more than this and cherish some latent intention. This in no way interferes with their skill in evoking natural sights; indeed, just because the singer has something purposeful in his mind, he takes care with his words and allows his senses to work at full stretch. But this should warn us not to treat these songs as we treat modern songs written on similar subjects but without these associations and half-concealed references.

Some of these innocent-looking nature-songs are charms, whose purpose is to secure the acquisition of fruits and like sustenance in due season. They are means of enchantment, but they make no show of it. No spirits are summoned; no hope or purpose is expressed. All that happens is that a scene is set before us with what is plainly affectionate care and cannot be taken for anything else. Such is a Semang song about fruit-buds:

> They swell and swell, the fruit-buds,
> To and fro wave the fruit-buds,
> Blown about are the fruit-buds,
> In the wind the fruit-buds,
> They turn round and round, the fruit-buds,
> And rock to and fro, the fruit-buds.[1]

The singer hopes to eat the fruits when they ripen, and this is his way of establishing a hold on them. The words are a charm with a definite purpose, but the only hint of this is that the singer watches the buds with so solicitous an attention that we suspect the innocence of his motives. The observation is keen and precise and even loving, but that is after all because the ripe fruit means much to the singer and excites his avidity. Another Semang song deals with a slightly different topic and envisages more closely the actual moment of achievement and satisfaction. It too has an innocent air, which masks its predatory aim, but from the start it reveals the singer as being more than a mere onlooker, and the portrayal of his actions shows that he has some serious task in hand:

> Our fruit grows plump at the end of the spray,
> We climb along and cut it from the end of the spray,
> Plump too is the bird at the end of the spray,
> And plump the young squirrel at the end of the spray.[2]

Here the wish, implied in the charm, is expressed as if it were already in process of fulfilment, and its purpose is to get not only the fruit but the bird and the squirrel as well. The calm, admiring approach to the unheeding victims need not surprise us. Because the hunter has such control of himself, he is able to lure them to their doom, and in his easy confidence he enjoys the spectacle of what awaits his skill.

The assumption, underlying these songs, that there is a special relation between man and nature, is not confined to their use as charms. It may be present for less practical and more enigmatic needs, as in the belief that events in the animal world, which seem to be quite independent of him, somehow affect him and must be heeded by him. For instance, an Australian song from Arnhem Land tells, with seemingly objective detachment, of a seagull called *gidgid'*:

> The white *gidgid'* bird is hunting fish,
> It stabs the fish with its beak and calls as it flies,
> It stoops low over the water looking for fish,
> As the fish leaps away in fear,
> "You and I, mother seagull, we fly."
> The bird saw the east wind blow as it hunted fish,
> And the fish leapt forward in fear,
> Leaping away from its beak as the wind came
>   blowing.[3]

This is not a charm devised for action, but none the less it has concealed implications. The relation between the bird and the fish is important to the singer because his totem is the *gidgid'*, and as he marks it in action, he identifies himself closely with it. In his brief dramatic lines we see how he has entered imaginatively into the bird's nature and watched it with the eyes of an admiring and deeply committed observer, since he is its own kith and kin and participates in its mood and understands it through an identity of nature. That is why he describes so vividly the behaviour of the fish. It is in fishing that the *gidgid'* reveals its character, and the difficulties that it has in catching its fish are for the song-man only another testimony of the closeness between himself and his totem; for this is the kind of problem that he faces every day in search of food. The sight of the bird extends the man's consciousness of himself and enables him to move imaginatively in a sphere which is not in the strict sense his own.

Even when nature seems to provide no more than a setting or a background for human actions, it may usually be surmised to be doing something more. Primitive man is so deeply rooted in his setting that he does not treat it as a mere setting but forms some more intimate tie with it in the belief that it affects his life. The Australian Laragia, who once lived by the sea but were driven inland by white settlers, have a song which they now sing as a lament for their old haunts:

> Waves, coming up against the rocks,
> Breaking, shi! shi!
> When the moon is high with its light on the
>   waters;
> Spring tide, tide flowing to the grass,

Breaking, shi! shi!
In its rough waters the young girls bathe.
Hear the sound which they make with their
hands as they play! [4]

Originally this song, as is clear enough, was not a lament, but
neither was it a straightforward account of a happy occasion
when girls bathed in the sea for amusement. The bathing by
moonlight has a ritual and religious significance, and the song
was connected with some ceremony. Water is a source and a
symbol of fertility, and that is why the girls bathe, and the
song celebrates this as a matter of some significance. But
just as the Semang hunter does not allow his concealed intention to obscure his picture of a visible scene, so the Laragia singer takes a positive pleasure in making the waves not
only an element in it but add to its mystery and fascination.
Though he sees a hidden significance behind the actual events,
he keeps strictly to the obvious facts and makes them catch
our attention for their own sake. Once this is done, the real
purport of the occasion is revealed through the ritual which
expresses it.

Such examples should warn us against taking these nature-
songs too lightly at their face-value or explaining them by our
own outlooks and prepossessions. Their special character is
more clearly disclosed when they deal with the animal world
and especially with animals that are hunted for food. Since
primitive man domesticates no animals except the dog, and
keeps the dog only for hunting, his whole attitude towards
the brute creation is quite alien to that of anyone who regards
a large part of it as something to be controlled for his
convenience and kept always available for his use. Civilized
man has indeed cultivated certain attitudes towards animals,
but they have been shaped by the conditions in which he meets
them. He may regard the horse and the dog as faithful, if
dumb, friends, cattle and sheep as patient props of his security, and even wild animals as worthy victims of his pursuit
who may be destroyed with a grudging admiration. Primitive
man makes no such distinctions, and even with his dog he
is not sufficiently sentimental to sing about it. His concern
is entirely with wild creatures, and he has his own highly
distinctive approach to them. It is based on the dominating,
inescapable fact that, if he is to survive, he must destroy
them. They are in the first place, his potential, coveted prey,
but they can also be his enemies or his rivals. Since he
eats what he kills, he regards most animals as food, but
this is complicated by their existing in their own right and
having their own instincts and strategy of survival. In his

wish to destroy them, he must pay attention to their ways and recognize that they will sometimes wish to destroy him, sometimes to grab the food which he wants for himself. He is forced to study them and know all their habits, and at this he is a master. He knows their haunts, their trails, their cries, their watering-places, their tactics and tricks in evasion, resistance, and counter-attack. In dealing with them he uses methods very like their own and makes up for his lack of fangs or tusks by using a bow or blow-pipe or spear or spear-thrower or boomerang. Physically he is much slower than deer or bucks or monkeys or ostriches, and much weaker than tigers or lions or elephants. His only real advantage is his knowledge of his opponents' habits, and his ability to outwit them, and even in this they are formidable rivals, since their senses are sharper than his and their immediate reaction to danger may be quite as acute and as quick as his own. Though the pursuit of each kind of animal calls for a special technique and encourages the development of appropriate tactics, such as striking spears into an elephant's belly from below, or killing monkeys with blow-pipes, or harpooning seals through the ice, in all cases primitive man is faced by problems which involve danger to limb or life. Even when he pursues a harmless buck, he cannot be sure that he has not a rival in some formidable beast like a lion or a tiger. Despite his human advantages, he is an inmate of the animal world and behaves in much the same way as its other inmates. For him, too, it is in the last resort a case of having either to eat or be eaten.

Just for this reason primitive man looks upon animals as much more than victims or rivals or adversaries. These indeed they are, but he knows them so well and has to study them so closely that he develops other feelings about them and takes at times a view of them which can hardly be quite impartial or detached but is to some degree independent of his hunger for their flesh. He does not hate them as dangerous enemies or despise them as predestined victims, but watches them with discerning eyes and forms his own expert view of them. If they are not exactly his friends, they are at least his fellows in a single world. He is far closer to them than a civilized man is even to his horse or his dog, for the good reason that he knows them in their unconstrained, unbroken nature and pays to them the respect proper to equals. He knows that, like himself, they have to struggle for a living, and he assesses them by their ability to survive, whether by courage or by cunning. This is why he interprets their actions as if they were human, and sees many resemblances between them and himself. When he sings of animals, he feels that he really knows them, and his songs are concerned with much more than the mere mechanics of hunting and killing. The study of animals is his most exact and most expert accomplishment, and he takes pride and delight in it. They exhibit a variety of behaviour beyond that of his human companions and are likely to yield at least equally rewarding results. This interest in them rises from constant warfare against them, but passes beyond the passions usual in such a struggle to a more detached and more imaginative outlook. There is no real contradiction between the desire to kill animals and a mixture of curiosity, admiration, and even affection towards them. Primitive man knows that he must at all costs kill them, but that does not make him dislike or despise them. That is why in his songs he appreciates the varieties of animal character and personality. When he uses the language of human actions and relations for them, it is because it expresses, as nothing else can, what he feels after long and close acquaintance and rivalry, and from his own point of view he is fully justified, since in most fundamental respects the lives of animals resemble his own.

Though many of these descriptive songs are charms to catch animals, they display an engaging disregard of this and present the victims very much as they appear to the admiring eye of the hunter. The Semang, for instance, have more than one song about a monkey called *kra,* and a comparison of two specimens will show what differences are still permissible in a theme which is standardized and even conventional, and through these differences we can see something of the general outlook of the Semang hunter. The first is the less dramatic of the two:

> He stamps with his feet, *kra,*
> He drags along, *kra,*
> He climbs up and away, *kra,*
> On the stalk of the rambutan, *kra,*
> He swarms high up the *semei* bamboo, *kra,*
> He swarms high up the *hamaleg'n* bamboo, *kra,*
> He climbs high up the *haur* bamboo, *kra,*
> He hangs down, *kra*
> He stamps, *kra,*
> They skip around, the children of the *kra,*
> He drags along, *kra*
> The rambutan fruits of the *kra,*
> The rambutan fruits of the *kra,*
> He drags along, *kra,*
> He bends the bough for a leap, *kra,*
> Lets the bough fly upward, *kra.* [5]

This song was composed by someone who knew all about the habits of the *kra* and recounts them methodically with the knowledge that comes from familiarity and experienced observation. That his observation is born from the needs of hunting and that the song is meant to assist it is not mentioned. The precise naming of the plants and trees which the *kra* frequents adds to the realism of the presentation, and the whole picture is admirably convincing, until the last line when the monkey's preparation for a jump is the moment when the hunter intends to kill him. The second song is conceived in rather a different spirit, though it uses several of the same themes, and indeed the two songs are variations improvised on a common stock, to which each singer makes his own small personal contribution:

> He runs along the branches, *kra,*
> Carries fruit with him, *kra,*
> Over the knotted seraya, *kra,*
> Over the knotted rambutan, *kra,*
> Running along the branches, *kra,*
> Running along the branches, he hoots, *kra,*
> He peers forward, *kra,*
> Among the young rambutans, *kra,*
> And shows his grinning teeth, *kra,*
> From every sapling, *kra,*
> He peers forward, *kra,*
> Dressed for the dance, *kra,*
> With the porcupine's quill through his nose, *kra.*[6]

This song also applies the language of human actions to the monkey, but differs from the first song in making him behave in a more specifically human way until in the last two lines he is treated as if he were a Semang got up for a dance with a quill through his nose for an ornament. The fancy, suggested by his agile antics, that he is a dancer brings him closer to the hunter and makes it easier to lure him to destruction. But in both songs what counts is the similarity between monkey and man. Both haunt the jungle and rely on their nimble movements to find food; both take their pleasures in a lively spirit. The singer enters into the nature of the monkey and sings happily of him because he understands him as a member of his own world.

Even when he is at open war with animals, primitive man does not abandon his friendly feeling towards them, or at least keeps up some pretence of liking them. This takes a special form in the charms which he uses for hunting. In many of them there is an implicit assumption that the hunter can lure his victim to death by speaking to it or about it in an admiring, amicable, even flattering spirit. The Eskimo, with a fine disregard for proprieties, offers to the caribou the shoes which he hopes to make from its skin and the lamp-wicks which he hopes to feed with its lubber:

> Wild caribou, land-louse, long-legs,
> With the great ears
> And the rough hairs on your neck,
> Flee not from me.
> Here I bring skins for soles,
> Here I bring moss for wicks;
> Just come gladly,
> Hither to me, hither to me.[7]

Yet even here there is a kind of affection in the opening words, playful perhaps and not free from mockery, but not hostile or contemptuous. The Veddas go even further and, with a keen appreciation of the cunning of the monkeys whom they hunt, speak in words of praise and welcome. One charm suggests that the hunter almost sees himself as a monkey when he tries to lure the female into his grasp:

> My mother, the lovely chief,
> Pops behind a cotton trunk,
> Crying "Ro! Ro!" Come, little dog.
> She goes behind a satin stem,
> Come playing, playing, running,
> Stop your game and come running.[8]

The hunter speaks first of the monkey in the third person that she may overhear his soft words, and then to her in the second that she may yield to his invitation and come to him. Another Vedda charm speaks of monkeys in the plural with adulatory admiration, as if they were likely to be pleased by it:

> They scratch off and throw down the branches,
> They spring on to that trunk,
> They come indeed saying "Ah! Oh!"
> They scratch off and throw down the leaves,
> They dance on this trunk.
> Why did they stop and look, both of them?[9]

At times politeness and praise come close to dissimulation and deceit or at least to a certain ambiguity of approach. So the Bushman approaches an antelope with a prayer that says the opposite of what he really means, even though it is sincere enough in his ambiguous attitude towards animals:

> Please don't kill my antelope,
> My darling antelope.
> My antelope is so poor,
> My antelope is an orphan.[10]

We get the impression that the kill hurts the hunter more than the hunted, and that for the creatures which he is forced to hunt he has a real admiration and even affection. Nor is this entirely wrong. The essence of such a charm is that the hunter enters into the life of his prey by telling of its habits and its haunts, and believes that by this he gets a hold on it. Such songs show the close relation which exists between primitive man and the creatures of his pursuit. He knows them so well and is so close to them that he assumes that, if he can only establish some personal ascendancy over them, he will have them in his power.

This attitude, which is both genuine and understandable, may lead to quite complex effects, when the hunter is absorbed in each moment of the chase and his feelings change as it develops. The Semang pursue the coconut-ape, and have a song which begins with a lively account of it in its forest haunts. When it is sung, it provokes laughter, and its dramatic character is emphasised by its performance partly by a soloist, partly by a chorus of three men. The song is not, of course, performed while the actual hunt is on, but is a social event designed to catch apes in the future or to celebrate their capture in the past:

> Proudly he walks up and down,
> From bough to bough he skips,
> He walks up and down,
> On the *anag*-tree, the ape,
> In his cheek-pouches he sticks
> The sweet fruit of the *manow*.
> > Father, mother, look at him,
> > His brothers look at him.
>
> He walks up and down,
> He peers into the distance.
> He sees the *bateg'n* fruit,
> He grinds them in his fists.
> > "You, give them to your father!"
> > His mother shrieks in warning.
>
> Silence! Was it a whistle of the ape,
> Or was it only a breath of wind?
> Silence! Tense, they all listen.
> They peer into the distance.

Soundlessly through the dusk of the *rimba*
The hunter waits and creeps.
On his shoulder the blow-pipe rests.
From the slim, smooth bamboos
Sharply loaded with the poisoned
Arrows, the pointed ones.

Hissing from the smooth pipe
Puffs the arrow, sharp, poisoned,
Pierces into the heart of the ape.
Alas, the mother has seen it! [11]

In this dramatic song the business of stalking an ape and
then killing it with a blow-pipe is presented with a keen
sense of what the ape is, even in its relations with its
family and in its mother's feelings when it is killed. Nor
need we be unduly surprised that the Semang find this amus-
ing. No doubt part of the fun comes from the actual words
and the music and whatever imitative action accompanies
them, but to a primitive sense of humour it is quite in order
to laugh at the doom of a poor ape, even if at the same
time it is felt to be almost human in its actions and the
affection which it inspires.

In these poems primitive man observes animals closely
and appreciates their essential character because they belong
to the same world as himself and are occupied with much
the same pursuits. In so doing he is liable to read into
their nature much that he knows from his own, and to interpret their motives by his own experience. This does not
mean a lack of imagination, but rises from a natural assumption that, since animals resemble man in so many obvious ways, their actions may be interpreted by the same
rules. This may be carried quite far, especially in dealing
with the struggle for survival between one creature and another. But the primitive poet knows animals so well that,
though he explains them in human terms, he never loses
sight of their more distinctive characteristics or forgets that
each kind has its own idiosyncrasies. When he sings of them,
he may well imply lessons for his fellow-men, but he keeps
his eye on his subject and presents it as he knows it really
is. So the Bushmen have a song about a cat and a lynx, in
which the cat is throughout the speaker, though it quotes
freely from what the lynx has said about it:

Ha, ha, ha,
Ha, ha.

I am the one whom the lynx derides,
I am the one who did not run fast;

For the lynx is the one who runs fast,

> Ha, ha, ha,
>   Ha, ha.

I am the one whom the lynx derides.
I am the one whom the lynx derides,
I am the one who could not run fast.

I am the one whom the lynx derides:
"The cat could not run fast.

"The cat is the one who could not run fast,
It was not cunning,
It did foolish things;
For the lynx is the one who understands."
But the cat is cunning.

The cat is the one about whom the lynx talked:
"It is the one who could not run fast."
It had to be cunning;
For the lynx is one who is cunning.

> Haggla haggla haggla
>   Haggla haggla
> Heggle heggle heggle
>   Heggli
> Heggli heggli heggli
>   Heggli n![12]

Behind this lies the well observed fact that, though the cat is not so fast as the lynx, it can escape from it by doubling on its tracks, and this justifies its claim that it is as cunning as the lynx. But the charm of the song is its agreeable presentation of the very cat-like character of the cat. Its calculating, cool manner, its confidence that it can outwit a crafty opponent, its quiet assumption that it is the better animal, its ironical, unperturbed treatment of the lynx's contemptuous criticism, and its final outburst into its own language, are all true to type, and the song shows how well the Bushman understands this enigmatic, independent, and self-assured creature.

The curiosity about animals which is forced upon primitive man by his struggle to live inspires a number of stories in which both he and they act in character and display their most characteristic features. A similarity between them is assumed, and may go deeper than we suspect. The Bushmen, for instance, have a story of an old woman who was left

alone in a hut because she was unable to walk with the
rest of her family when they changed their home. A hyena
came and carried her off, but when it was about to kill her
by casting her on a pointed rock, she sprang aside and
not only saved herself but killed the hyena. This has prompted a song which makes a nice point, even if it is not very
complimentary to the determined and resourceful old woman:

> The old she-hyena,
> The old she-hyena,
> Was carrying off
> The old woman from the old hut;
> The old woman in this manner,
> She sprang aside,
> She beat the hyena;
> The hyena herself,
> The hyena killed the hyena.[13]

The fantastic situation is certainly believed to be true, and
may even be based on fact, but the singer makes use of it
to enforce his own conclusion. In his society old women
are, for unflattering reasons, often compared with hyenas,
and the comparison comes aptly enough here, where it gives
a final point to the song. But the song has something like a
moral. The old woman, who has been abandoned as unfit
to travel and therefore unfit to live and suffered the uncouth fate of being carried off by a hyena, asserts herself
at the crucial moment, and the struggle is between similar
and well-matched opponents. It is hard to say whether the
old woman is like the hyena or the hyena like the old woman, but there is certainly a common element between them,
and conclusions can be drawn from it.

This song comes from the end of a tale told in prose
and clinches it in this summary form. Bits of song are common in Bushman tales and often mark a crisis or draw a
lesson. Some of these tales are concerned with mythological
origins and turn on the belief that some animals were once
men. In their original state before transformation they
display the characteristics both of men and of the animals
which they are going to become. So one tale tells how the
kwai-kwai bird was once a man and put some children into
a net. At this point the children burst into song:

> Mother, mother
> The Kwai-kwai
> Is taking us to kill,
> Though we stayed at home!
> Mother, mother,

> The Kwai-kwai
> Is taking us to kill,
> Though we stayed at home![14]

The children are delivered and in revenge for their treatment
roast the *kwai-kwai*. The song has its own human aspects,
and the *kwai-kwai* may be a familiar enough type of bogey
in savage societies. The drama of children who are abducted
and then saved gains in verisimilitude because the abductor
is a bird which may be expected to behave in this kind of
way. Another tale tells of the lizard who climbs a thorn-
tree:

> Oh, oh!
> The lizard lives on the thorn-tree.
> Oh, oh!
> Oh, oh, the lizard lies on the thorn-tree.
> Oh, oh!
> The lizard was lying on the thorn-tree.[15]

The point of this primaeval little jingle is the careless indif-
ference of the lizard to the dangers which encompass it.
Though it is menaced by both men and beasts, it lies in a
tree and pays no notice to either, with the result that, as
the change of tense in the last line shows, it is destroyed.
The moral is clear, and the function of the song is to convey
a familiar mood of insouciance in a very simple form. By
attaching it to a lizard instead of to a man, the singer gives
it a certain detachment and adds a small touch of humour.
A third tale tells of a beetle and a mouse. The beetle has
killed the long-nosed mice, and the striped mouse comes to
avenge them. When he finds the beetle, a singing-match and
a slinging-match take place, in which each creature, while
it sings, throws missiles at the other. The beetle begins:

> Get out of the way,
> The beetle is throwing,

and the mouse mockingly replies:

> The beetle is throwing,
> Get out of the way.[16]

In the end the beetle knocks the mouse down and kills it.
The song echoes the contemptuous hostility in which the
adversaries engage one another, and the mouse, who is the
aggressor, throws the beetle's own words back at it in ironical ridicule. These little songs are crystallized pieces of
proverbial wisdom and display recurrent situations in a new
light by relating them to stories about animals. The animals

are true to form and act according to the rules of their own being, but in so doing they illustrate situations in human life and draw attention to their paradoxes and contradictions. They come from a world where animals are so well known that they can be made to provide a commentary on human society, and have a certain small dignity because they are thought to be related to mankind through descent from common ancestors in an undated past.

If primitive man understands animals because he sees them as like himself, he also interprets men through their likeness to animals. When he wishes to stress some point about his own kind which excites his wonder or his mockery or his amusement, he often presents it in a tale about animals. These are the first fables in the long tradition connected with Aesop, and the secret of their appeal is that they presuppose a real similarity between men and beasts. They thrive best when men really know animals from close, competitive contact. Fables stretch the range of understanding because they make men look more closely at themselves in a medium in which they are thoroughly at home, and so become more critical of their actions. The advantage of primitive fables over more sophisticated ones is that the beasts are not merely disguised human beings but keep most of their own essential nature, and the foibles and the follies of men are made to look more absurd or contemptible by their closeness to those of animals. Such songs imply a thorough knowledge of the animals who are given parts in them and of the life which they lead, but this is not difficult to grasp, and the result is often terse and pointed.

Songs of this kind are popular among the Eskimos, who sing them to illustrate their disagreements with one another. There is a dexterous, if not very assertive, art in them, and they are admirable instruments of derision. The issue is usually presented with some air of detachment and objectivity, and this makes the point sharper when it comes. Let us take a dialogue between a raven and a gull:

Raven   You big dirty-white gull,
        Where do you think you are plumping
          yourself?
        You are no match for me.
        So leave me in peace.
Gull   When the ice breaks
        In the rivers,
        I take with me my pronged spear.
        What then is impossible?
Raven From those who go out in the icy cold
        You are mostly absent!

One picks up dung, another berries.
Nothing is impossible
For him who can![17]

Since the raven cannot catch salmon, while the gull can, the
gull mocks the raven's none too polite approaches, but the
raven wins the round because it is more courageous and
more enterprising than the gull. The animal-setting only just
contains the human parable, but there is no difficulty in allowing the gull to speak of its beak as its pronged spear,
since this merely stresses its character as a fisher. The two
types of bird stand neatly for two types of hunter, and there
is real insight in the comparison between them. The fable
not only clarifies the nature of the contrast and the rivalry
which it engenders but throws light on the professional pride
on which hunting thrives. Since the raven has the last word,
the singer himself may be presumed to be on its side, but
he recognizes that the gull also has something to say for
itself.

This art provides openings for humour and satire, and the
Eskimos' sly appreciation of each other's foibles and faults
finds a happy outlet in comparisons between men and animals, even though these are implied and not explicitly stated.
The conclusions are by no means obvious or easily foreseen.
For instance, another Eskimo song tells of a water-beetle
and a blow-fly, who, as the singer explains before he begins,
were "going to box." He then sings his song of the two small
creatures who pass from verbal controversy to a comic conclusion:

So said the blow-fly:
"Because you have no belly, perhaps,
You cannot reply at all!"
The little water-beetle said:
"No belly? It may be so!
Still you may be sure that I shall answer back!"
He made a grimace
And turned his back at once,
Without trying to answer back.
He was a bad one at arguing.[18]

The water-beetle is neither courteous nor dignified, but he
defies his critic and routs him by an insulting indignity.
Here too the animal frame is stretched as far as the singer
dares, and the behaviour of the water-beetle is more true
to a human being than to its own kind. But there is verisimilitude in it, and a human relation becomes sharper by
being cast into this shape.

The animal world can also illustrate and elucidate human feelings in a more subtle spirit, and secure a complexity which adds strength and interest to emotions which are not easily described in common language. This is the art of the psychological poet, who watches himself carefully and records his feelings faithfully. So an Eskimo sings of his lack of success in love, and is able to give shape to his otherwise amorphous conflicts by showing how they are affected by his experience of hunting, and to disclose how well he understands himself and how his manner of life enables him to define the character of his failures and defeats:

> While I stood longing for women,
> While I yearned for them,
> My comrades, yes, then it was,
> Yes, then it was that their women
> Swam past me
> Out in the great sea out yonder.
> By day it was,
> Early in the forenoon,
> That I took into the camp
> One with dark hair on her face,
> A companion, Inugtigjuaq.
> Yes, it was I,
> I, who have no children running to meet me;
> A poor dog and nothing else
> Is all I know of.
> While one yearns for women,
> While one longs for them,
> It was a tiny little calf and no more.
> There, where I had found the trail
> Of cows with calf,
> In vain I was annoyed,
> I came upon it from behind, and it was not afraid.
> And I was not to give it
> The skin of the great-bearded seal,
> The one for making into seal-things.
> I came upon it from behind, and it was not afraid.
> And I did not give it
> The skin of the big white bear.
> Yes, it was I.[19]

The song has two movements. In the first part the singer, obsessed by the thought of beautiful women whom he does not possess, sees them in his mind as he watches seals swimming out to sea. This embodies his obsession and his conviction of failure, since the seals are as much out of his reach as women are, and he makes no attempt to catch them or to do anything but look at them. The second part turns to hunting on land and tells how, when he found caribou, he contented himself with taking a calf from behind. For this he gives no reason, but in retrospect he sees it as characteristic of his lack of enterprise. He treats it in the language of a bridal, but with a bride whom he does not value at all highly or honour with appropriate wedding-gifts such as the skins of seals or bears. It is his nearest approach to success, and it is a pitiable achievement, whose character is sketched by the implicit parallel with getting a wife. The two parts of the song hang together because the first part tells of the hunter's dreams and the second of his actual performance. He has an urgent need to sing about himself as he really is, and he does so with an engaging candour and with no attempt to excuse himself. To describe his humiliating experience he uses the best instrument at his disposal, the world of animals in which he lives, and shows through his relations with them and his unaccountable failure in simple situations, how his defeatism has entered into his nature and weakens his capacity for action. The point of the poem is the contrast between his own defeats and the successes and satisfactions of other men. To make this clear he sets his song in the one sphere in which everyone is interested—hunting, and thereby displays his inferiority to his fellows and his melancholy dissatisfaction with himself.

In these several ways primitive man turns the animal and natural world into material for song because it is inextricably interwoven into his own existence and his struggle to live. When he treats of such subjects in this secular spirit, we can easily share his way of thinking, and though he is much closer to nature than we can ever hope to be and lacks our prepossessions about it, he thinks of it very much as we do and in action does not trouble about his complex religious assumptions concerning it. But this is only one side of his approach. Though he knows what natural things are and has no illusions about their behaviour, he also sees them in other lights with other implications, and his songs of them often take their colour from these, and the result is strange and mysterious. Physical nature provides him with many of his religious beliefs, and when he sings of it, he shows how he interprets much that is ultimately unintelligible to him. So long as he deals with nature for purely practical ends, his approach to it is also practical and hard-headed, but once he begins to think about it in itself or to relate it to a scheme of things, it takes on new appearances, each of which contributes something to the variety of his songs.

First, in his sense of kinship with animals and indeed with

all nature we can detect a more considered, more mature relation than mere contiguity or association or even similarity of behaviour. Animals are often used to explain human origins and play a large part in the rites connected with them. A clear case of this can be seen in totemistic beliefs such as are held, for instance, by Australian tribes and brought by them to a far greater degree of elaboration than by anyone else in the world. A totem may come from almost anywhere in the natural scene. It may be an animal or a bird or an insect or a tree or a stone. Whatever it is, it provides the central point of a group, in which every member shares the totem and is in some sense identified with it. If the totem is a kangaroo or a wallaby, the members of the group are themselves kangaroos or wallabies. This does not prevent them from pursuing their lives in an ordinary human way, but it imposes duties on them, such as not eating the flesh of their totem, and at certain festivals they become vividly conscious of their identity with it and sing of it in ritual songs which are accompanied by mimetic gestures and dances. In these songs the imagination is set to work with an almost automatic readiness. The totem is placed in his appropriate setting and made to live before the audience as he looks and is. His part is taken by actors, suitably painted and adorned, and a song explains what they do in their presentation of him. So in an Aranda song a wallaby is neatly introduced:

These acacia seeds
They crunch with their teeth.

The cold wind runs
Through the cane-grass bushes.

The acacias have white flower-buds.
They are decked with white flower-buds.

He has a bent back,
With his hair standing up he goes with a
    bent back.[20]

After this introduction the song proceeds to perform its ritual duties, but it has already shown its skill in giving a verbal picture of a wallaby on the run. Once the totem has been described and presented to the company, it is but a small step to make it speak in the first person through the actor who takes its part. So a song about a totemic mouse called *tokia* soon makes its chief character come to life:

> This mouse will scrape earth from the hole,
> This mouse will scrape earth.
>
> This mouse has bright spots.
> This mouse has bright spots.
>
> "This soda bush, I gnaw it through,
> I myself gnaw it through.
>
> "The damp earth I break up,
> The head laid on cushions I break up.
>
> "The cotton-bush, I gnaw it through,
> The leaves on its top I gnaw through."[21]

If a man really thinks for the moment that he is a wallaby or a mouse, he will sing about it in the most natural way, and his song will be unusually straightforward because he knows all about his subject and gives his powers to making himself as like it as possible. He is not obstructed by reservations or doubts or even by a desire to impress; he aims simply at giving a lifelike representation of his totem. So those Aranda who have an eagle for totem sing in the first person of two eagles in the air:

> "One above the other we are hovering in the air;
> Both of us are hovering in the air.
>
> "Off the edge of the mountain bluff we are hovering in
>   the air;
> Near the jagged mountain we are hovering in the air.
>
> "We, the two young eagles, are hovering in the air;
> Near the jagged mountain edge we are hovering
>   in the air." [22]

Here for the moment an identification between men and eagles is secured by the imagination and aided by imitative disguises and gestures, while the repeated phrases stress the notion of hovering and keep the attention on it. Through their totemistic beliefs some peoples, notably Australians, evolve a special poetry of nature, whose strength is that it keeps very closely to actual facts and is not encumbered by too many mythical references. Just because the singer believes that he really is an eagle, he feels no call to go beyond his knowledge of eagles from his own observation, and since he feels that he is one with them, he presents them almost from within with the easy confidence of familiarity.

HUNTING

1
Cave-paintings of the Late Stone Age at Alpéra, Spain, showing
(*right*) a dancer-sorcerer, hunters with bows and arrows and
(*center*) a honey gatherer climbing to take honey from a nest of
wild bees. See page 17.

2

A Bushman from South West Africa aiming a poisoned arrow from his bow. See page 17.

3

A Bambuti Pygmy from the Congo, the leader of a hunting party, with his hunting dog, the only domestic animal of primitive man. See page 20.

4
An Australian aboriginal hunter from the Liverpool River area of Arnhem Land, returning from hunting with a young kangaroo. See page 17.

5
In Ceylon the Veddas live in the deep jungles, living by hunting and by poisoning fish. See page 116.

6
A Vedda chief; these people are now nearly extinct. See page 19.

7
The Tierra del Fuegians of southernmost Chile live by hunting and fishing; when Darwin saw them in 1834, he wrote "I can scarcely imagine that there is any spectacle more interesting and worthy of reflection, than one of these unbroken savages." See page 31.

8
HMS *Beagle* in Jemmy Button Sound in 1834, illustrating the savage country in which the Fuegians live. This picture, and the fisherman above, were painted by Conrad Martens, who accompanied the voyage. See page 22.

9

The Selk'nam and Yamana Indians of Tierra del Fuego wear skins and build flimsy shelters of boughs and skins against the icy winds. Darwin thought the difference between them and civilized men "greater than between a wild and domesticated animal." See page 19.

10

The last-known canoe of the Yamana, hollowed out of a tree trunk. There are now almost none of these people still alive. See page 248.

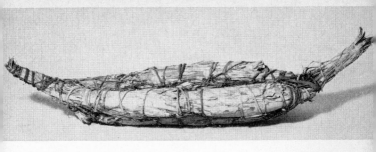

11 and 12
British settlers systematically exterminated the Tasmanian aborigines; the last Tasmanian died in 1876. A Tasmanian fishing canoe of Eucalyptus bark and reeds (*above*). See page 18. Eskimos of the Arctic also fish and hunt seals and reindeer; (*below*) a Padelmuit Eskimo from the Perry River, Canada. See page 45.

DANCING

13
At Cape Bessov-Noss on Lake Onega in the USSR a Bronze Age
carving illustrates a dancing figure in an animal mask following an
elk, probably connected with hunting magic. See page 243.

14
Bushwomen dancing;
once frequent all over
South Africa, the Bush-
men now live mainly in
the Kalahari Desert. See
page 243.

15
Veddas of Hennebedde
in Ceylon dancing to the
Noe Yakku, spirits of the
newly dead. See page 246.

16

A Pygmy encampment in a clearing in the Congo jungle. The Pygmies pray to the "Father Elephant" that he will not tread on their fragile huts of leaves and sticks. See page 19.

17

A Bambuti Pygmy of the Congo plays the drums. See page 37.

18

The *Batu Rib'm,* or magic mountain, home of the gods of the Semang people of Malaya. See page 58.

19

Two young Semang leaping in a spring dance; only the men take part in the dancing, while the women clap or beat a small drum in rhythm. See page 210.

An Eskimo drummer repairing his open-sided drum. See page 111.

21 and 22

Many corroborees of the Australian aborigines are concerned with animals; (*above*) dancers mime animals in this ceremony, recorded by a traveller in the late eighteenth century. (*Below*) Aborigines waiting to begin their dance in the Bandicoot Ceremony of Ilhal-rntja in Central Australia. See page 243.

23
An aboriginal from Arnhem Land, singing a sacred tribal song, the night before a corroboree is to take place. The women are warned by this and leave the area until the corroboree is over, otherwise they would be killed. See page 161.

24

In this circumcision and initiation ceremony, a huge pattern is
drawn on the ground and men enact the tribal creation story. They
are seen pushing a mythical snake back into the well in which it
lives. See page 62.

25

Aborigines taking part in a *Rom* ceremony, a corroboree which lasts for three days. The dancers' body painting is in earth colours, white, ochre, red and black. See page 243.

26
Children imitate the corroboree of their parents, as a game. Adults encourage them, and in this manner the traditions, ritual and movements are passed on to the next generation. See page 170.

27 and 28

(*Left*) A herd of bison, painted by prehistoric artists of the Late
Stone Age, at Niaux in the foothills of the Pyrenees. Some beasts
are wounded with arrows. (*Above*) The Bushmen hunt antelope
with bows and huntings dogs; a cave painting from Barkley East,
South Africa. See page 13.

29 and 30
The Bushmen of the Drakensberg in Natal painted the animals and incidents familiar to them; (*above*) a rare painting of a python. (*Below*) A fight between two tribes, probably over disputed hunting grounds. See page 131.

31
In this Bushmen painting a group of men dance round a central
figure in an animal mask. See page 243.

32

In the Arctic Circle there are carvings made by Bronze Age man thousands of years ago, which represent animals with many anatomical details; a rock carving of an elk from Åskollen in Vestfold, Norway.

33

Similar anatomical details appear in the paintings of the Australian aborigines; this drawing of a kangaroo in a cave in the Wellington ranges is probably about seventy-five years old. It is reproduced here for the first time. See page 212.

34 and 35
Vedda paintings (*above*) show a leopard attacking a dog, and stylized human figures. See page 19. (*Below*) Carvings on walrus ivory made by Eskimos, showing scenes from their daily life; hunting, fishing and drying skins for clothing. See page 118.

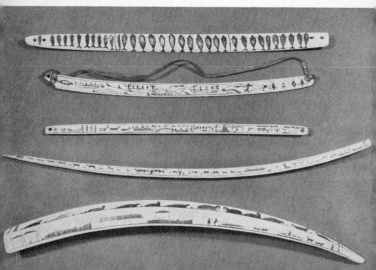

A second use of animals is not unlike this but has a special character because it is connected with the belief in shamans, who are thought to take the shape of animals and behave like them. In this state they gather knowledge which is concealed from common men and reveal it on high occasions. The assumptions in this are different from those of totemism in more than one way. First, the shaman is a favoured being who learns his lessons for himself, not a member of a group which shares a common belief. Secondly, his ability to change his shape means that in effect he is above both men and beasts and moves in a superior order of being where he is close to the gods. So shamanistic songs, which have many touches drawn from nature, pass beyond it into theology and myth. For instance, among the Semang the shaman may become a tiger and perform special duties as an intermediary between gods and men. Yet even so he is seen with a clear vision in his tiger-body, which he has assumed as he enters a hut from which he delivers his message on a ceremonial occasion. As such, he is the *bidog*, whose acquaintance we have already made in a primitive drama of the Semang, and whose movements are described in another song:

> With great strides the *bidog* marches into the hut,
> With lightning in his eyes he marches into the hut,
> With glittering stripes he marches into the hut,
> On the shore of the Sengon he marches into the hut,
> Turning round in circles he marches into the hut. [23]

This takes full advantage of the tiger's relentless, unfaltering advance and his striking, impressive appearance, but it goes beyond this and suggests that in his supernatural being the *bidog* is even more formidable than an ordinary tiger. He is so easily and so successfully presented because the Semang know all about tigers, which abound in their jungles, and are able to catch the impressive determination with which they stride to their tasks. Here the shamanistic belief, enhanced by the seriousness which the elementary dramatic performance gives to it, adds something to what is already known and felt about a tiger but still keeps within the bounds of verisimilitude. The belief that some tigers are divine beings means that they are more like tigers than ever.

A third, more advanced, more elaborate, and more decorative use of natural things may be seen in some Australian ritual song-cycles from north-eastern Arnhem Land. The cycles of Kunapipi, who has some of the characteristics of a primitive earth-mother, and of the Djanggawul, who are mythical ancestors responsible for almost all forms of life, both make full use of natural things because these are their first and most serious concern. The Kunapipi songs are shorter and more concentrated, and may well be older. They deal with the journey of Kunapipi as she moves over the land and gives life to it. Though their compass is small, they contain many vivid glimpses of nature; such as

> This lizard, with body poised,
> Watches the rain-waters swirling past,[24]

or

> The black shag moves along, the shag, among the paper-
>   bark trees,
> Catching fish there in the stream, [25]

or

> There are the eagles crying, swooping from side to side,
> Pecking in play at each other's feathers, their feathers falling;
> Crying out and flashing there in the sun;
> Soon in their nest there will be young eaglets. [26]

Though the songs are accompanied by expressive rituals, which indicate more than the words say, yet the words show a lively eye for nature and a feeling for its abundant powers which never cease working. In them the belief that nature is sustained by divine beings gives to it an enhanced interest and makes everything in it worthy of notice because it displays the spirit of life, represented by Kunapipi, at work. Yet though she is responsible, the whole array of living things seems to go on apart from her, or at least to have its own individual splendour and attraction. Our attention is turned much less to her than to her works, and in these each element is seen with discerning appreciation.

In the Djanggawul cycle the songs are longer and more elaborate but not in principle very different from those of Kunapipi. The Djanggawul, who are believed to give life not merely to all living things but also to earth and water, are suitably celebrated in songs about many forms of nature. These songs serve a double purpose. First, some natural objects are seen as ritual or symbolical things which illustrate the powers and the activities of the Djanggawul; secondly, many actual creatures, on land or sea or air, are described because, though they owe their existence to the Djanggawul, they now exist in their own right and are presented largely for their own sake. It is this second purpose which now concerns us, since it shows how fully and freely a primitive people can depict natural sights and what observation and acquaintance can do for this kind of art. In general these natural elements are related to the central theme, but the relation need not be very close and the songs often go beyond it and enjoy themselves in irrelevant but not superfluous description. Such scenes are brought legitimately into the picture because they have a part in the whole process of creation and the maintenance of life, but their connection with the main theme may often be slight and introduced in a rather off-hand way, as if it did not matter very much. Of course it does matter, but in dealing with natural powers like the Djanggawul, a single, visible object, which almost speaks for itself, is far more important than any underlining of its relation to them. Everyone knows that the relation exists, but the main interest is in the particulars which embody the general laws. For instance, the songs often mention an emblem called *rangga*. It stands for fertility and is indispensable to the whole round of rites, but it is usually enough for it to be present and mentioned without too much ado. It is the archetype of trees and other upstanding objects, and therefore to be found everywhere. So it is appropriate that, as the Djanggawul paddle their canoe to land, they should see it as a sacred tree, but its peculiar interest is that it is a nest of flying foxes:

> What is that? What is the cry?
> Flying foxes suspended there in the tree, comrade
>   Djanggawul, crying out from the tree,
> We saw the sacred tree, the sacred *rangga*. Flying foxes
>   in the sacred tree!
> Little flying foxes crying, as they hold that sacred tree!
> They cry from their home, where they hang among the
>   branches of the sacred tree.
> Cry from the topmost branches, from all the branches
>   of the tree . . .
> They cry from their home: crying, comrade, from the
>   sacred fig-tree . . .[27]

To the average member of the audience the account of the flying foxes, as they are seen from afar, is at least as interesting as their relation with the sacred tree or its special place in the ritual. The song catches their movements and their cries, and their appearance to seafarers coming to land certainly gives a right impression of the fauna and flora which await them.

Yet, though these symbolical associations do not obtrude themselves too aggressively on the attention, they must not be missed and are indeed indispensable, and it is because of them that various living creatures and natural phenomena are presented with such faithfulness and care. This is the furthest limit reached by primitive song in its attempts to give an ulterior significance to physical nature by attaching it to unseen powers. It is they which give life, and therefore everything in nature is relevant to them and must have an honourable place in song. It is this conviction which gives such vivacity to these natural scenes, and the method shows how man is able to combine his belief in unseen powers with a practical knowledge of the visible world. His sense of their presence and their influence makes his accounts of it more lively, and at no point do we feel that his interest in the supernatural background dims or distorts his physical vision. Again and again, we notice with pleasure the delighted skill with which some creature is introduced in a characteristic and revealing role. So the turtle swims in the light of the morning star:

> Paddling we saw that turtle; saw its eyes open, its flippers outstretched, as it floated.
> Sea-water lapped at its shell, spreading across its back.[28]

A plover hangs above the canoe of the Djanggawul and cries at them:

> Its screeching cry sounds over the waters from Bralgu, mingling with roar of the sea, spreading across it.
> Sound as it skims the sea's surface, sound from its plashing and foam![29]

It is soon followed by a gull:

> The female gull, with its beak, cries out as it sees the dark rain clouds rising.
> The seagull cries out at the time of the wet season; it thinks of nesting.
> Gliding along, it thinks of its home at Bremer Island.
> Diving, it skims the water, sending out spray. Its eyes can see in the night. It shakes itself dry.[30]

At sunset the glow of the parakeet's feathers are caught in the evening light:

> There, on the tree, it saw the sun's rays and the glowing sunset sky,
> Saw the rays of the sun setting, in the west beyond Milingimbi.
> Drying its red feathers in the glow of the sun, it claps and scratches at the tree, with its claws.[31]

Trees, growing by water, watch its movement:

They see the water splashing, roaring, as the spray comes
    up . . .
Roaring as it pushes the silt along, flowing strongly . . .
Well water, bubbling and splashing, among the wild
    banana palms . . .[32]

The skill with which each feature of the rich and varied scene
is presented is ample evidence of the primitive Australian's
love of the world in which he lives. It expands far beyond
the practical calls of hunting, and, though it is ultimately derived from the needs of his belly, it has come a long way
from them and has a different appeal for him. He is inspired by affection and wonder to assume that at every point
a divine power is at work.

The Djanggawul songs carry to an accomplished finish an
art implicit in the humblest charms which seek to control
nature by understanding the supernatural powers at work in
it. At almost every stage primitive song gains this belief.
Because of it, singers assume without effort or trouble that
what they see before them has indeed some wider and grander
significance than its immediate usefulness in the struggle for
life, and that the hold which nature has over them comes
from unseen powers within it. If some Australians are the only
primitive people who have succeeded in turning into a full
artistic form what this means for them, it is the logical conclusion of what most primitives to some extent believe, and
the expansion and clarification of their feeling for unnamed
forces to be evoked from the natural scene. Their intimate
contact with living things calls for a unifying system, and this
they find in the assumption that all such things are in some
strange but not impossible sense divine. Dwelling, as they
do, with nature for their background and foreground and the
source of their survival, primitive singers need such a scheme
and are at times able to express their imaginative sense of it
by a sharpened vision which comes from seeing it as the in-
carnation of unseen powers and presences, of associations
and affinities with something beyond its visible self.

CHAPTER 7 *The Human Cycle*

THE LIFE of primitive man, from birth to burial, resembles a sequence of events in a single ceremonial. At each stage he recognizes that something important is happening and that he must celebrate it in a full and fitting way. The process of birth, growth, maturity, decay, and death has its own marked stages, and these summon him to songs which take him away from the customary calls of hunting into another sphere where he can look at his human condition from an independent angle and see beyond its immediate necessities to more embracing issues. Inside this frame he takes things as he finds them and expresses himself freely in song, which has a distinctive appeal because it is concerned with his hopes and his fears, his personal attitude to birth or death and therefore to family life with its affections and its claims and its anxieties. His sense of omnipresent gods and spirits in no way hampers or distorts his human feelings; rather it gives to them a new interest because it relates them to the unseen world. Even when he placates the gods at the birth of a child or after the death of someone whom he has loved, the claims of religion do not interfere with the force of his emotions. Indeed, even those songs which have been established through traditional usage and might be called conventional have clearly been composed by men who felt strongly all that is involved in such occasions, and turned into words their own acquaintance with joy and suffering. Just as hunting-charms are tied to the thrills and worries of the chase, so songs about the cycle of human life are based on what each stage demands in anticipation or retrospect and rise to meet the challenge with a full understanding of what it means and costs to its participants. Whether primitive man sings what he knows to be the customary, appropriate words for some stage in the human cycle, or bursts into extemporary song from a sudden inspiriting impulse, he shows the same qualities and finds a similar outlet for his emotions. Just as he enters with his whole being into the rites of formalized ceremony, so he is no less wholehearted in his reactions to events which suggest large issues beyond themselves and must be treated with all the attention that he can give to them.

The close relation between personal feelings and the calls of the supernatural can be seen at the start in songs of pregnancy and birth. To primitive man birth is indeed an astonishing mystery, and he must do his best to see that all goes well with it and that the expectant mother is not exposed to perils from the unseen. She must look on no sinister or menacing sights and give all her care to her unborn child. So in a song of the Gabon Pygmies strong injunctions are given against her looking at either tortoises or lepers:

> When the child in your womb
> Already leaps and moves,
> Let not your look stop,
> Young mother,
> Let not your look stop
> On the trailing tortoise,
> Which moves its scales on the pathway!
> Look not at the leper who strays in the village!

> Let your child,
> Young mother,
> Let the child who comes forth from your womb
> Not see, as he sucks the nourishing milk,
> Not see either the tortoise which moves its scales on
>   the pathway,
> Or the leper who strays in the village.[1]

This song has a severely practical purpose, which is that the child shall not suffer from evil fortune either before or after birth. We are not told why the tortoise and the leper are singled out for special injunctions, though it is quite understandable that the sight of a leper might hurt the child and its mother. Such prohibitions are common enough in primitive societies and are by no means confined to pregnant mothers. But the charm of the song is that it is composed in a mood of tender care for herself and her precious burden. The song-maker knows what it means to be a mother and how fatal a sudden shock may be, and his sense of evil forces at work beyond his knowledge does not prevent him from speaking with an entirely natural solicitude. Indeed his affectionate attention is enhanced and made more responsible by his fear of the dangers which menace the mother, and he distils his feelings into this ingenuous and touching form.

The birth of a child is an occasion for delighted pride and confident hope, and primitive parents feel these with even greater force than others, because birth is never easy for them, and all too often children die from the many diseases and mischances of the forest or the desert. So the Gabon Pygmies have another song which welcomes a child into the world and, in giving him his name, wishes for him beauty and a long life:

> A man-child is born,
> A man-child is born.
> May he live and be beautiful.
> A man-child is born,
> A man-child is born.
> May he become old, very old.
> Joy, joy, praise, praise!
> Ngongonabarota, know it, is his name.[2]

The rite of naming the child, with all the consequences that a name has in such a world, is suitably combined with wishes for him. The gods are not directly invoked, but of course it is only they who can grant such wishes, and the song has an unassumingly religious character. Yet here too behind the obvious purpose there is an instinctive movement of hope and delight. This is its human side; its divine side emerges when the new-born child is placed outside the hut, and his father dances to the sound of the tom-tom, while the rest of the family make a circle round him and sing to the accompaniment of varied cries from the women:

> The tree has given its fruit, and the fruit is good to
>   eat.
> Oh! Oh! Oh! *yélè, yao, yao!*

> The day is bright, and the night is black.
> Say nothing, do not speak, those who pass this way!
> Oh! Oh! Oh! *yélè, yao, yao!*

The *nkula* turns to dust at the foot of the tree,
The animal runs and man eats it,
The bird flies and man eats it,
The fish darts and man eats it.
Oh! Oh! Oh! *yélè, yao, yao!*

Say nothing, do not speak, those who pass this way.
Oh! Oh! Oh! *yélè, yao, yao!*[3]

In contrast with the preceding song this is not domestic but
public, not personal but social, concerned not with an individual but with the whole process of bringing life into the
world. That it is a holy occasion and makes no attempt
to hide it is clear from the repeated demand for silence,
which is the silence of awe and reverence. The song deals
with man's unique place in the world, with his power over
other living creatures, and the arrival of such a being is
spoken of in images which are also symbols. The comparison first with the fruit of a tree and then with the light of
day suggests that here is something pure and sacred which
is properly spoken of in exalted riddles. The mood is more
of awe than of delight, and the awe is due to the inexplicable, peculiar position of man in the scheme of things.
Though the gods are not named or even mentioned, this is a
religious song. The singers are possessed by a sense of the
holy, of something happening which calls for amazement
and veneration, and this strikes a solemn note in which even
joy is kept in a subordinate place.

The young child is born into a privileged order of beings,
and has to be trained to take his place among them. As he
grows up, his mother or his grandmother will strengthen and
correct him by magical incantations and rites. Though primitive peoples are unusually indulgent to their children and
hardly ever say harsh words to them or punish them, they
take care that they are properly trained and instructed. So
among the Euahlayi of Australia, when a child catches hold
of something as if to give it away, an elderly woman, usually his grandmother, takes it and croons over the child:

> Give to me, baby,
> Give to her, baby,
> Give to him, baby,
> Give to one, baby,
> Give to all, baby![4]

As soon as the child begins to crawl, the mother finds a
centipede, half cooks it, and then catching the child's hands,
beats them with it to the accompaniment of a song:

> Be kind
> Do not steal,
> Do not touch what belongs to another,
> Leave all such alone,
> Be kind.[5]

Such songs, so plain and forthright, are far clearer than the
rites which they accompany, and show how primitive song
makes articulate what would otherwise be lost in an almost
mechanical rite, which is indeed prescribed by custom and
probably obligatory, but certainly would not in itself convey
anything explicit. Indeed what is surprising in these Euahlayi
songs is their instructive tone. The mother is so eager for
her child to be all that a man ought to be that her songs
over him are unashamedly educational. The child does not
understand them, but in a world where anything can be
done by words they are aimed at an end, and this is such as
any mother might wish for her child. Short and elementary
as they are, they convey very firmly the mother's affectionate
desire that her child should take an honourable place among
his fellows and behave according to their best traditions.
The song purveys instruction, but it is also a charm; for if
the mother speaks in this way, it is because she feels that
her words will have power and that her child will do as she
tells him.

The Gabon Pygmies express their hopes for their children
through lullabies and other songs in which, as in songs of
hunting, a wish is presented as a future event, and of course
this too is a charm uttered on the assumption that, if a
wish is felt strongly enough and set forth in the right words,
it will influence unseen powers and be fulfilled. Yet this sense
of magical efficacy is infused throughout with purely human
feelings, which the mother expresses as she sings over her
child:

> Sleep, sleep, little one, close your eyes, sleep, little one!
> The night comes down, the hour has come, tomorrow it
>   will be day.
> Sleep, sleep, little one! On your closed eyes day has fled.
> You are warm. You have drunk, sleep, sleep, little one!
> Sleep, to-morrow you will be big, you will be strong.
> Sleep, to-morrow you will take the bow and the knife.
> Sleep, you will be strong, you will be straight, and I bent.
> Sleep, to-morrow it is you, but it is mother always.[6]

The ideal which the Pygmy mother cherishes for her son is
that he should be large and strong, and though no doubt
her standards are relative to other Pygmies, who hardly

ever reach five feet, for her it is the right ideal. The future rises before her as she watches her sleeping child, and while she foresees his growing strength, she foresees also her own decline into old age. This price she is prepared to pay for her son's future, and in the mysterious words of the last line she hints at what she has in mind. The child has indeed to-morrow before him, and in it he will grow to manhood and perform a man's actions, but, though this is his special time, his mother is still with him, if not in presence, at least in her thoughts, and, more insistently, in his physical being. The theme of the song is the relation between a mother and her child, and it deals with this in truthful, imaginative, loving pride. The bond which binds her to her son is stronger than mere affection. It is indeed rich in hope and ambition for him, but at its roots it is physical. She knows that he is flesh of her flesh, and that there is a bond between them which nothing else can equal, and this gives him a unique place in her love.

At the age of about twelve both boys and girls are subjected to initiation ceremonies, which do not so much indicate that they have grown up as enforce by magic the process of doing so. Such ceremonies are treated with the utmost seriousness, and the songs in them attempt to bring out their inner significance as well as to draw attention to some of their external aspects. An Australian song from Arnhem Land deals with circumcision and shows, with some elaboration, what the rite means both for the eyes and for the understanding. The woman addresses her son who is being circumcised and her uncle who does it:

Ah my son, uncle—
Ah, my son, blood and the red sky of the sunset!
The blood of the kangaroo flows . . .
At Gamarala, Burginbugi, and Nuga . . .
Who struck it down? It was a *wanud* man, a *gamarag* man . . .
He killed it with his jungle spear.
Ah my son, my son! Ah, the kangaroo . . .
It jumps from the rock to the ground, that creature with claws . . .
Blood is flowing, the red sky of the sunset . . .
Ah, my son, a small flow of blood from a small penis.
He is young, he has not grown big!
Ah, the wallaby small and young!
My son, a small flow of blood, this well and my son's penis—
The rays of the setting sun and the blood-red sky . . .

Ah, my son, a little penis, a little blood and the red
sunset . . .
Our son and our uncle.[7]

Here the religious parts of the rite take pride of place, but
they too are infused with human feelings, as the mother laments what happens to her child and does not shrink from
relating the physical act of circumcision, which is done with
a sharp stone, as if it were a form of destruction and death.
She feels that the child whom she has known has now become someone else, and this is her way of describing it. At
the same time the action is of profound significance in more
than one way. The boy's totem is a kangaroo, and through
this rite he turns from being a wallaby into a fully fledged
kangaroo. His uncle, who performs the change, is identified
with a kangaroo leaping savagely on him, as indeed he
does in the rite, which is necessary but none the less hard
and painful. Secondly, the flow of blood is likened to the
blood-red sunset, no doubt because it takes place in the
evening. But the comparison has also a symbolical purpose.
As the sunset proclaims the end of one day and foretells
the coming of another, so it is with the boy's life. He leaves
childhood behind him and enters upon manhood. The comparison underlines the extent of the change for him and
gives to it a certain supernatural quality, since the setting
sun is a divine being. The action is seen alike in its human,
its dramatic, and its religious aspects, and the result is a
poem which does nothing to dissimulate the callous nature
of the operation but at the same time exalts its importance
by relating it to the whole scheme of things as known in
totems and in nature.

After his initiation a boy is treated as a more or less
grown-up person who takes part with his elders in the essential duties and labours of his family. In many ways
primitive children mature early. They have already learned
the techniques of getting food and join in the pursuit of it,
and they have been well trained in the ceremonies and
relaxations of dance and song. This does not mean that they
never feel the limitations and disadvantages of their youth.
In fact they are not shy of singing about it, and certainly do
not feel it improper to do so. Some hint of this can be seen
in a song composed by an Eskimo, Norqaut, when he was
ten years old:

There are people there
With enormous strength,
And one gets strength from them.
Their teeth there

They bare in a grin.[8]

Norqaut recognizes that his elders are stronger than he is and that they can help him to succeed in his ambition to be a hunter, but he feels a slight resentment at their smiling condescension towards him. Neither he nor they could be expected to behave otherwise, and the little song is true to the aspirations of a boy who wishes to be treated as a grown-up among grown-ups. Norqaut also composed another song, in which with primitive frankness he discloses his precocious interest in matters of sex:

> Young men want wombs
> That make them want to piss;
> Inviting, pleasant things
> Are always sensual.[9]

Reticence is not to be expected from a boy who spends his time with his elders and hears their talk, and Norqaut wishes to show that he knows all about women and is quite as mature as his elders in his interest in such matters.

Primitive society looks after children so long as their parents are alive, but if anything happens to break the scheme, the child may suffer not only neglect but isolation and contempt, since nobody is responsible for him or willing to look after him. He may have some sort of place in his group, but it is unlikely to be dignified or comfortable, and he may be subjected to slights and humiliations. An Eskimo tells of such a situation:

> When I was orphaned, I had always to stand up,
> But, since I was not yet ill-treated,
> It was not hard for me to keep on standing up
> In the ship's fore-room.
> When I was orphaned and not yet ill-treated,
> I could easily keep on standing up,
> And my eyes gazed everywhere about me.[10]

This is said to be an old song, though we cannot tell what exactly that means, and evidently deals with a not uncommon situation. Whoever composed it recalls his first years of orphanhood, and though he hints that things got worse later, when he was actually ill-treated, yet at this time his only humiliation was that he had to stand up in the kayak, while the others sat down. This is a social discrimination which evidently counts in Eskimo society, but the boy was able to endure it and prides himself that he did not find it difficult. Indeed, he even turned it to a good purpose, for it was this that taught him to keep his eyes open so that noth-

ing escaped them. The song shows how a boy can overcome
his hardships and be proud of his triumph over them. The
dignity of his attitude casts a comforting light on the ability
of primitive peoples to live up to their ideas of what a
man ought to be, even when circumstances are against them.

With puberty comes love, but it is remarkable that on the
whole primitive songs about love are in short supply. This is
in marked contrast with peoples who have just passed out of
the stage of hunting and gathering and begun to settle down
to an agricultural routine, as the Aëta of the Philippines have
a number of love-songs, which speak with open passion and
draw their imagery from their new way of life. This is not
to say that primitive peoples do not fall in love, but simply
that, since it is not connected with any religious rites or even
assumptions, it receives less attention than other subjects which
have a supernatural ambience. Of our few specimens one
from the Eskimos is remarkable in being composed by a
woman who speaks with tart candour to the man she loves:

> Kangiak, while you take me for a fool,
> I take you also for a fool.
> Kangiak, take nothing on yourself.
> Take three women to yourself.
> One of them can get no children.
> You must try to get her.
> You must use her as usual.
> It is not in the least difficult.[11]

She is wounded by his neglect of her and tells him scorn-
fully what he really needs. The song is not quite so cynical as
it sounds, but is the chiding reproof of a woman who feels
herself badly treated. Its spontaneous frankness can be found
in other songs with a very different temper. The tenderness
which men feel for women comes out in those songs of parting
which they sing before they go on expeditions. In these we
find a real warmth and tenderness, and an Eskimo example
again sets the form:

> My betrothed,
> My beloved,
> I leave you now.
> Do not sorrow too much for me.
> I cannot forget you.
> Your eyes full of tears
> Are the image of your heart.
> All who love one another
> Find it hard to part from one another.
> And when we have held our marriage,

We shall never part from one another again.[12]

This frank approach to the ups and downs of love means that these songs are not hampered by the usual conventions that cluster round it, and are free to touch on topics which are certainly relevant but lie outside the limits of more stereotyped song. In some primitive peoples serious obstacles may arise to marriage because a man belongs to the wrong group, and what this means is stated with delightful frankness in a Dama song:

> Be not abashed, you with the black face! Do not weep!
> I am a man of another stock.
> Young men have shining cheeks.
> Am I one who is gazed upon and desired?
> You with the graceful thighs, I go away.
> In this year I go away.
> I go and linger around. Call me not.[13]

The lover skilfully depreciates his own charms and thereby stresses the genuine fidelity of his love, and with perfect tact he suggests that he will leave his beloved for a while and asks to be left alone by her, no doubt in the hope that in due course she will come round to him and marry him.

Love may lead to marriage, which is a much more serious subject since it is hardly less mysterious than birth or death and provokes religious considerations. The straightforward, secular act of making love is transformed into an almost metaphysical activity. Marriage is connected with the supernatural world and has its own seasons and rules. Spirits are at work in the courting-season, and in north-eastern Arnhem Land the aborigines associate love with the season of the monsoons, when the flashes of lightning in the sky are identified with snakes, which are symbols of mating among many peoples. At such a time courtship becomes a ceremonial appropriate to the time of year and evokes far-reaching associations:

> The tongues of the Lightning Snakes flicker and twist, one to
>   the other . . .
> They flash across the foliage of the cabbage palms . . .
> Lightning flashes through the clouds, with the flickering
>   tongue of the Snake . . .
> It is always there, at the wide expanse of water, at the place
>   of the sacred tree . . .
> All over the sky, their tongues flicker: above the place of the
>   Rising Clouds, the place of the Standing Clouds,
> All over the sky, tongues flickering and twisting . . .

They are always there, at the camp by the wide expanse
    of water . . .
All over the sky, their tongues flicker: at the place of the
    Two Sisters, the place of the Wauwalak
Lightning flashes through the clouds, flash of the Lightning
    Snake . . .
Its blinding flash lights up the cabbage palm foliage . . .
Gleams on the cabbage palms and on the shining leaves . . .[14]

Here love-making is intimately associated with supernatural
powers, not merely with the Lightning Snakes but with the
mythical Wauwalak, who, like the Djanggawul in other parts
of Arnhem Land, are ancestors responsible for the origin and
maintenance of all living things. Yet this association with the
unseen only makes the occasion more exalted and gives to it
an additional dimension of excitement and delight. Courtship becomes even more dramatic because it is associated
with formidable natural powers and partakes of their strength
and magnificence. The air is full of them; a man enters into
the supernatural pattern of things and makes his own contribution to it.

Marriage, which is entered upon so solemnly, has of course
its human side, of which primitive peoples, to whom it is a
necessity, are well aware. The narrow frame of their existence
makes them keenly awake to its possibilities, because any
change in the course of life evokes undivided interest and attention. They know very well what it means to pass from
childhood into maturity, from single to married life, and they
see what risks and anxieties lie before the newly wedded. So
the Gabon Pygmies sing to the bride a song which has a
melancholy sweetness as it dwells upon the break which she
must make with her family and her past life:

> Slowly, slowly,
> Child, counting your steps,
> Go away, go away with tears,
> With a large heart, with a weary heart,
> Without turning your face,
> From the house, from the village,
> Where your eyes so gaily
> Laughed at every comer.
>
> Counting, counting your steps,
> Today you go away.
> With a large heart, with a weary heart,
> Go away, go away below!
> Counting, counting your steps,
> With a large heart, with a weary heart,

Today you go away.

Keep on your heart
And guard well the flower
Of your mother's garden,
The flower which will say to you:
"I am still loved below!"
Keep on your heart
And guard well the flower
In memory forever.

Counting, counting your steps,
Today you go away,
With a large heart, with a weary heart,
Go away, go away below!
With a large heart, with a weary heart,
Today you go away.[15]

The grave grace and the tender understanding of this song
are a tribute to the warmth of family feeling in a primitive people. The bride's family and friends know what marriage means to a young girl who leaves her own kin, and
comfort her by showing how well they sympathize with her
feelings, and advise her to be faithful to what she has
learned at home, as it is symbolized by the flower *mvi*, which
she wears in memory of it. The primaeval device of repetition is used with accomplished effect to stress the salient
elements in the situation and to make the young bride look in
a serious spirit on what lies before her. Here, indeed, there
is no specific mention of gods or spirits, and the whole
song seems to be set at an exclusively human level. Yet in
the flower and the ritual wearing of it some evocation or
symbolical gesture is intended. It is not an empty pose but
relates the occasion to an order of unseen powers who look
after the home and insist that the bride shall remember it.

Once married life begins, it is of course a normal state
and attracts its own range of songs. It is taken so much for
granted that it seldom calls for anything special in the way
of celebration, and its vast significance is revealed only when
disaster or death deals it a mortal blow. Even when all
seems to go well, it may have its rifts and troubles, and then
it is as likely in primitive society as in our own to become a theme for comedy. The Gabon Pygmies tell stories
in which the more dramatic moments are compressed into
songs, and these illuminate the chances and surprises which
await married couples in the equatorial forest. One such story
tells of Ki and his wife Lütshi. Ki loves his wife and is not

too fond of his mother-in-law, and the song-maker not only pays special notice to this but draws his own conclusion from it:

> Ki loved his wife very much,
> He scarcely loved his mother-in-law,
> Indeed he did not love her at all,
> Oh! Ki had a very good reason.
>
> Mothers-in-law are like acid plums,
> Like plums all green and hard.
> You eat them, and they put your teeth on edge,
> Your tongue is rasped.
>
> Young women, tasty plums,
> Are full of delicious juice, so good to crunch!
>
> Ki loved his wife very much.

Lütshi is torn between her mother and her husband, and the song poses the question and examines her position when she decides to leave her:

> To leave a mother to find a husband, to leave a husband
>   to find a mother.
> Which is the greater joy or sorrow?
>
> To leave your mother, to leave your village, *ohé, hé!*
>   Your heart gives you pain, *O, yo, lo!*
> To come back to the village, to see your husband again,
>   *ohé, hé!*
> Your heart is content, *eh, yé, lá!*
>
> To leave your daughter, to stay in the village, *eh, yé lé!*
> Your heart gives you pain, *eh, yo, lo!*
> To see your son-in-law far away, *eh, yo, lo!*
>   Your heart is content, *eh, yé, lé!*

Lütshi then goes out with Ki's brother, Ntiô, and they meet a tiger:

> Lütshi is much afraid, much afraid,
>   For she has seen the tiger, and the tiger would
>   eat her, *eh, yé, lé!*
> Lütshi is much afraid and wishes to save herself,
>   But fear fastens her feet to the earth, *oh, yo, lo!*

She is saved by Ntiô, who is badly wounded in the process, and she decides that, as he has done so much for her, while Ki has not even given her children, she will kill Ki and mary Ntiô:

> Ki despised Lütshi,
> He had not given her a child, *oh, yé, lo!*
> Lütshi preferred Ntiô,
> Ntiô, who had saved her, *oh, yo, lo!*

Ntiô rejects Lüshi's proposal. Instead they evolve an ingenious plan. Lütshi gets under the tiger, and Ntiô runs to the village to tell Ki that his wife is in deadly danger. Without taking any precautions or even preparing himself properly Ki dashes out to rescue her:

> He has not taken his spear,
> He has not taken his bow,
> He has not taken his knife,
> He has gone, he runs, he runs.

He finds the tiger and hurls himself on it, taking it by the throat. The tiger rolls over, and Lütshi comes out and tells Ki that the tiger is already dead and that she has wished to find out if Ki loves her:

> She wished to see if he loved her,
> She wished to know if he loved her.[16]

After this all is well, and the couple have many children born to them. This little cautionary tale is illustrative of Pygmy life with its strains and its compensations. It provides material for discussion and instruction about the relative bravery of Ki, Ntiô, and Lütshi, and is a secular myth of married relations, with their risks and disagreements and reconciliations.

Another Pygmy tale, told in the same way with patches of song, discusses the qualities that a man seeks in a wife, and relates how a young man called Ephra, in search of a wife, hears of three possible candidates in three different villages. At the first he meets Ekhui, who has been out fishing:

> The basket was full of fish, the basket of Ekhui,
> Full of fish, the basket of Ekhui,
> Of big fish, of little fish, of fresh-water shrimps,
> Of crabs, of shell-fish it was full,
> Quite full the basket of Ekhui.

Ekhui makes her mother cook the fish, on the grounds that she herself is too tired, but takes and eats a large portion. Ephra sets out with a full belly:

> For the second village Ephra has set out,
> Ephra has set out,
> At the first he has eaten well, Ephra has eaten well,
> His belly was quite full, his belly was heavy.

On his way he kills a squirrel:

> Ephra was a skilful hunter,
> His wife will always have something to eat,
> Happy wife, happy Ephra,
> Plenty at the hearth is a very good thing.

At the second village Ephra seeks a girl called Pâmo. She is out fishing, but when she comes back, her basket is half empty, and it is clear that she is not good at fishing:

> Pâmo was not a good fisherwoman,
> The fish laughed under her nose,
> The crab pinched her for amusement,
> Pâmo was not a good fisherwoman,
> Her mother was always tired.

However, Pâmo makes up for this deficiency by being an excellent cook. She gives Ephra an admirable meal, and after it he sleeps:

> When he has drunk the warm drink, he goes to sleep.
> Ephra has said: "My belly is full, I am content."
> Pâmo knows very well how to cook meat;
> Her husband will be happy.[17]

On the third day, at the third village, Ephra meets a girl who is good neither at fishing nor at cooking but knows very well how to make love. After some reflection, in which Ephra weighs her claims, he marries her. This story too provides ample material for discussion as to which of the three girls he ought to have married, but both in this and in the first tale the passages of song throw a lively light on marriage among the Pygmies. A wife must look after her man, but there are more ways than one of doing this, and in return he must treat her properly and love her. Once these principles are accepted, it is permissible to discuss details and alternatives. The songs provide a lively commentary on the incidents told in the tales. They are texts for argument, but they would not be discussed at all if they did not have their own vivid little art and their keen appreciation of human characters and their situations. They take us away from the world of spirits to the everyday world of men, and make their own contribution to the philosophy of how to be happy though married.

So long as he is strong and healthy and able to hunt, primitive man does all that is asked of him and is able to face his companions and himself with ease and honour. But when his powers begin to decline, and he ceases to be a help and becomes a burden, his lot is hard. The Bushmen and the Eskimos have a short way with the old and leave them to their deaths or accelerate the process. Before this final fate overtakes them, those who have ceased to be good hunters are sadly aware of what they have lost and suffer all the pathetic helplessness of advancing years. They do not always surrender and may show a certain defiance in the face of their new deprivations. But even when they face their difficulties frankly and boldly, we see how formidable these are and how a man's confidence is undermined when he can no longer set out in pursuit of game. An honest and touching revelation of such a condition informs a song composed by an old Eskimo called Nujialiaq:

Avunga, yayiya, aya!
Avunga, it is not for me to catch anything
With my poor dog on the ice.
Avunga, to my hunting companions
It simply leads me;
Avunga, I who can never make a catch
I turn my thoughts to hunting-companions on the ice.
Avunga, I am guided empty-handed
To the neighbours, to those with pretty women!
To those who are clever with the needle.
Avunga, I can never be one nearest the animals,
In a place by the sea, where there are animals and
    onlookers,
I would like to be the one nearest to them.
To a big bull and a fat cow with no calf,
Out in the water, I would like to be the nearest.
    Avunga, yayiya, aya![18]

For men like this the present is not worth having, and there is no future. They can only turn their thoughts to what others can still do and they themselves once could, but though they may find a momentary consolation in memories, in the end they cannot fail to be discouraged by the contrast between these and their present impotence. The doom of primitive life is that it depends too closely on a single form of activity and on the qualities which are demanded for success in it. Once a man is unable to maintain his own capacity for it, he is ruined, and there is no place for him even in his own family.

Sickness is hardly better than old age, and is regarded

with alarm and dismay. It is understandable that Australian aborigines, who naturally cannot comprehend it, should attribute it to the malignant magic of enemies and believe that even death may be caused by a spell laid from a distance on an otherwise healthy man. The *xon,* or medicine men, of the Selk'nam claimed to have power to harm their enemies by such means, and even the Anglican missionary Thomas Bridges, who incurred the wrath of a *xon* and found such a spell put on him, confessed that it gravely affected his health and that it took a long time to recover from it. Such spells are purely magical, and magic must be used to dispel them. So the *xon* of the Selk'nam, after crooning for a long time *wubwubwubwub,* makes various gestures, till he feels that he knows what the trouble is and utters his charm:

> Here is the curse . . .
> It is like a rat.[19]

Any sickness or disaster may be attributed to such a curse, and this belief makes primitive man even more uncertain of his security. The whole sphere of the supernatural is so far beyond any forecast that he surrenders to it and blames himself for anything that goes wrong. This is not to say that he gives up his own kind of struggle. Even when he thinks that his case is indeed bad, he may still face the facts bravely and hope for the best. There is an authentic note of confident defiance in a charm which the Gabon Pygmies use to send away sickness. While the medicine man brandishes in his left hand the tail of an elephant and shakes it all round the sick man, at the same time he pronounces an invocation which gives sense to the rite:

> Go away, spirit, worker of evil,
> Go back to the forest, to the night,
> To your own place, father elephant!
> Retreat, leave this hut,
> Leave this man alone, wicked spirit![20]

Since the elephant is the lord of the forest, he is thought to be responsible for sickness prevalent in it, and, when he is summoned to leave the sick man and let him recover, he is treated not with respect or reverence but with stern dismissal. What a similar situation looks like from a human angle without any recourse to magic may be seen from a long Eskimo song composed by Orpingalik, himself a well-known shaman, when he was stricken with illness. It begins with an account of his present state:

Unaya, unaya,
I sing a song, loudly I sing:
Since autumn I have been as helpless as my own child.

At times I wish that my house and its mistress were
gone,
She does not deserve to stay with him
Who should be her refuge and provide for her.
I would she were gone,
Now that I can no longer get up.
Unaya, unaya.[21]

From this sad mood in which Orpingalik thinks more of the
trouble which he brings to his wife than of his own afflic-
tions, he recovers some sort of cheerfulness by thinking of
his hunting prowess in the past. No doubt many primitive
men face sickness in this spirit, but we cannot doubt that
for them it is a hideous menace. Not only does it mean
that they are unable to look after their families by finding
food for them but it rots their confidence in themselves and
their place in the scheme of things. It is not surprising that
a crisis of this kind calls for the utmost courage and resistance and provides a test of their ability to face the worst
when it comes. Decay and disease hang over primitive man,
and when they strike him, he has to summon all his strength
and all his self-command to face them. If he does not, he
is lost, and nothing awaits him but emptiness and failure.

The impact of sickness makes primitive people feel that
something has broken violently into the customary round
of their activities, and this makes them conscious of the in-
stability of their lives. There is almost nothing that they
can do except pray to their gods and hope that succour will
come from them. So in a time of famine a Dama tries to
appease them:

O fathers, listen!
Temper your anger!
Have kindly thoughts!
You have left them behind on the earth.
What have they greedily refused you,
That the people are always sick?
You have ceased to give, and, as it is said,
The people die while you eat up their store.
Why did you injure them?
Temper your anger!
Have kindly thoughts, all of you![22]

What makes this prayer impressive is the sense of the in-

justice of the gods who have sent the famine, and the old
man who utters the words asks, indeed, if men have left un-
done something that they ought to have done, but his questions are almost rhetorical; he does not admit that men have
neglected the gods, and for this reason his approach to
them has a powerful undertone of indignant complaint. He
has enough tact not to charge the gods openly with greed,
but he is not far from hinting at it, and bravely asks them
to cease their anger and show mercy.

When sickness passes into death, primitive peoples do not
find in it any of the sweetness with which romantic fancies
sometimes contrive to console civilized man, and in the moment of loss find no consolation in the thought of life beyond
the grave. In this, as we shall see, they often believe, but
the recognition of it comes slowly, and the actual impact of
death is always a cause of bitter grief. Their reactions to it
are violent, disturbed, and distressed. They sometimes suspect
that it is due to the magical action of ill-wishers, and they are
always appalled by its presence, even though they live in conditions in which it is to be expected every day. In the small
unit of the family, in which everyone has a task to perform
and even children do something to help, death means not only
personal loss but menace to the whole group in its struggle
for subsistence. The worst thing that can happen is that a
father of a family should die; for this means that its main defence and refuge is gone. What this costs in grief and desolation can be seen from the laments which Dama women sing
for their husbands. In most of them the shock of death is at
first incredible and incomprehensible. The widow can hardly
begin to grasp it, and clings to any hope that puts off its
final recognition. As she comes to realize the truth, she sees
what an enormous change it means in her life. So in one
song a widow, who realizes that her husband is dead, and
begins to see what his absence means, is still ignorant of the
manner of his death and cannot but ask how it came:

> Father of my little son, black as a pigeon,
> You go no more on the way of the chase!
> No bad young man was he.
> Our store was full of flesh, my husband!
> Is then the father silent?
> On the way by which he was wont to come back
>   there is darkness.
> Has a scorpion hurt him?
> Has he been caught by a lion?[23]

So, too, just because a woman's tasks are in their own sphere
as indispensable as a man's are in his, the death of a wife

may be no less destructive of a husband's security and happiness. Another Dama song shows what he feels when this happens to him:

> Daughter of the woman with a low brow, my
> companion,
> Come and kiss me!
> When will you arise and speak to me?
> My companion is dumb and silent.
> Instruct me then in singing
> That I may help you to sing!
> Arise, and let us look for caterpillars!
> Arise and let us dig up wild onions!
> Like one who could now arise, you lie there.
> Cease to sleep, and arise!
> Arise and kiss me![24]

The bereaved man is so accustomed to his wife's presence that he can hardly believe that he has been robbed of it. The strict rules of his existence have imposed a pattern on his habits and his thoughts, and when this is broken, he feels that it cannot be true, that he has only to summon his wife to her customary duties for her to get up and rejoin him. His horrified surprise is closely connected with all the activities which he has shared with her, and it is to these that he vainly calls her back. So too a child's death may create an almost equal conviction of hopeless deprivation; for a child too has its place in the close economy of the family, and its death is no less unexpected and horrifying, as a third Dama song shows:

> He who was wont to give me beautiful things, the
> son of Noworb,
> He is dead.
> Arise. Why do you lie there?
> Do what your companions do, go and play.
> Son of my beloved, why do you lie there?
> Arise, run and play, that I may see you.
> Your companions go away from you.
> Whom shall I now send to fetch water?
> Whom have you left behind for me?
> Son of Gakhubes, arise that I may carry you on
> my back.[25]

Primitive life is so fragile and so precarious that almost any mischance may destroy its shape and the confidence of those who live by it, but just because it is so uncertain, it makes men cling more closely to what they know and value and especially to the affections, which are among the very few things which have a certain stability in their unstable world.

Living in a world which calls for the full exercise of their bodily gifts and the satisfaction of their bodily needs, primitive men see with more than ordinary horror what physical corruption means in its ugly immediacy and its merciless haste. Indeed their vision of it is all the sharper because they lack the protection with which civilized man protects himself against the facts of the flesh and his kinship with the beasts. Though the Australians of Arnhem Land have many songs about death, the most distressing of them are those which deal not with beliefs in what happens to the departed spirit but with the actual shape of death when they see it in their midst. Though these songs hint at supernatural influences they remain close to the first horrified consternation which men feel when they see a dead body. So a Djapu song runs:

> Ah, my daughter, my grandson,
> Whence does the south-east wind come blowing through
>   Dagaljagal and Wanumaru?
> Maggots grow and fly at Mauwimana . . .
> Ah, who is that flying away? It is the maggots.
> They have eaten the limbs and arms of a Djapu body
>   and flown away . . .
> Whom does the wind blow there, and the maggots
>   attack?
> There they are striking a Djapu body, a Djapu skull
>   lies broken.
> Whom does the wind blow there, and the maggots
>   attack?
> There at night they are striking at Darlijabi.
> Ah, my daughter, my grandson![26]

Here there is an echo of the supernatural in the mention of the south-east wind, which is thought to blow from the island of the dead, but the rest is drawn from the visible scene and shows how attentively the singer has observed the sudden irruption of death and how deeply it has affected him. The maggots are correctly reported, since they quickly turn into blow-flies and fly away from the corpse which they devour. The dominating mood is horror and dismay at the corruption of the flesh, at a dead body eaten by vermin. The sense of abhorrence and alarm is enhanced by the belief that supernatural forces are at work and that therefore nothing can be done. Primitive peoples are acutely aware of what corruption means, and it lies at the root of their views of death. Whatever explanations they may find for death, and whatever relation they may imagine between it and supernatural agencies, its physical aspect obsesses them and provokes an indignant reaction against it.

This sense of corruption is intimately interfused with a sense of personal loss, which it makes more bitter by the visible, unavoidable abomination. Behind it and around it lies an angry sorrow for someone snatched away, without reason and without purpose, by unseen powers who are seldom friendly and now reveal their inscrutable, murderous will. What death means in this aspect may be seen from some rhythmical prayers, which the Yamana, who in their last days knew in full measure its omnipresent menace, have to say about it. These prayers are not songs, but they are a true form of poetry in their passionate concentration on their subject and their gift for setting this in an impressive order. Many of them are of a poignant simplicity, cries of complaint uttered by widows and parents who have lost their nearest and dearest, and their normal form has a terrible nakedness as they lament a loss:

> My Father alone above is angry with me, alas!
> Truly the slayer on the mountain is angry with me, alas![27]

or

> Alone I stand in my hut, where I should be happy;
> Silent is the hut, and the hut of my children, alas![28]

or a woman who has lost all her other children is afraid that the last one left will also be lost:

> I am afraid because of my Father, alas!
> My only child is in danger from above, alas!
> I am afraid, alas![29]

When unexplained disaster falls on him, primitive man denounces his gods for their cruelty and treachery, and suspects them of base or brutal motives, as here the god is suspected of callously wishing, for no definite reason, to kill a whole family. These outbreaks show how the Yamana stand in relation to their Father above, what they expect and demand from him, what they fear they will actually receive. The agony in the words is plain for all to share, and their compression into a short space makes them more touching and more tragic. The god, who should look after his people, is angry with them and robs them of their children. This is no time for subservient humility or patient acceptance. Death is too serious a matter to be taken so lightly, and the Yamana show that, even when it is all around them, they resist and denounce it and feel that they have been tricked and betrayed. They turn on their god and try to force him to listen to them.

Primitive men hardly regard death as a natural event which is bound to come sooner or later, but tend to ascribe it to some evil power, whether the callous anger of a god or the evil designs of an enemy or some more mysterious agency. This last is sometimes the case when they live in a totemistic system, which explains what might otherwise be inexplicable and conforms to convictions about the closeness of man to other natural things. Totems are as open as men to attack by evil spirits, and a song from Arnhem Land shows what can happen:

> There at Dungulmu stands the stringybark tree.
> "Ah," says the tree, "I shall keep standing here,
> Where the little green birds are living."
> Ah, far away stands the stringybark tree.
> "I will cut down that tree," says the Wijar spirit.
> "That tree that has for so long been standing there,
> The home of the little green birds."
> Crying he goes and cuts the stringybark down.
> "Those flowers are mine, that stringybark is mine,"
>   says Wuda'l.
> The tomahawk cuts the tree, the leaves come falling.
> The tree falls into the water at Iurmiiurmi,
> The water is swirling there where the stringybark
>   falls . . .
> Ah, daughter, grandmother, grandchild,
> It was there you lost all—dead!
> Ah, you lie there as if you were only sleeping.[30]

The lives of a family are tied to the life of a tree, and when the tree dies, three of them die also. This is how the Australian song-man sees it, and for him it is all perfectly simple and natural. He dwells at length on the fall of the tree not only because it is the cause of the catastrophe, but because when this comes, it explains why the disaster is so great. It does not matter that the tree is far away; it is still inextricably bound with the human beings whose totem it is. Its fall is attributed to a malign spirit called Wuda'l, and it is clear that his motives are purely destructive, that he simply wishes to show his power over the tree by cutting it down. Against such evil influences men cannot struggle, and that is why the song ends on a note of pure grief for the dead. But even in the presence of such frightening powers the human tone is still free and unrestrained, and sorrow finds an outlet in lamentation.

Such songs on the sudden incursions of death show how deeply it affects primitive men. Living as they do in the moment, absorbed in its needs and its relaxations, they take little thought for the morrow, and anything so disrupting as death comes as an annihilating shock. Yet they must struggle to go on living, and somehow recover their balance and their confidence in themselves. Sometimes they do this by speculating about what happens to the dead; at other times they master their emotions enough to see that, however strange death may be, it is still after all natural and must be accepted even without any understanding of its meaning. Though the Gabon Pygmies hold lamentations over their dead, yet, when the body is ready for burial, they sing over it a chant in which grief gives place to awe and wonder, and the personal sense of loss is merged in a recognition that death is part of the unfathomable mystery which envelopes human life. Though the occasion is indeed solemn and reverent, it is not one of unmixed grief. The eldest son of the dead man begins, and the maternal uncle replies:

A. The animal runs, it passes, it dies. And it is the
    great cold.
B. It is the great cold of the night, it is the dark.
A. The bird flies, it passes, it dies. And it is the
    great cold.
B. It is the great cold of the night, it is the dark.
A. The fish flees, it passes, it dies. And it is the great
    cold.
B. It is the great cold of the night, it is the dark.
A. Man eats and sleeps. He dies. And it is the great
    cold.
B. It is the great cold of the night, it is the dark.
A. There is light in the sky, the eyes are extinguished,
    the star shines.
B. The cold is below, the light is on high.
A. The man has passed, the shade has vanished, the
    prisoner is free!
    Khvum, Khvum, come in answer to our call! [31]

Though this song suggests that the spirit of the dead passes to another realm of existence, its actual feelings are true to human nature in the moment when it recovers from the first shock and pang of bereavement. Death is then seen as a natural process, as is right for men who live among animals and birds and fishes and share their world and in so many ways resemble them. The first part of the song states the incontrovertible truth that man perishes like the beasts and passes into darkness and cold when the warmth leaves his stiffening body. The second part changes directions towards a glimmering of hope set in the imagery of light. Whatever awaits the dead man's spirit, it is thought to be good, and comfort is found in it. The bereaved hope that, if the god answers their prayers, all will be well and the spirit will be freed from its earthly trappings and go to the place of other spirits. By such means the Pygmies master their grief, and, because they are able to face what death means in its physical setting, they are ready to ask what else it can mean when the spirit is loosed from the body. It is all reasonable and consistent. Death raises troublesome questions, but they can to some degree be answered, and it calls for certain actions to ensure that all is done that custom and belief prescribe for the passage of the spirit to another order of being.

These songs, which mark the different stages of the cycle of existence, have indeed their full portion of human feelings and speak for emotions and states of mind which are perfectly intelligible to us. This is the more remarkable because in the first place they are often accompanied by rites which we cannot understand easily from inside, and which seem to come from a much more primaeval outlook than the songs which illustrate them, and in the second place, though they usually imply belief in gods and spirits and indeed in a whole encompassing order of supernatural beings, these do not diminish but enhance their strictly human aspect. Primitive man sees the main events of his life as stages in a natural process akin to what he knows from animals and plants and as suitably illuminated by them. Despite the ignorance which encloses him on every side, he has a firm hold on the elemental ties which bind him to his own kind and on the obligations which these impose upon him. The strength of these songs lies in their closeness to common experience, their uninhibited response to the calls and climacterics of living, and their straightforward handling of them. Each has its own temper, and this gives unity to it and helps it to carry conviction, but the emotions are always kept in control as they are reduced to their essence and presented in shapely concrete forms. This is only one class of primitive song, and to see it in its proper perspective we must take it with songs of the supernatural which forms its background and its sequel. Yet, taken in isolation, it has its own appeal and unlocks a consciousness which might at first sight seem to be very remote but is proved on acquaintance to be surprisingly sympathetic and understandable.

CHAPTER 8 *Primitive Imagination*

IN MODERN usage imagination normally means a capacity to form a mental image of something which is not present to the senses. What it represents may exist somewhere else in the actual world, or it may exist nowhere; it may belong to the past, the present or the future, or to no specified time. In any case it is presented to the eye of the mind, which accepts it on the assumption that it is real, even if it is known not to be. The process is applied not only to the forms and appearances of things but to thoughts and feelings, which give meaning to them and, though absent, can be shared and absorbed and understood. This faculty is almost indispensable to modern poetry, which deals with matters outside the immediate purview of most of its readers and takes a professional pride in extending experience by creating through words "forms more real than living man" and making them hold our attention by the intensity of insight and feeling incarnate in them. Once this process begins, there are almost no limits to it. The poetical imagination can be used to seek for transcendent realities behind the visible scene and to give them a convincing actuality, to create whole orders of beings and events which may incidentally illustrate known behaviour but are intended to be taken for their own value and their own sake, to re-create scenes from the past with a convincing persuasiveness, to see more in ordinary things than is commonly seen in them and so to give them a new character and a new relevance. Primitive imagination does nothing of this kind. It is resolutely and rigorously concerned not with what is absent in time or place but with what is believed to be present but invisible. So far from creating its subjects out of nothing and making them live in their own authority, it assumes that they exist already and that the singer's task is simply to show what in fact they are, how they work, what is their appearance or character or behaviour. Its sphere is confined to the supernatural, and to this it gives its attention and its insight. This means that its activities are limited and almost prescribed, but though it is thus limited it is extremely active and lively and purposeful. Primitive beliefs are often so strange that they call for a powerful imagination to make sense of them, and most myths would be lost in indeterminate shapelessness if they were not presented with a firm grasp of what matters most in them and can be made vividly present to the mind. Such an exercise of the imagination is almost forced on the song-maker by his attempt to understand what certain beliefs and myths mean. He looks at them from his own outlook and interprets them through it, with the result that even the most impalpable presences are brought into the orbit of his factual art and find a place in the familiar world.

The absence of conscious effort in setting the imagination to work and its almost instinctive response to calls made on it are particularly clear in those beliefs which primitive man takes for granted as the most natural and most obvious in his universe. Such is the case with the innumerable presences with which he thinks that he is surrounded. Since he does not begin to question their existence and feels them at work everywhere, he develops towards them an attitude which makes them as familiar as the figures and phenomena of every day. Yet though this is admirably natural, it calls for an ability to see them in their true character and to deal with them accordingly, especially when they are wanted to do, or to stop doing, something which lies in their power alone. Such a task is neatly demonstrated in some Eskimo weather-incantations. The Eskimo who wishes something to be done about the weather approaches his guardian-spirit and speaks so intimately to it that to us he may seem to omit matters of some import. Yet from his own standpoint this is entirely reasonable, since the spirit will probably know in advance what is going to be asked and will certainly be well acquainted with the man who asks it. Such an approach implies an active use of the unforced, unpremeditated imagination. The Eskimo imagines his spirit so clearly that he has his own methods of dealing with it, and he knows that he must be both firm and conciliatory:

> Come, he says, you outside there: come, he says, you
> outside there,
> Come, he says, you outside there: come, he says, you
> outside there,
> Your Sivoangnag bids you come,
> Tells you to enter into him,
> Come, he says, you outside there.[1]

All that he does is to bid his familiar to enter his breast, but this he does with all the authority that he can command. Behind this lies his assumption that if the spirit enters into him, he himself will be able to control the weather. He associates himself with the spirit as his own special guardian and does not think it necessary to say all that is on his mind. That is left for the spirit to infer and is a courteous tribute to its helpfulness. The Eskimo leaves much to be taken for granted just because he is comfortably at home with unseen presences and believes that they understand him. He naturally omits what is obvious both to himself and to his spirit. Even when the situation is rather more complex than this, a similar method of approach is used:

> My great companion, my great guardian spirit,
> My great companion, my great guardian spirit,
> Hear our fine incantation, our fine cries.
> There is no snow-hut; it is empty of people.
> He is not a real man; it is empty of people.
> Beneath it, down there, let us two search.[2]

Here the singer summons his spirit to help him in finding and expelling some other, less well-disposed spirit who is tinkering with the weather and must be stopped. The song hints at his disposition when it says that he is not a real man and in fact has no hut, but is working underground. This oblique and allusive method is a testimony to the complete understanding between the man and his spirit, and it is in its way purely imaginative, just because the imagination gets to work on the unquestioned assumption that its task is real.

Just as many songs elucidate rites which are otherwise hardly intelligible even to those who take part in them, so in dealing with the supernatural the imagination has not only to see and understand what it is, but to help in finding the proper way to handle it. Thus the Gabon Pygmies believe that the chamaeleon is a messenger from friendly spirits and must be welcomed and treated with care and good will. If by mischance anything harmful happens to it, men cannot reject all responsibility and must take steps to avert the menace of vengeance. The actual rite consists of throwing the body on a fire, but while this is done, a song is sung:

> Chamaeleon, chamaeleon,
> To him who sent you
> Go back quickly,
> Chamaeleon, chamaeleon!
> Your eyes are dead,
> Your ears do not hear,
> Chamaeleon, chamaeleon,
> You have delivered your message,
> Go back to him who sent you.[3]

The imagination has no difficulty in adjusting itself to the belief that the chamaeleon has brought a message from the unseen and that, after being burned, it will go back to the spirit which sent it. This is easily taken for granted and forms the background of the song. But a special effort is needed to secure the right tone and temper in addressing the dead chamaeleon. It is assumed that, since it is dead, there is nothing for it to do but to return to its master, and this is put to it in a friendly and familiar tone, which establishes an easy relation in awkward circumstances. The repeated "Chamaeleon, chamaeleon," and the polite, if firm, injunction to go back catch the temper of the rite and show what it means. The chamaeleon is assumed to have enough sense to see that this is the only thing to be done, and it is hoped that it will depart without causing any trouble. In such a case the existence of the rite forces the imagination to work on certain lines, and it does so not merely correctly and appropriately but with a tactful understanding of what is at stake. The relation with the chamaeleon is not very different from that with a friendly stranger who has come from far away and is now sent off when his errand is finished. The song insists that, even though the chamaeleon cannot now hear or see, yet in the world of spirits, to which it belongs, it can be approached by human entreaties and expected to respond to them.

In such cases the imagination works not so much pictorially but emotionally, not so much by forming a visual image as by catching exactly the right tone for a special occasion. But in other cases the pictorial element is often needed, if only to give body and presence to what might otherwise be too elusive or disembodied. Primitive peoples use images, which are not, like most of our own, literary devices to stress one or another aspect of a subject, but a means to make sense of what is otherwise hard to grasp. They are the elementary stuff of myth and are taken quite literally, even if it is recognized that their present function is not quite the same as in more commonplace spheres of action. For instance, the Australian Jajaurung conjure a man's ghost to get up and fly away:

> Rainbow spirit, cutting like a knife,
> Fly like a swallow, a curlew.[4]

The expressive, apt images catch the character of the spirit's emergence from the dead body and its departure to the place of other spirits, and each image says exactly what is intended. The words evoke visual impressions, and each is assumed to be a true version of reality, conveying the diaphanous nature of the spirit, its eruption from the corpse, the swiftness of its flight. In a similar way the Bushmen believe that dead men ride on the rain, and call out to them when they need their help:

> O gallopers,
> O gallopers,
> Do you not know me?
> For you do not seem to know my hut.

The Bushmen regard the dead as friends and helpers, and speak to them with an easy freedom as they express surprise that as yet no rain has come. They see them galloping through the sky, but this does not interfere with their sense of intimacy with them. Then they address the rain itself as if it were an animal which does not know how to behave itself:

> You should put your tail between your legs,
> For the women are looking shocked at you,
> You should put your tail between your legs for the
>   children.[5]

The rain is chidden for its impolite behaviour. The pictorial imagination which sees it so clearly prompts the tone of the reproof and makes the song both reproachful and playful.

The imagination has a large field of enterprise in dealing with spirits, and since evil spirits are in richer supply than good and need to be dealt with decisively, they set the imagination in action with some force. They have to be persuaded to give up their fell designs and depart, and though it does not matter whether this is done by argument or by abuse, it must none the less be done and calls for a powerful effort against them. Such are often spirits harming the dead, who return to earth with the intention of harming the living, and they have many ways of doing so. Among the Gabon Pygmies, when an elephant ravages the forest, it is because malicious ghosts have stung it on, and to keep them quiet a song is sung, which has in it a note of expiation and, while it deals primarily with the spirits, addresses the elephant, which is their unwilling victim:

> Driven by the wicked spirits of the forest,
> The old elephant, father of the herd,
> He, who wanders alone, whose females no longer
>   want him,
> O father elephant, where is your manly force?
> The force of which you were so proud?
> Driven by the wicked spirits of the forest,
> The old elephant draws near to our huts,
> May your eye not see them, father elephant,
> May your ear be deaf to the small child who cries
>   *gnian, gnian,*
> May your foot, which is too big, not crush our huts,
> O father elephant, O father elephant![6]

The evil spirits are dealt with at one remove. The immediate task is to placate the elephant which has been set on the rampage by them and menaces the safety of the village. The elephant is addressed not in a spirit of servility or even of courtesy but rather with a pitying contempt, on the assumption that his present rowdy behaviour is due to senility and declining powers and that he would not have been so ill-mannered in his prime. This is an indirect jab at the spirits, who are treated as if they could master only an elderly and impotent elephant, but equally it does not spare the elephant's own feelings. In this there is an element of bravado, of bluff, of pretending that the elephant is not all that he might be thought to be, but there is also an undercurrent of genuine fear of what an enraged elephant can do to the flimsy shelters of the Pygmies and to the unprotected children in them. The Pygmies have no difficulty in imagining either what the spirits have done or what the elephant will do at their instigation. They treat the whole situation in a matter-of-fact temper and hope that by arguing with the elephant they may stop him from doing his worst. Their knowledge of his habits enables them to speak with confidence, and they are not shy of doing so. The elephant is still called "father," as befits the lord of the forest even in his decline, but even fathers have sometimes to submit to the candid strictures of their children, and such are the comments made to him here.

The Pygmies also believe in ghosts who appear as white spectres in the forest, often in the form of skeletons with burning coals in their eye-sockets, while they snap their teeth as if they were cracking nuts. Such evil spirits have an evil past and maintain its habits in their new guise. The Pygmies are frightened of them and make this clear enough in a prayer to one of them to go away:

> Ogiri, you who on earth were an eater of men,
> Ogiri, do not draw near to our huts!
> We have seen your eyes shining in the black night,
>   O Origi!
> We have heard your teeth which made *kra, kra,*
> You, who on earth were an eater of men,
> O Ogiri, who we have known well,
> Do not try to draw near to our huts![7]

Ogiri is treated with more respect than the rogue elephant, because his powers are more frightening and more mysterious. Here primitive imagination is at the service of a world-wide belief and conforms easily to it. Such creatures as Ogiri are known to most simple peoples, as they are to children, and it takes no suspension of disbelief to accept them, especially when they lurk in the impenetrable gloom of the equatorial forest. Because Ogiri's habits are well known, there is no need to describe him in detail, and the characterization of him through his eyes and teeth and cannibal diet is quite enough to give a blood-curdling impression of him. His appearance is nothing new, and when the Pygmies admit that they have known him before, the implication is that this makes him all the more formidable. The song is an apotropaeic prayer, and its purpose is to turn Ogiri away to other haunts before he attacks the village, but it is cast in a manner which might seem to be almost too conciliatory to have any decisive effect on such a monster. But even this is true to the imagination. Though Ogiri is a horrific brute, the only hope of keeping him off is to appeal to him in a human way and to trust that this will move him.

Ogiri is an exceptional ghost, who has to be handled with unusual tact. The ordinary ghosts of the Pygmy dead do not wander during the day but hang like bats from the walls of caverns. A man may go into a cavern and fail to see them, and this enhances their weird character. It is not surprising that men should ask where they dwell and whether anyone has seen them, and the questions are indispensable if the ghosts are to be countered and controlled. It is assumed that they exist, and it is certainly strange that they cannot be seen; so a song catches the paradox of the situation and shows what wonder it evokes and how curiosity about these elusive beings clamours to be satisfied:

> Spirits of the forest, ghosts of the night,
> Who during the bright day,
> Like the bat which sucks the blood of men,
> Dwell hanging on the slippery walls of great caverns,
> Behind the green moss, behind the great white stones;
> Tell us who has seen them, the ghosts of the night,
> Tell us who has seen them.[8]

So far from shirking the presentation of such ghosts, the song-man is fascinated by them and forms a clear picture at least of their hiding-places as they hang on their perches. For him, of course, the identification with bats presents no problem, but his strength is that he understands exactly what this means, sees it firmly and clearly, and deals with it in a straightforward way. If such creatures live in caves, it should be possible to see them, and, without irony or ulterior purposes, he asks whether anyone has actually done so. Such a curiosity is not hostile, but it may well conceal an element of fear. Ghosts usually excite both fear and curiosity, and at times stir also a friendly attention, even if they themselves are far from friendly, and this contradictory but quite understandable mixture of feelings is present in this song. When Pygmy ghosts are released to wander at night by the light of the moon, the possibility of their presence stirs anticipation and wonder. It is true that, since they bring fever, they are not without menace, but this is not mentioned in a song which refers to them:

> Glittering stars of the white night,
> Moon shining on high,
> Piercing the forest with your pale beams,
> Stars, friends of white ghosts,
> Moon, their protectress![9]

The song's aim is to enlist the help of the moon and the stars against any possible harm from the ghosts, and its intention is so obvious that the ghosts are only just mentioned, and then in an apparently neutral or even friendly way. The Pygmy sees no need to underline his intention, but he takes care to praise the moon and the stars in appropriate words. His imagination finds it easy to see how the powers of the sky at night can keep the ghosts in control, and he sets about his duty in a respectful, conciliatory spirit.

The ease with which supernatural powers are brought into the human orbit is due to the assumption, never seriously questioned, that they are active and present in the physical world and belong to it quite as much as man does. The same is true of more mysterious forces like those which are set in movement by the spells of medicine men and shamans on their enemies, often from a distance, or are themselves thought to work harm if they are not placated in advance. The effects are real enough, and there is no need for the song-man to relate them, since everyone who has seen their victims suffering knows what they are. But the reality of spirits at work must be made obvious and, if it is to be pictured at all clearly, calls for a considerable effort. It is imagined not visually but through its effects, and this is wise, since the effects are what matter and are patent to everyone. So the Australian Euahlayi knock out a tooth that they may not be attacked by a spirit, and their notion of the advantage brought to them is stated in a forthright, practical way:

> Now you can meet the Boorah spirit,
> Now he will not harm you.
> He will know his spirit is in you.
> For this is the sign,
> A front tooth gone.
> He will know you by it.[10]

Here there is no imagery, and indeed no need for it, and though we do not know, any more than the song-man, why the removal of a tooth should have this result, it is sufficient that it does, and there is no more to say about it. The spirit has entered peacefully into the man at his invitation, and all is well. A similar temper sometimes inspires charms which summon spirits to give help. One of the Australian Wurunjerri was believed to have had a spell put on him from the Dullur country beyond Gelong, and his brother Wenberri, who was a medicine man, tried to exorcise the curse from him with a song in which he invoked a powerful spirit, called Bunjil, to help:

> We all go to the bones, we all go to the bones,
> They shine white in this Dullur country;
> Our father Bunjil comes with a rushing noise, singing,
> Into this breast of mine, inside my breast.[11]

The spell begins by speaking of the danger which comes from the Dullur country, and the reference to the bones indicates the imminence of death. It continues by invoking Bunjil to enter the sick man's breast that he may protect him at his most sensitive point. The pain is already there, and

Bunjil must follow it if he is to exorcise it. His arrival is loud and joyful, as befits the rescue of an injured person, and the whole proceeding is fully thought out and understood and expressed with a keen eye for its different stages and aspects. To us it may all be imaginary, but to Wenberri both the curse and the rescuing spirit are entirely real, and he has no difficulty in imagining how they work.

In this case the patient died, but this is not a song of death. Such songs exist and find their richest scope in considering what prospects it offers to the departed spirit and what happens to it. On this matter every primitive group has its ideas, and though the Yamana and the Andamanese are reported to be not very interested in survival after death and even to doubt its possibility, it certainly occupies much primitive attention and invites imaginative consideration. This after all is a subject on which nothing is known for certain, and though firm beliefs are held on it, they can only be brought home through a full use of the material which primitive man has collected in his long and lively observation of the living scene. If he is to speculate at all clearly or confidently about life after death, he must bring it into relation with life as he knows it and build up his own pictures of what myths about survival mean when careful thought is applied to them. A bridge must be thrown from the immediate and unanswerable presence of a dead body to the realm whither the spirit is believed to have passed. Such beliefs are not always very clear or detailed or consistent, and most primitive peoples maintain a certain reserve in speaking of them. The practical test for the imagination is how far it goes in dealing with a matter on which there is bound to be considerable uncertainty and a general refusal to say too much. Songs which deal with such topics must remain faithful to accepted beliefs and do neither more nor less than they allow.

What is said about the after-life must conform in temper with the laments which are everywhere sung over a dead person. It need not echo their sentiments, but it must take account of them and not ignore the anguish of loss which they proclaim so bitterly. The Semang believe that all spirits of the dead alike go to a world of shadows, and they forecast what this is when they pronounce a lament at a funeral, at which incense, made of a resin called *keminin,* is burned in the grave over the body:

> The incense smokes in the grave,
> You have vanished, you are at rest on the sea-shore,
> You crown yourself with *tanyong* flowers;

If only you had been just sick!
Who of us would wish to make you angry?[12]

The imagination works easily and quietly in the notion that
in its journey over the sea the departed spirit crowns itself
with flowers for its entry into a new existence. Though
Semang myths might well allow more than this, no elaborate
mythology is even hinted at, and the vision of what happens
arises naturally from the sense of farewell and separation,
and is concerned mainly with it. Because the dead man is at
peace, the living wish to be at peace with him and to do
what he desires by carrying out the proper rites. The moment of parting is caught in its dual nature, in the thought
of what happens to the dead and in the expression of what
the bereaved feel about him.

The transition from life to death is by no means free
from anxieties and regrets, especially when the after-life is
thought to provide not something better than this life but a
restricted or impoverished version of it. If the dead are de-
prived of much that they have known and enjoyed, it must
be spoken of, and any song about them must state the facts
fairly and even pass its human comment on them. An instructive example comes from the Australian Euahlayi, who
look on death as a feebler version of life, and when, for
instance, they lament the death of a woman, her oldest male
relative pronounces words in the grave, while women mourners wail in the intervals:

She has gone from us; never as she was will she return.
Never more as she once did will she chop honey,
Never more with her digging-stick dig yams.
She has gone from us; never as she was to return.

Mussels there are in the creek in plenty,
But she who lies here will dig no more.
We shall fish as of old for cod-fish,
But she who lies here will beg no more oil;
Oil for her hair, she will want no more.

Never again will she use a fire.
Where she goes, fires are not.
For she goes to the women, the dead women.
Ah, women can make no fires.
Fruit there is in plenty and grass seed,
But no birds nor beasts in the heaven of women.[13]

The Euahlayi have evolved a peculiar but quite lucid notion
of what happens to women after death, and to this the singer
is faithful. He is keenly aware of the negative aspects of

their after-life, and he makes clear what they will *not* have. He matches his sense of the pathos of death and of its deprivations with his belief that these will largely continue after death, and works up to his climax of a poverty-stricken afterworld. He makes no attempt to palliate its drabness, and his imagination works steadily and sympathetically as he tells exactly what he thinks will happen.

This close interaction of the emotions and the imagination is no less obvious among peoples who have more elaborate notions of the after-life than this. In some places departed spirits are thought not to leave the scenes of their earthly labours but to survive in them close to those who were their partners. Such a belief calls for an unfaltering grasp of what it means to associate a disembodied spirit with his old haunts and his surviving companions. Some women's songs from Bathurst Island, off the Northern Territory of Australia, show how powerfully and convincingly this can be done. These songs, which are invariably short, are sung by widows, whose actual compositions they often are, and some of them take the form of a dialogue between the widow and her dead husband, in which she acts both parts as she sings. In all there is a candid, outspoken temper, as we might expect from a people who make no attempt to conceal their feelings especially on such a matter as death. The songs almost form a series in which different states of mind are embodied as they get further from the actual moment of death. At the start a widow sings immediately after her husband's death, when he is not yet buried, and she can still draw a distinction between his dead body and his living spirit:

> Your grave is ready now,
> But I don't know where you have gone.
> Your body is lying there wrapped in bark,
> And your body must stay in the grave.[14]

Here her imagination has just begun to work but has not come to any conclusions; it is enough for her to grasp the immediate situation and prepare herself for burying the body wrapped in bark before she turns to ask where the spirit has gone. Soon enough she begins to think about this and imagines that her husband's spirit is present and conscious and that, finding himself in an unknown place, he asks her where he is, and she tells him. She puts this into a dialogue with him, no doubt believing that she hears him speaking to her:

> *Woman.* I am like a turtle,
>   And I'm coming close to you quickly.
> *Man.*   I don't know where I am.
> *Woman.* Look, it is Mutanumpi.

He left his country and came here.[15]

She assures him that he is still himself, though he feels lost in a strange land, and this helps him to resume his former personality. The first move comes from her and from her desire to meet him again, and this is how she does it. Once their relation has been renewed, it continues and thrives and starts new associations suited to the changed conditions in which husband and wife communicate with one another. In a third song the wife feels that the dead man's spirit has sung to her, and she answers him:

> What is that singing?
> That spirit went past me.
> Don't go with other women.
> Or we, your wives, will stop you.[16]

She feels that she is still his wife, and that he still has obligations towards her, which she is prepared, if need be, to enforce. She assumes that her dead husband is near to her and liable to behave as he would have behaved when alive, and to this her reactions are delightfully quick and spontaneous. Her first care is that he should continue to be faithful to her, and that is why she asserts her rights and her powers. In a fourth song the woman begins a conversation, almost a confession, as if something were hanging heavily over her mind, and in answer the man promises to be with her and to continue the life which they used to lead:

> *Woman.* I've been sweetheart with lots of men.
> *Man.*   You leave our camp.
>   We will play and talk together all night,
>   And you will tell me who are your sweethearts.[17]

In this there is a charming little surprise. She confesses her loves to him, and he with playful tolerance makes little of them but promises to look after her and hear what she has to say. The singer does not elaborate how his promises will be kept, though no doubt she believes or hopes that somehow they will be and has no difficulty in envisaging it. It is enough that they are given and reveal how the dead man still maintains a lively curiosity about the living woman. In a fifth song the widow makes her husband alone speak and assumes that he knows how heavily her grief has borne on her and how he wishes to give her comfort:

> Why are you so bony and thin?
> I am sorry for you.

No man will give you food,
You come, quick, here to me,
I will give you a child who looks like me,
For I'm putting blood on myself.[18]

In this a sad tale has almost a happy ending. The dead
man's compassion and comforting words are highly practical,
even if the singer has no notion how they will be fulfilled.
Through the power of her imagination and her vivid
sense of the dead man's presence, his widow believes that
she can still converse and live with him and even enjoy
again the joys of wedlock and motherhood.

Other songs from Bathurst Island lead to a somewhat
different kind of climax. Just as in this world human relations between man and wife have their own surprises and
their own strains, so they may still have them when one
or the other has passed beyond the grave. Though these
songs beat with a sincere affection, they have sometimes a
touch of crudity, which indeed reflects what death means to
people who are not in the least ashamed of their physical
appetites and speak frankly about them. In one place a
woman sings of her dead husband:

Let us sit down here together,
We'll stay here, no matter how hot the sun.
It was by the mango-tree that he shot you this morning.
It was close to your father's grave at Partarapu.
I have plenty of hair between my legs,
And that man's going to grab me.[19]

The woman sees herself as the destined prey to her husband's
murderer, and is not entirely hostile to the notion, but for
the moment she wishes to share her husband's company in
the sunlight and appease him after his violent death. She tells
him what has happened, as if he were not yet fully aware
of it, and proclaims her own helplessness before her coming
lot. The sudden violence of the last two lines shows how
closely death and life are interwoven in such a moment, and
how the lusts of the flesh are too powerful to resist even in
the agony of grief. Indeed, it is this very sense of the body's
power that makes these songs so real, as if what means so
much in life could not possibly be annihilated by death. A
second song certainly breathes a real affection, but the husband holds out no comforting promises to his wife. Rather,
he warns her of the dreary existence which is now his, and
which, if she also dies, she will have to share:

Man.   Why do you come here every day?

> *Woman.* Because your posts are painted and ready.
> Come on, get out of your grave!
> I saw you dancing there just now,
> Shaking yourself in the dance.
> *Man.* Why not come to me here?
> *Woman.* I'm not old, I'm too young.
> *Man.* Well, I'm waiting for you here . . .
> I'm glad my wife's coming near me.
> You will be thirsty. I can't give you water.
> I'm taking you to a dry and waterless
> country.[20]

The conclusion is left in the air, but the wife is torn between her desire for life and her husband's summons to share his death, and this conflict in her is the point of the song. The dispute between them has the strangeness of their strange relation. The wife comes every day to his grave because she believes that her husband is still active at it and that she has seen him dancing. Once we allow that she believes this, and it is obvious that she does, the rest follows easily and comes to an appropriate close in which she prefers to stay silent rather than to make up her mind to join him. The dialogue is by no means badinage and is more like a serious dispute between man and wife, in which the man knows his own mind but the wife is not sure that she shares it. A third song is not ultimately very dissimilar. The wife hears spirits singing, and from them comes her husband's voice:

> *Woman.* All those spirits are singing.
> *Man.* Tipula'mwareiju, why are you crying for me?
> Why not sleep here with me one night?
> *Woman.* No, we'd better look after our child.
> *Man.* Stay with me, be my wife again.
> Why didn't you give me food?
> Why have you all come up today to my grave?
> Whatever I tell you, you tell to somebody else.
> *Woman.* Why are you thinking of me and what I say?
> *Man.* Sneak up to her while she sleeps at night.[21]

The husband nags his wife, who has good reason for staying at home, and his last words are addressed not to her but to a spirit whom he sends to keep an eye on her. This song too is a kind of dispute between man and wife on the vexed question whether she should be with him or with her child. It is all presented very realistically, and it is based on the woman's fears that her husband is angry with her for neglecting him. That is why she fears that he will keep a watch on her. In these three songs the sense of existence beyond the grave is informed by the belief that is very much the same as here, but rather narrower and more constrained. The dead husband wishes to re-establish close relations with his wife and behaves to her very much as he must have behaved in life. The imaginative strength comes from the ease with which a dead man's presence is felt and his form seen and his voice heard. Of course this is absolutely sincere and rises from the lonely widow's brooding and troubled thoughts, but it is remarkable how sharp and firm a form it takes. We might expect such spirits to be but dimly apprehended, but such is the belief in them that they behave like living men, and the songs which their widows sing of them stand for a relation which may be imaginary to us but is certainly not imaginary to them. In all these songs from Bathurst Island the imagination is set to work by beliefs and feelings beyond the singer's choice, and for this reason it has a greater assurance and firmness of touch and makes no mistakes in its realistic delineation of a supernatural state.

In general, though primitive peoples face prospects after death with some caution, they allow a certain freedom of speculation within acknowledged limits, as the different songs from Bathurst Island show. Shamans and medicine men may put forward elaborate theories, as they do among the Semang, but these scarcely pass into popular currency or gain the circulation which comes from being echoed in song. Song is rather concerned with what everyone feels and believes about death, with the speculations which its impact has inspired and canonized, and these often turn on the uncertainty which wraps the fate of the dead and itself calls for an imaginative treatment. Doubts on so important a matter must be presented candidly and clearly, and the song-man is free to state how far speculation may go and what can be made of it. So the Gabon Pygmies, after a body has been buried in a cave or a tree, sing about the spirit's fate:

> *Leader.*   The Gates of Dan are shut.
> *Company.*   Shut are the Gates of Dan.
> *Leader.*   The spirits of the dead flit hurrying there.
>   Their crowd is like the flight of mosquitoes.
>   The flight of mosquitoes which dance in the
>   evening.
> *Company.*   Which dance in the evening.
> *Leader.*   The flight of mosquitoes which dance in the
>   evening.
>   When the night has turned completely black,
>   When the sun has vanished.[22]

> When the night has turned completely black.
> The dance of the mosquitoes.
> The whirlwind of dead leaves,
> When the storm has growled . . .

Company. When the storm has growled.
Leader. They await him who will come.
Company. Him who will come.
Leader. Him who will say: You, come, you, go away!
Company. Him who will say: Come, go!
Leader. And Khmvum will be with his children.
Company. With his children.
All. And this is the end.[23]

This song in no way rules out a life beyond the grave, but is concerned only with the preliminaries to it, when the departed spirits have gone to the cavern of Dan, where they wait for their future fate to be settled. The comparison of the spirits with mosquitoes or dead leaves catches their state after they have left their bodies and before they have been turned into fully fledged ghosts. Their fate will be determined by the god Khmvum, who will soon join them in the Gates of Dan. The song conveys the faint and unsubstantial being of these spirits between one life and another. Those who hear it may well have their own ideas of what happens later to the dead, but for the moment this must suffice. It sees very clearly what this intermediate state is, and with instinctive tact leaves the main questions unanswered. The general impression of the passage from light to dark, from storm to calm, from the solid earth to fluttering in the air, is what the singer intends to make, and he succeeds in his task because he has pondered the matter very carefully and seen exactly what it means.

If death provokes the primitive imagination to notable flights, of equal importance is the nature of gods and other divine or superhuman beings, and just as death is made more real by being presented in imagery drawn from every day, so gods are made to live on the familiar earth and conduct their activities on it in a recognizable manner. Beliefs about them may often be based on dreams or vague associations which are hard for us to grasp, but in the songs which tell of them there is a solid core of intelligible matter just because they are meant for the instruction or comfort of ordinary men. From elaborate beliefs something is extracted which is seen and felt and brought within the scope of normal understanding. Such songs are seldom direct cries from the heart like songs of death; they are built round systems of rites, which are themselves traditional and performed with scrupulous care. In them the singer's task is to make explicit many half-formed or half-revealed hints and to see that these are presented in their full worth. Even when much is taken for granted and the words are not fully intelligible without reference to the rite, they still add something to it, and in this lies the singer's opportunity. He can rise to the height of the occasion by stressing something which he thinks specially significant and making the most of it by a deft use of words. It is here that imagination is needed. It alone can give life to many of the myths behind the rites which he illustrates and set them in a living context. Such a gift is required particularly in those songs which are based on shamanistic or totemistic assumptions. In the first class the shaman really believes that he has knowledge of the unseen world through intercourse with gods and spirits, since he can change his shape or travel through the air; in the second class the connection between men and animals and other totems is seen as a physical relation, and in Australia this often extends beyond the cult of living totems to the cult of mythical ancestors, who are sources of life and actually present somewhere on the earth. It is obvious that, though both of these systems raise many difficulties and obscurities, they provide rich matter for song. What the myths really mean does not for the moment concern us, and we must accept them as they are revealed in the songs, and try to see how they are brought home by the exercise of the imagination. Here too, as in songs about the dead, the imagination works within prescribed limits, but that does not prevent it from doing its utmost within them. Its task is to make as palpable as possible the assumptions which lie behind the rites. Many of these may elude it altogether, and these it neglects. Others may not seem to be of sufficient importance to trouble about and the accompanying gestures may be left to take care of them. But there is a substantial residue which incites the imagination and may well be rewarding if it is handled with a vivid sense of its possibilities and its relation to the common world.

Among the Semang a number of songs are connected with the Chenoi, divine beings who lurk in nature and are the powers behind many growing and active things. The success of such songs in convincing their singers that they are close to the gods depends on an ability to imagine the gods with an instinctive, unfaltering, unquestioning vision and to convey something of them as dwellers in nature and yet able to move to loftier and more august realms. The way in which this happens and the gifts which it demands can be seen from a song connected with fruit-blossoms in the spring. In these

the Chenoi are busily present and indeed have come down
from the sky to create them. The Chenoi are gay and friendly creatures, and their descent to earth has a happy, even
boisterous character:

> Beat on the Sun's Road,
> Clap on the cord-rope,
> Start storms rushing,
> Strike on the Sun's path,
> Clap your hands.
> My grandmother is glad
> That joy should laugh
> Under the path,
> The path which we beat.[24]

The theme is the descent of the Chenoi to earth by the rainbow, which is called the "Sun's Road," and their explosive
delight as they strike their hands on it and climb down it like
a rope. They are visiting their grandmother, who is a spirit of
the earth and shares their excitement. The song fits the season when the fruit-trees blossom, and embodies the mood
of spring when the sap rises and life stirs and things happen,
and the clapping hands are a preliminary sign of the thunder
and storms which they summon to action. The song, in its
breathless exhilaration, echoes the mood of the Chenoi as
they come rapidly and noisily down to earth, and exalts to a
supernatural gaity the emotions which spring inspires in both
gods and human beings. In it there is a reckless, almost violent element, which is admirably true to spring with its sudden, devastating storms and its incalculable moods, changing
without warning from sunshine to thunder. Such a song, like
others of the same kind, is usually improvised from stock
themes and phrases, but that does not spoil its artless freshness. It catches the spirit of spring and exalts it to a divine
level. So, too, another song of a similar kind concentrates
on the descent of the Chenoi to earth, and here again the
actors take their part and identify themselves with them in
an excited, exultant mood:

> Ah! Oh! Wa!
> We glide down from the rocks.
> With the music of flutes we glide down from the rocks.
> Ah! Oh! Wa!
> We glide down from the rocks,
> We, the maidens of the Ple, glide down from the rocks,
> Glide down the rock-face, glide down from the rocks.
> Let the weapons clash. We glide down from the rocks.[25]

The Chenoi glide down from the rocks because it is the way from the sky to the earth, and their song does little more than proclaim their coming. Their action is illustrated by gestures, and though in its simplicity it resembles a children's game, it is faithfully imagined and kept going by an enthralled excitement. Conversely, when the Chenoi have finished their tasks, they return to their place in the sky, and then they sing:

> Companion, up and away on the Sun's Path,
> On the Sun's Path,
> Toss your weapons to the east,
> Companion, go up and away
> On the swing in the east.[26]

Once the storm has burst, the Chenoi are free to return by the way by which they came, and the moment is of relief after the storm, when the Chenoi no longer need their weapons of thunder and lightning and swing themselves up to the sky. Other Chenoi remain at the bottom of the rainbow, which is also a divine snake and a source of life from above. They too are closely connected with flowers, and their gay pastimes reveal their nature:

> They rub flowers together in the meadow,
> They play in the waterspring,
> They are glad to follow one another,
> All Chenoi together
> All rise up and away,
> Wander together,
> Loud is their laughter,
> They love the scent,
> The fine scent of their Chenoi,
> They rub together,
> They rub the fibres,
> The Chenoi are happy,
> The Chenoi fondle
> Them in their breasts,
> They seek fruits as they rise up and away.[27]

Since the Chenoi are spirits of flowers and fruits, they enjoy one another's company in an innocent sensuous way. The poet recognizes this essential quality in them and sets them to work in a flowery meadow where they can savour all the scents which are their special domain.

In their small compass these songs succeed because each concentrates on a single imaginative idea—the joy of the Chenoi at arriving in spring, at returning to the sky, at smelling the flowers which they have made to grow and whose

scent they enjoy almost as part of themselves. The song-
maker has caught the spirit of these comings and goings and
made his supernatural beings as delightful as the physical
world for which they are responsible. The art of the songs
lies less in conjuring up a visible scene, though this they
certainly do as an aid to the rites, than in suggesting the
mood which pervades the spring. This is the mood of the
Chenoi and reflects all that they mean in nature. The composer follows his fancy not so much by describing their actions, which come from tradition and must be observed in
the rites, as in interpreting these actions in an understanding
and sympathetic spirit. With a clear notion of the Chenoi
in his mind he pierces the external appearance of nature to
its inner temper and significance, and he presents this without
much care for anything else. This is quite natural for a
primitive poet, but here it takes a special form. The earth is
so full of spirits that it cannot be dissociated from them
or understood without them. The songs act on this conviction and bring natural and supernatural together in a set of
single scenes, but their unusual claim is that they reveal something which is really identical in the Chenoi and their physical
manifestations, and from this they extract a sprightly poetry.

Shamanistic songs call for this kind of imagination, at once
visual and psychological, since they expound the inner
meanings of religious beliefs, but totemistic songs, which
superficially have something in common with them, are less
concerned with inner meanings than with establishing the
reality of their subjects in the actual world. They are
much interested in mythical ancestors, who are believed to
exist in the known scene and to perform specified functions
in it. They are greatly honoured, and their powers are
evoked through ritual dances accompanied by songs, particularly among the Aranda, who in a large number of such
songs give a vivid picture of ancestors as their devotees
imagine them. They may indeed be remote and peculiar,
but, since they have a place on the earth and belong very
closely to it, they partake of its nature. This art need not
concern itself in detail with the actual functions of the ancestors, since these are already known and taken for granted.
What is wanted is to make the ancestors themselves more per-
sonable, and this is done by describing them in language
which makes them visible and intelligible in a human way.
Certain ancestors, for instance, stand to one another in the
relation of fathers and sons as they live on a mountain, but
a song which celebrates them is not troubled by the precise
meaning of this relation and is much more interested in their

physical situation as they watch the sunrise from their moun-
tain-crest:

> The spinifex tips on the mountain are glowing;
> The bold forehead of the mountain is glowing.

> "Fathers and sons, upon us before all others,
> The greying sky is hurling its spears of light."

> "Fathers and sons, upon us before all others,
> The sun is hurling its spears of light."

> The miners, to be sure, are twittering;
> With their merry beaks they are twittering.

> The messengers of the birds singing soar to the sky;
> When the morning is young, singing they soar to the
>   sky.

> The chattering messengers of the birds singing soar
>   to the sky;
> Yes, the chattering messengers of the birds singing
>   soar to the sky.

> Without a break, to be sure, they are singing their
>   song;
> The birds to be sure, are singing their song.

> Yes, when the young morning furrows the sky
> The birds are chirping in noisy throngs.

> The carpet snake is sunning himself
> On the soft soil before his hole.

As the earth grows light, wallabies can be seen everywhere
among the rocks:

> "Along the path under those dense bushes
> They are hopping upwards in the gully."

> They appear from the broken heaps of rubble;
> They are standing still, watching intently.

> The baby joey on the nose of the precipice
> Looks down without a move.

> The great sire is basking in the sun;
> His legs resound on the rock-plates.[28]

Here an affectionate observation gives solidity to the world
which the ancestors see in the dawn from their mountain-peaks.
But to use observation in this way on such a scale implies a

fine exercise of imagination. The song-maker has clearly asked himself what it is like to be seated on a mountain at dawn, and he shapes his own picture of it. Though his actual details are gathered from the sights of every day, his use and organization of them are truly imaginative in that he not only sees the world through the eyes of the ancestors but understands what in it will catch their attention. We feel that we are in their presence and look on the scene from their lofty outlook. This brings them closer to humanity and places them firmly in the physical setting to which they belong.

The life of ancestors on inaccessible summits has indeed its own majesty and mystery, and it is right and suitable that they should be able to see the wide lands over which they exert their strange dominion. But just because they are inextricably tied to their duties, they may suffer for it. The primitive mind has its own ruthless logic and is not prepared to underestimate what their functions impose on them. Their powers imply duties, and their duties enforce restrictions. On the mountain Iloata, in the Central MacDonnell Ranges, a number of women ancestors are believed to have lived in the beginning of time, and a long song tells of their position with its splendour, its hardships, and its pathos:

"Among the boulders of the peak we shall be sitting,
A band of sisters we shall be sitting.

"Among the boulders of the peak we shall be sitting;
Sisters all, let us recline here!"

From the north the wind is blowing fiercely;
From the east the wind is blowing fiercely.

The north wind blows incessantly;
The east wind blows incessantly.

The east wind blows incessantly;
The south wind blows incessantly.

The mountain hawks scream as they come swooping
    down;
In the vault of the air they scream as they come swoop-
    ing down.

From the vault of the sky they are swooping down;
The mountain hawks are swooping down.

The mountain hawks are descending with whirring
    wings

From the vault of the sky they are descending with
  whirring wings.

They come swooping lower and lower;
With hoarse cries they are settling on the ground.

The mountain bluffs are running in parallel ridges;
The mountain valleys are running in parallel grooves.

The mountain bluffs are running in parallel ridges;
The mountain bluffs are falling down in sharp
  precipices.

Towards the foothills they are descending tier by tier;
Into the depth below they are descending tier by tier.

Into the depth below they are descending tier by tier;
The little mountain peaks are descending tier by tier.

The kangaroo grass is descending tier by tier;
Into the depth below it is descending tier by tier.

Thick stands of mountain grasses are descending tier
  by tier.
Towards the foothills they are descending tier by tier.

"The holly trees are standing with intertwined branches;
Our own fruit trees are standing with intertwined
  branches."[29]

So far the technique is that of the preceding poem. The place
of the ancestresses is made visible in its remote majesty, and
the earth opens up before it. But at this point the tone
changes, and a new theme is introduced. The sisters see the
poles of other ancestresses rising from many peaks both
near and far and know that these present invitations to visit
them. But this the ancestresses cannot do, since they cannot
leave their seat:

"With bandicoot-tails she beckons me to come;
With furry tail-tips she beckons me to come."

From the crest of the mountain she causes her to
  weep—
A flood of bitter tears she causes her to weep.

On the edge of the precipice she bows low her head;
The tear-drops are chasing each other down her
  cheeks.

The tear-drops are chasing each other down her
  cheeks;

Searing her brain, they are chasing each other down
   her cheeks.

The tear-drops are chasing each other down her
   cheeks;
Tears upon tears, bitter with grief.[30]

The ancestresses, who, despite their august powers, cannot
leave their mountain, have a helpless pathos. We might at first
think that this is simply a bold fancy of the song-man, that,
when he turned his mind to considering their manner of
existence, he saw that it had its disadvantages and, judging
them by human standards, made an effective use of them.
This may be true so far as it goes, but it is surely right to read
into the words more than a purely dramatic effect. The ancestresses are fastened to their places by the very nature of
their functions. This is where they have been since the beginning of time, where they dream that timeless experience
through which they effect the living world. But because they
are women and share the essential being of women, the song-
maker, knowing how other women are tied to their duties
and their tasks, sees their position and interprets it from what
he knows of human beings. His imagination has got to work
in a purposeful spirit and seen beyond the visual scene to
its inner significance, and he is able to do this because he is
a keen spectator of his own society and moves, without
noticing it, from this to another order of things.

Though primitive imagination works mainly on the supernatural and the unseen and is inspired to action almost un-
consciously by the demands which are made on it by its
subjects, it none the less deserves the name. It presents to the
mind something which can almost be seen, and it does this
by applying to the unseen and the unfamiliar what is
known from the seen and the familiar. Its great asset is the
keenness of primitive senses, and on these it relies for its
vigour and its verisimilitude. It would certainly not be so
successful if its results were not so solid and so visual. Not
only are the senses of primitive man sharper than ours, but
he relies much more on them. In his daily round he develops
a remarkably acute and precise knowledge of the physical
scene and, since both his religious and his totemistic beliefs
are largely concerned with it, it is right that his songs should
keep in close touch with it. Despite his almost unlimited
belief in the supernatural, he lives in a single world. Even
the dead are close to him, and everything is both natural and
supernatural. Since he makes no real distinction between the
two and assumes that they are in effect one, he uses what he

knows to shape his ideas about what he does not know but whose existence he does not dispute or doubt. His imagination is an extention of his observation, a special application of it beyond its usual task of noticing things to creating other creatures and other scenes which fit naturally into what he and his kind absorb from the perceptions of every day.

A MYTH is a story whose primary purpose is not to entertain but to enlighten primitive man on matters which perplex him and cannot be made intelligible, as they can to us, by analysis or abstraction, since these are beyond his linguistic and mental resources. He is presented instead with a story which attempts to illuminate obscure subjects by providing a kind of historical antecedent or parallel to them. Something happens in the present because something not very unlike it has happened in the past or happens outside the familiar scheme of time. In a world where science and the scientific outlook do not exist and every natural event is shrouded in mystery, myths serve at least to make phenomena less formidable by relating them to more or less intelligible stories. In primitive societies myths perform the duties of cosmology, theology, history and science, and have a special round of duty in connection with the weather, the recurrence of the seasons, and the cycle of procreation, birth, growth, and decay in all living things. Primitive myths are often hard to understand because they assume connections which mean nothing to us and operate by emotional or visual associations in which we see little coherence. They are not conceived in a rational spirit of explanation but appeal to half-conscious and unconscious elements in human nature. To grasp their relevance we must not think logically of cause and effect but try to capture a mood or an atmosphere or an emotional frame of mind, in which individual images count for everything and must be allowed to make their full impact with all the echoes and implications and associations which they evoke.

Myths are closely related to the primitive conception of time. Our peoples have indeed a sense of time, but it is not quite the same as our own. Their languages distinguish between past, present, and future, and the distinctions are perfectly clear even in Yamana, Andamanese, and Tasmanian, while Eskimo and some Australian languages make fine discriminations between contingencies and possibilities and wishes. But all these stem from the present. They look forward only to an immediate future, and the past has no meaning beyond immediate memories of it. What we would consider a remote past, whether historical or mythical, is treated differently and set almost outside the temporal scheme. Time itself is regarded as a recurring cycle, in which events repeat themselves in a definite, regular sequence, as the seasons of the year with their appropriate growths of animals and plants. Anything that recurs in this way is thought to have a permanent character and to be to that extent outside time. Though immediate events are seen in a limited time-scheme, recurrent events are seen as belonging to cycles, and in trying to clarify the nature of such cycles myths play a large part. The permanence and the constancy of nature lie beyond even the cycle of the seasons or the rhythm of individual lives. So primitive peoples pass beyond the conception of time as a recurring process to the notion that certain powers are outside it and unaffected by it, and that they cause or control or influence what happens in the world. Such powers may be gods, who live in a timeless order and are always to some degree present on the earth, even if their presence is more marked at some seasons of the year than at others. Some gods have marked personalities and defined duties; others hardly have names and may even not be imagined with fixed characteristics. Some peoples, like the Yamana, the Selk'nam, the Pygmies, and the Semang believe in a supreme god, who lives in the sky and is responsible for the main structure of things and for much that happens in it; but other peoples, like most Australian tribes, scarcely believe in any powers that may be called gods. Their universe depends on mythical ancestors, who exist forever in the actual world and keep it going by being what they are in their timeless and unchanging being. They are in a constant state of dream, and their dreams are the phenomena of the familiar scene. But whether primitive men believe in gods or in ancestors, the whole array of physical phenomena, with its changes within predictable cycles, is ascribed to the dominion of supernatural powers, each of whom has his sphere of authority, while all of them are responsible for what happens here and now and for the pattern to which it conforms. It is the task of myth to make these supernatural beings comprehensible by turning their activities into stories which can easily be understood and so to bring them closer to the experience of men.

Song is not a normal means for telling myths. They are usually told in prose tales of a very simple kind with none of the elegance or the artifice of song, no doubt because this presents less dangers in a sphere where errors must be avoided and precision and correctness are paramount. Nor indeed is the primitive manner of composing songs well suited to anything so elaborate as a myth. Its tendency to concentrate on a single, limited topic rules out a full handling of what may well be complicated both in substance and in temper, while the brief scope of most songs forbids the narration of long and intricate events. That is why primitive song lacks the large cosmological and theological themes which play so striking a part in the early poetry of the Middle East and are born from a desire to clarify beliefs about the gods and to present them in a full, impressive, and detailed way. On the other hand primitive song is closely allied to myth in more than one respect. First, since myths deal with the supernatural, they inevitably inspire a large number of songs, especially charms and hymns and ritual celebrations, which cannot be fully understood or appreciated or understood without some knowledge of the myths behind them. Secondly, just because songs do not tell myths in their completeness, their task is to cast on them a special light from a special angle, to select and emphasise what the song-maker thinks most relevant in them, and to give to this a full imaginative attention. This means that the songs concerned with myths are usually more coherent and more orderly than the myths themselves, simply because they deal with chosen sections or aspects of them and present these in striking isolation. Thirdly, songs move in a mythical way of thinking, not indeed always, but usually, when they deal with some subject beyond the immediately visible scene. Such thinking operates neither with abstract notions nor with straightforward accounts of individual actions or events, but with something between the two, in which visual images convey associations beyond their immediate selves and contribute to the emotional and imaginative effect of a song by lifting it to a more mysterious level than its immediate occasion.

Since song approaches myths from a restricted angle and

does not attempt to present them in their completeness or to confer any doctrinal authority on them, it is free to indulge itself in handling them, and the song-maker can concentrate on what catches his imagination most strongly or exerts a peculiar fascination. Myth gives to song a dimension outside the present moment by relating it to unseen powers which enhance the majesty and the mystery of human life. When it deals with physical phenomena it does not describe them for their own sake, though it is well aware of this, but seeks for the powers at work in them, and these it presents as closely to human experience as it can. It is after all natural that primitive man should use his own experience to interpret natural phenomena which in fact lie far outside it, but his attempt to do so brings something into play which is truly imaginative and illuminating. A simple example of this may be seen in the Gabon Pygmies' treatment of the sun, which is connected with Khmvum, the father of the forest and their chief god. The myth tells that Khmvum at times visits the sun to keep its fires burning, and this has the advantage that it distinguishes him from the sun and leaves him free for other, multifarious duties. When he does this, a rite is performed and a song is sung:

> The fire grows dark, the wood becomes black,
> The flame will go out, misfortune will fall on us!
> On us misfortune, O Khmvum!
> Khmvum sets out on a journey,
> A journey towards the sun,
> In his hand the bow shines,
> The bow of the hunter on high.
> He has heard the voice of his children.[1]

The main outlines of the myth are taken for granted, but they are clearly implicit in the song. Khmvum, as we might expect among a hunting people like the Pygmies, is a hunter who sets out on an expedition with his bow, but his special task is to renew the light of the sun, which in human terms resembles a fire which seems likely to go out and needs replenishing. There is nothing obscure in the presentation of Khmvum's task, but the strength of the song, as opposed to a careful account in prose, is that it puts all its emphasis on a central point and gives this a vivid actuality which anyone can understand. The renewal of the sun, like that of any other fire, brings it within the orbit of human experience and explains why it does not go out. At the same time the song rises from a deep anxiety that, unless something is done to it, it will in fact go out, and in taking care that it does not Khmvum acts on behalf of his earthly children. The song gives both the essential meaning of the occasion and its inner lesson in the god's care for mankind. By simplifying the myth the song makes it more dramatic and more impressive and closer to the common consciousness.

Another Pygmy myth tells that the Milky Way is made from the dust of broken stars. It is called *dzi-ko*, which means "the road of the sky," and the god travels along it gathering the stars, as Pygmies gather insects, and returns with them to the sun, but he gathers too many, and some fall by the way on his return:

> In armfuls he gathers them, *viss, viss, viss,*
> In armfuls he piles them up,
> In armfuls, *viss, viss,*
> Like the woman who gathers locusts,
> And heaps them in her basket,
> And the basket is full and brims over.[2]

We are not told explicitly what the myth in its full version tells, that the stars are needed to provide fuel to feed the sun, but that is why the god gathers them, and the song-maker, true to the rule of one theme at a time, is concerned only with the Milky Way as he sees it, and for him it is made of star-dust. This is the point which concerns him, and he gives a full force to it by putting into human language what is thought to happen in the tropical sky when stars flicker or fade. The song brings the celestial scene closer to earth by its comparison of the god who gathers stars with a woman who gathers locusts. The image is not demanded by the myth, nor indispensable to it, but it gives a freshness and an immediacy which reduce the myth's remoteness. The song-maker sees the god's action from his own point of view and communicates his special notion of it. A myth, which has already a considerable charm and even splendour, is enhanced by his treatment of it. The task of song is to bring home the essence of a myth by stressing what is most striking in it.

This art of selecting the salient point becomes more elusive when the song is accompanied by ritual actions or is part of an elaborate ceremony. Then much which is done by gesture need not be mentioned in words, and it is normal practice to leave much of a rite without comment on it. Elements which are obvious to the performers or the spectators are less obvious to us who do not see what is happening. Yet the connection between words and dramatic action is so established and so fundamental that this kind of song is in every way as straightforward and immediate as the Pygmy examples which we have just examined. The Semang songs about the divine creatures called Chenoi derive their being from the conviction that the Chenoi are busily at work in the physical world. In any song about them the actors identify themselves with them and believe that they are themselves partaking in a celestial action, in which the Chenoi are present. This gives the songs their immediacy and urgency and their air of dealing with a real situation. One song accompanies a ritual in which the actors garland themselves with flowers and run around gaily and boisterously. It claims to be sung by Chenoi and to show what they feel on this uninhibited occasion:

> They hang down, hang down, the long garlands from the brow.
> The young man runs, the children run,
> The voice of the nightingale sounds, the nightingale on the *gopal*,
> White and dappled.
> They hang down, hang down, the long-scattered rain-clouds,
> They drift, the unmarried man runs, the maiden runs,
> The married man runs, the old man runs,
> The garlands drift and turn,
> The young man runs, the maiden runs, the young man runs.[3]

Here the myth and the rite are closely interwoven. The Chenoi, being spirits of nature, are busy in the springtime, and its bursting life is mainifested, with no distinctions of age or sex or married status, in the putting on of garlands and running. This enacts a myth of nature, whose rebirth is explained by reference to divine beings at work in it. The rite and the song take an exuberant form, displayed in high spirits and exemplified in the song of the nightingale, which is itself one of the Chenoi, and in the presence of the rain-clouds, which indicate the time of year and the appropriateness of the rite of it. These are the essential ingredients, and each complements and completes the rest. The song brings the performance into a world of celestial gaiety, and through it they not only share the exhilaration of the spring but participate in the work of the gods. Such songs shed a bright light on the familiar scene by their suggestion of divine beings present in it, and bring men closer to the gods by making them act as if they themselves were divine, and therefore believe that in some sense for the moment they are.

Though mythical ancestors are not the same as gods or even as such beings as the Chenoi, they have a place in the scheme of things as the first performers of this or that activity, and every subsequent activity of the same kind is connected with them, because in their timeless existence they are responsible for it whenever it happens. Thus they are often thought to be present on occasions which are their concern, and the song-man must refer to them and show what their presence means. This happens even among peoples who have not brought the belief in ancestors to the almost exclusive dignity which it enjoys among most Australian tribes. For instance, the Semang believe in a man and a woman called Jamoi and Jalan, who are the first of their kind and once lived on the earth, as their descendants still do. In their fear of the two traditional enemies of their race, the thunder and the tiger, they were taken to heaven, where they work constantly on behalf of men and intercede with the thunder-god when he is too hard on them. Their influential position makes their presence desirable on more than one kind of occasion, and the song which introduces them must make clear which among many possible parts they are playing. One song is, on the surface, exclusively about them:

It hangs down, the long garland, from the brow,
Of the newly wed Jamoi and Jalan,
Hair ornament, ear ornament of the young man,
A scent, a wind, a cyclone straight ahead,
Young man, chew lightly, maiden, chew well . . .
The sun rises on his path,
The storm brings cloud,
And in it the rambutan turns red.
Girdle of pearls and sash on the breast,
The maidens like the young man very much,
A string links their hands, plugs in the young man's nose,
The newly wed bow down.
Good is the waterfall,
The crash of the river Rekam
Falls down, deep down. Old man and young married man run.[4]

Two themes are combined. The first is the young couple, dressed for a wedding in their ornaments and finery; the second is the menace of storm and cloud-burst. Both are the business of Jamoi and Jalan. As the first human beings and the first man and wife, they are appropriately present at a wedding, whether as original ancestors or, in some places, as Chenoi, and it is right that the young couple should identify themselves with them and see in their wedding a repetition of the first wedding on earth conducted with a like solemnity and exhilaration. Moreover, since Jamoi and Jalan protect men from the thunder, this too calls for mention, since the wedding takes place in the spring when thunder is in the air. The two themes are in fact united and brought together for a single purpose in a single scene. The significance of Jamoi and Jalan is that they embody the spirit of marriage and guard the newly wed from natural dangers. They represent not only marriage but its protection by celestial powers. The song emphasises the two aspects first by the ornaments worn by the young couple, which make them look like divine beings, and the second by the menacing sound of the thunder, and then it closes by showing that all is well when young and old run together in safety and happiness. The myth of Jamoi and Jalan has many variations, but in this case the song-man has selected those which are specially demanded by a wedding and makes use of them to put it in its right perspective in the relations of gods and men.

When myths pass into song, the actual contents count less than the spirit and the general intention. Jamoi and Jalan have a part in many myths and are credited with a variety of functions and duties. They have their place in the natural world, where Jamoi is the protector of fruit-trees and Jalan is the mistress of the wind. The difference between their tasks may even bring them into friendly conflict, and this notion lies behind a song in which the Chenoi play a game by throwing at one another a fruit called *galel*:

Throw the *galel*, hit one another with it, drop downwards,
Throw away the head-dress, the head-dress of Jalan,
On the meadow of Jalan throw the *galel*.
Go hence to your dwelling, to your dwelling and abide there,
Throw the *galel*, pick it up, throw it away,
Throw the *galel*.
This is the place of Chenoi;
They are lively together, some of them are silent.
Throw the *galel*.[5]

In the song the actors impersonate the Chenoi, who play a lively game as they come down from the sky to the meadow of Jalan, whence after play they will return to their celestial home. The game suits their characters as spirits of flowers and trees, and they enjoy its ebullience. Jamoi is not mentioned by name, but his presence is implied in the repeated mention of the *galel*, and Jalan inspires the riotous nature of the occasion in throwing away the head-dresses made of blossoms, for this is what the wind does. But though Jamoi and Jalan are present, they are not more important than the Chenoi who hold the stage. The purpose of the song is to make the company share the excitement of the Chenoi in the season when the wind blows the blossoms from the trees, and this the words do gaily. But for the myth the song would have no point, and it remains faithful to the myth by making its own choice from the possibilities open to it and giving a lively attention to a mood which is familiar to everyone in the spring.

In such songs, and in the myths from which they are derived, the main purpose is to give reality to the belief that divine beings, like the Chenoi, are at work in the familiar world. This presents few difficulties to a people who take such a matter for granted and feel no inclination to question it, but the reality conferred by such songs is of a special kind. They catch the nature of gods and spirits and the temper behind their activities with a special understanding of what it means for the emotions, and in this lies their specifically poetical appeal. It reinforces an imagination which is already at work by giving it a wider field for its exertions and moves easily from the bare facts of myth to their realization in practice. The strength of such songs comes from an unquestioning belief in the presence of divine beings on the earth among men and women, whose actions are inspired and guided by them and receive through them a divine sanction. The primitive conviction that divine beings are at work everywhere is displayed in a concrete form, and we see what advantages it brings. Such songs are to primitive peoples as indispensable as the myths which they represent, just because they show what the imminence of gods and spirits means to the sentient and sensitive human self. They catch aspects of divine activity in the world, and what begins by being a myth and therefore sometimes obscure and remote becomes part of human experience and displays its worth in the setting of mankind.

Not all mythical songs conform to this pattern. Often enough gods and spirits and mythical ancestors are conceived as living apart from mankind and yet shaping its fortunes for good or ill. Just as the Pygmies sing songs about the sun and the stars, so some Australian tribes tend to place their ancestors in some remote and inaccessible place, which may indeed be on the earth and have a known geographical home but is none the less outside the range of human movement and acquaintance. When song deals with myths of this kind, it adopts a technique rather different from that of the Semang songs about the ever-present Chenoi. The Australian ancestors tend to have strong and highly personal characteristics, and to make them vivid to their devotees calls for a bold effort of the visual imagination. As their functions and their appearance are often by human standards highly unusual, a nice tact is needed not to make them too uncouth or repellent.

Ancestors so presented not only fulfil their proper duties in a convincing way but have their own dignity and distinction. The ability of the Aranda in this is remarkable. They not only avoid many possible pitfalls in pathos or absurdity but create situations which catch the eye and stir the emotions. In the song of the honey-ants, they are described in their cells under the roots of the mulga trees and are given certain human characteristics, as befits the ancestors of men and makes them more approachable:

> The ant-workers yonder dwell, ever dwell;
> In ring-tiered homes, they dwell, ever dwell.
>
> With down-hooded heads they dwell, ever dwell;
> With stripe-banded chests they dwell, ever dwell.
>
> With cobweb-closed eyes they dwell, ever dwell;
> With down-hooded heads they dwell, ever dwell.
>
> In cellarèd cells they dwell, ever dwell;
> With bodies ring-rimm'd they dwell, ever dwell.
>
> In cellarèd cells they dwell, ever dwell;
> Like pebbles pile-heap'd they dwell, ever dwell.
>
> Where far-flung their hollows stretch
> With firelight aglow they dwell, ever dwell.
>
> Where far-flung their hollows stretch
> With firelight aflame they dwell, ever dwell.[6]

This is just what an ant-ancestor should be, and the song-man's imagination is at work strongly and convincingly on them. He sees not only what they are but what they must be, and his little human touches add notably to their plausibility.

Another Aranda song is concerned with rain and tells of the mythical ancestor Kantija, who sits on the cracked rock-plates whence the water flows in spring. Above him the sky is always dark with clouds, and his hair is tightly bound with a string lest the rain that continually falls from it turn into violent cloudbursts. This, we might think, is not a very promising start, since the picture is in itself a little unattractive, but in fact Kantija is an impressive figure:

> Among the rippling waters he sits without a move,
> It is Kantija who is sitting without a move.
>
> Moveless like a boulder he is sitting;
> His hair bedewed with rain he is sitting.
>
> On the fissured rock-plates he is sitting;

On rock-plates welling with water he is sitting.

Bedrizzled with rain he sits without a move;
Among the rippling waters he sits without a move.

Bedrizzled with rain, a reddish glow overspreads him;
Among the rippling waters a reddish glow overspreads him.

The sky is clouded with water-moss;
The sky sends down scattered showers.

Over the rock-plates the flow is echoing,
Over the rock-plates green with moss.

"Moss-covered one,
Spread forth your waters!

"Come, moss-covered one,
Pour forth your waters!

"Come, foam-crested,
Come, spread over the waters!"

Over the darkened river sand calls the voice of the thunder,
   the voice of the thunder;
From billowing storm-clouds calls the voice of the thunder,
   the voice of the thunder.

The first storm-showers,
The first storm-showers are falling here and there,
   are falling here and there.

The first storm-showers,
The first storm-showers are pouring down in torrents,
   are pouring down in torrents.

A flash of lightning
Shivers trees in pieces.

A flash of lightning
Shocks and terrifies.

Overflowing its banks into side-channels
The flood rolls down its waves.[7]

Kantija, despite his remote station and supernatural functions, is inextricably part of the physical scene. The song
breathes a vivid understanding of what rain means to a land
where it is always scarce and its failure means death to
men and animals. The lines are quoted from a larger
whole, but even in this part we may distinguish three main
sections or movements, each of which has its own charac-

ter. First, Kantija is pictured as he is before the rain comes,
as the source of water, and embodies its nature and its powers. Next, in four short couplets the people pray for rain
and show how ardently they desire it and how vividly they
foresee its effects when it comes. This sudden personal appeal
to him starts a new section and brings him closer to the human scene from which his fastnesses might seem to sever
him. The prayer is the more impressive because it is so short
and direct and conveys a genuine awe before the unseen
powers of Kantija. Thirdly, the lightning and the thunder
announce that Kantija has heard the prayers and the
downfall is coming. We are back in the familiar world,
and the ancestor has done his work. Though the song is
both a hymn and a prayer and has even a share of narrative, it moves not among remote theological abstractions
but in the world that we know, and gains enormously from it.
Its central theme is rain, and this is broken up into the
source whence rain comes, the need of men for it, and its
effect when it comes. The song-man tells of rain with the
passionate commitment of a man who knows that without it
human beings will perish, and his observant, sensitive account
of it gains from its association with a mythical ancestor,
while the ancestor in his turn becomes more intelligible
because he is what we should expect a spirit of rain to
be, with his whole being bound to it. In such a song the
myth is treated both seriously and literally, and its more
wayward moments are kept in check. The song-man, true
to his beliefs and his art, creates a series of scenes which
do full justice to the rite as a means to get rain and at the
same time have their own lively independence as an account
of a being beyond the ordinary acquaintance of men.

Kantija has the advantage that his duties are entirely intelligible and that he has a recognized place in a physical
landscape, even if nobody has actually seen him in it. In
his myth there are no awkward, irrational elements of
which sense has somehow to be made. But this is not always the case with ancestors or other divine beings. Many
myths are far less tractable and present difficulties even to
those for whose benefit they exist. First, some myths attempt
to explain rites which have existed long before them, and
the rites have in the course of years lost their original intention. In their efforts to deal with them myths may be inconsequent and incoherent. It is clear that there is a discord
between them and the rites, and in the end we may
understand neither the one nor the other. Secondly, other
myths, which are not intended fully to explain rites but
rather to accompany and illustrate them, may seem to be

no less inconsequent because they contain irrational elements derived from the unconscious self, sometimes through dreams, which are treated with reverence as messages from the unseen world. It is not easy to distinguish to which class some myths belong, and the obstacles which they present to our understanding remain unsurmounted. Even to the song-maker they may present difficulties, since his art is expected to emphasize and clarify what he thinks important, while the rest is left to explain itself, as best it can, through the action of the ritual. The result is that songs derived from myths are usually simpler than the myths themselves and certainly much easier to grasp than the rites which they accompany.

The way in which a myth is simplified and made more attractive may be illustrated by the Aranda song about a mythical ancestor called Ankotarinja, who follows a scent underground from one place to another and on his way devours inhabitants of the underworld. The myth is not an explanation of cosmic phenomena but tells of a dog-ancestor, who embodies the activities of dogs in a series of dramatic actions. If no actual dog behaves in quite this way, it is not out of character in a primaeval, archetypal dog such as Ankotarinja is. The main part of the rite is taken by a single man painted with coloured stripes. He has on his head a *tjurunga,* a magical object used to symbolize violent acts, including killing, and at his side is a *tnatantja,* a pole with somewhat similar intentions, but rather less powerful and less commonly set in action. These symbolical objects are both visible to the eye and mentioned in the song, and their appearance is to stress the destructive character of the dog-ancestor. They may interfere a little with the narrative, but they give a hint of its nature and contents. The song itself is more coherent than the complete myth and makes a brave attempt to weave chosen elements into an intelligible narrative. The actor who takes the part of Ankotarinja describes his adventures in the first person, and at intervals other singers fill the gaps in his journey by telling what happens to him:

"Red is the down which is covering me,
Red I am as though I were burning in a fire.

"Red I am as though I were burning in a fire,
Bright red gleams the ochre on which I have rubbed
    my body.

"Red I am as though I were burning in a fire,
Red, too, is the hollow in which I am lying.

"The red *tjurunga* is resting on my head,

Red, too, is the hollow, in which I am lying.

"Like a whirlwind it is towering to the sky,
Like a pillar of red sand it is towering to the sky.

"The *tnatantja* is towering to the sky,
Like a pillar of red it is towering to the sky.

"A mass of red pebbles covers the plains,
Little white sand-rills cover the plains.

"Lines of red pebbles streak the plains,
Lines of white sand-hills streak the plains.

"A cavernous pathway lies open before me,
Leading straight west it lies open before me."

He is sucking his beard into his mouth in anger,
Like a dog he follows his trail by scent.

He hurries on swiftly like a keen dog;
Like a dog he follows the trail by scent.

Irresistible and foaming with rage
Like a whirlwind he rakes them together.

"Out yonder, not far from me, lies Ankota;
The underground hollow is gaping before me.

"A straight track is gaping open before me,
An underground hollow is gaping open before me.

"A cavernous pathway is gaping open before me,
An underground pathway is gaping open before me.

"Red I am like the heart of a flame of fire,
Red too is the hollow in which I am resting." [8]

This is not the whole poem but it gives a fair sample of its
manner and method. The song-man has produced something
like a story and given it a notable verisimilitude. He dwells
with delight on the physical scene as it presents itself to
Ankotarinja on his journey from east to west, where eventually he devours the inhabitants and is himself killed for it. As
he lies in a hollow, he looks up and around and sees the
first of his enemies whom the song-man calls simply "them,"
as Ankotarinja "rakes them together." They are not of sufficient importance to deserve more attention at this stage of
the story, which is mainly of the actual journey. Then he sees
an opening in the earth, and this lures him on in high excitement. This is not a trip to the centre of the earth, but
it has at least the thrill of a dog hunting down a burrow.

All this implies a good deal of selection and simplification, and to this extent the song is a heroic tale, comparable with tales in more advanced societies about shamans and medicine men who go under the earth to visit the dead. As such the song provides its own adventures, and no doubt its audiences enjoy the art which conveys the excitement of an expedition into the unknown from the bright, shining earth with its pebbles and sand-rills.

At the same time the song-maker intends to provide more than a mere story and is aware that he must suit his methods to the ritual which he illustrates and pay attention to significant elements in it. The first sign of this is his emphasis on the colour red, in which Ankotarinja paints himself, and which is repeated in the *tjurunga* and the *tnatantja*, instruments of destruction, in the pebbles on the plain, in the hollow where he lies. This is done on purpose. Red ochre is commonly used in Australian ceremonies of more than one district and is a symbol variously applied for the warmth or the rays of the sun, heat from a fire, blood from afterbirth or wounds. It suggests, in general, heat and life, and when the actor daubs himself with it and sees it all around him, he stresses his connection with the sunlight and the living world and his own abundance of vital force. The song-maker takes advantage of this element in the ritual to make a special point in the narrative and to reveal something of its importance for the imagination with its hints of full-blooded activity. Secondly, when he names both the *tjurunga* and the *tnatantja*, it is as symbols of destruction, and their appearance is calculated and purposeful. They stress the destructive character of the dog-ancestor Ankotarinja and at the same time point to his courage as he descends into a world which is alien to everything that he knows and where his boldness and strength will stand him in good stead. Thirdly, Ankotarinja is a dog-ancestor; that is, he is both a man and a dog and possesses qualities which are common to both. He has not yet taken the form of a dog, but he is already behaving like one and has the temper of one. Hence his eagerness on his journey, his lying in a hollow for something to happen, his sudden outburst of temper, his quickness on the trail, his rapid despatch of his enemies, his dash down the burrow into the dark. Moreover, because he is at heart a dog and behaves like one, in the end he goes too far and is destroyed. The identification of a man with a dog is very skilfully managed, and in Ankotarinja we see how a dog's most salient qualities are not after all very different from a man's.

In this poem the use of red ochre and of the *tjurunga*

and the *tnatantja* is justifiably called symbolical if we recognize
the limitations of the word in this context. Such symbols
come from objects and practices in ritual, where they have
a prominent place because they suggest in an individual,
visible, concrete form, powers and forces which are none of
these things and cannot be easily presented through words
alone. Primitive man is acutely aware of invisible powers at
work in nature and himself, and his favourite way of trying
to come to terms with them is to find examples of them
and to make these serve as representative instances or symbols. When he uses something visible as a symbol of something invisible, he asserts not similarity between them but
identity. He works not so much by association of ideas as
by association of impressions, whether visual or emotional
or merely evocative. A matter which means much to him
but of which he can speak only through pictorial images
gains in strength through the other associations which such
images may evoke. Thus the use of red ochre may in the
first place suggest strength, but it also suggests warmth of
blood and eagerness of purpose. The fundamental purpose of
symbols is to bring the remote and the intangible into the
range of human consciousness, and this is all the more necessary when the subject itself is beyond factual speech and
can be conveyed only through hints of resemblance and
association. Because primitive language uses images without
the least effort or premeditation, it falls easily into symbols,
but symbols are not the same as images. Whereas an image illustrates one single theme by another, a symbol illuminates an occasion by relating it to something vaster outside
itself, to which in some way it belongs. Both are indispensable to primitive song, but symbol is more adventurous and
advances into less familiar fields.

Symbols stand in a special relation to myths. A myth
may even be regarded as a single, long, coherent symbol,
in which every detail is worked out to a given end, but just
as some myths are not symbolical but historical, so symbols
may do no more than stress and amplify some elements in
myths by drawing attention to their significance. This is
not difficult for primitive man, since he tends to interpret
the powers of nature as if they were in some sense human
and to ascribe to them characteristics like his own. When
the Bushman addresses the moon as if it were an old
friend, he conforms to a common practice, and a like approach is to be found in much other treatment of natural
things. Once it has begun, it can be enhanced and strengthened by other associations and especially by the attribution of
characteristics which have a symbolical significance. For in-

stance, the Mudbara tribe of Wave Hill in the Northern
Territory of Australia have a song which celebrates the sun:

> The day breaks—the first rays of the rising Sun, stretch-
> ing her arms.
> Daylight breaking, as the Sun rises to her feet,
> Sun rising, scattering the darkness, lighting up the
> land . . .
> With disk shining, bringing daylight, lighting up the
> land . . .
> People are moving about, talking, feeling the warmth,
> Burning through the gorge she rises, walking westwards,
> Wearing her waistband of human hair.
> She shines on the blossoming coolibah tree, with its
> sprawling roots.
> Its shady branches spreading.[9]

The Sun is introduced, more or less, as a goddess in human
form. She has indeed her disk and her rays, but she stretches
her arms and rises to her feet, and in this the Mudbara
would see no more contradiction than Homer's audience
would in the rosy fingers of the dawn. But this anthropomor-
phic conception is combined with other suggestive associations.
Both the waistband of human hair and the coolibah tree with
its sprawling roots are brought in with set intention, since
both are symbols of fertility in man and nature. Hair plays
a large part as a male emblem in the ritual songs of the
Djanggawul and kindred rites, and the roots of trees are
connected with the male function in procreation. The Sun,
who is herself female, is thus associated with male activities,
and the implication is that she gives life to the world
because she promotes these activities in men and animals.
The waistband and the roots of the tree are symbols which
stand for something large and comprehensive beyond themselves. They are introduced unobtrusively, perhaps because
the song-maker does not wish them to interfere too much
with his picture of the Sun rising and warming the world, but
they cannot be ignored and are indispensable to the full
sense of the song. The Sun is a female principle, and that is
the reason for her waistband, but she stirs the male activities of the world, and that is symbolized by the roots of the
coolibah tree. The song-maker is not content to present her
simply as an object of beauty or even as a source of
warmth and comfort; he is well aware of her natural functions in the scheme of birth and growth, and he introduces them quietly but firmly. He starts with a great
advantage in the common belief that the sun resembles a
woman, and he advances beyond this to hint what it means

in the order of natural things. This is an authentic symbolism because the symbols are visible emblems of powers beyond the reach of the senses. They are known to exist, but their character can be conveyed only by the indirect means of hint and allusion.

Against this form of symbolism, which gives significance to familiar things by relating them to invisible forces, we may set a second form, which aims at making the invisible significant by relating it to visible things. The procedure is reversed, and the second type is quite as important as the first, because it is primitive man's way of coming to grips with many matters which he cannot properly understand but which he hopes somehow to control or use. The problem which beyond all others obsesses him is that of procreation and fertility, not merely in men but in the whole range of life. For him it is just as important that beasts and birds and fish should multiply and that wells should be replenished as that he himself should find food and beget children. It is this conviction which imposes a special character on the Australian cycles of the Djanggawul and Kunapipi. Both deal with mythical ancestors, who are responsible for the creation and the maintenance of life, and both explain what this means, not by general statements but by a series of symbols, which are indeed symbols in the full sense of being visible emblems of invisible forces. The songs do this by accumulating images of various kinds round a single theme in the hope that they will suggest the common character inherent in them. Some of these symbols are objects made by men and given functions in ritual; others are present in the natural scene and constantly mentioned. What we get is a symbolical presentation of certain fundamental processes connected with fertility, and though man is the first concern, it is clear that his processes are similar to those of other creatures and that all alike presuppose the same kind of supernatural powers at work. The symbols are chosen on a basis of association through their obvious resemblance to one another, and their relation to the central issue. This happens constantly in the Djanggawul cycle, as when the Djanggawul plant a sacred emblem called *djuda* that water may flow:

Here is another: come, put the *djuda* roots into the well!
We make the well calling the invocations ...
Put them in quietly, with shining feathers, as we invoke the
  sacred names ...
They see the water bubbling up, splashing and spraying ...
Quietly they stand, watching the rising water rushing
  through the wild banana palms:

Roaring along, pushing the silt, with waves splashing
   together . . .
They come within the transverse fibre of the mat . . .[10]

Here the Djanggawul re-enact, through their human represen-
tatives, a timeless past when they established life in the world.
Everything that they do is symbolical and hints at wide associations. The *djuda,* which is a pole decorated with bright
feathers, and the mat, which is like a bag, are emblems of
male and female organs. The well stands not only for water
on the earth but for physical processes in man and woman.
Even the banana trees evoke similar echoes on the male side.
The vivid description of the visible objects calls up the invisible powers which they represent. In this song the words
follow the ritual closely and do not advance much beyond
it, but they reveal that even so technical a business as this
can have an imaginative side and that the notion of an ulti-
mate identity between life in water and life in man is aptly
presented in this concrete manner.

In these ritual songs there is a tendency for the symbols
to take command and inspire what look like independent
themes which do not advance the main meaning and might be
regarded as decoration for its own sake. Yet, when this happens, we are probably expected to see that the decoration is in
fact relevant to the central theme and does something for it,
not indeed in the way of explanation, but by making us see
how it interpenetrates the living scene. For instance, when
the Djanggawul are still at sea in their canoe on their way
to land, they encounter a whale:

What is this which blocks us? The whale!
As we paddle, we see its gaping mouth. What is that?
Spray and sea splash as it moves.
We paddle gently, for we see the open mouth of the whale.
What is this swimming? Our *ngainmara* mat, swimming un-
   der the water!
Water swirling! We hear the noise of the water, and of its
   spray.
We saw it out at sea, a long way from Bralgo, spray from
   the swimming whale.
Water rises and swirls, with noise caused by the whale;
   spray and foam from the whale!
As we paddle, see it swimming. Bralbral calls to the Djang-
   gawul,
It is our mat, our basket! Let us take some. The others
   we leave in the sea!
Waves rise from the large *ngainmara* mats that they leave
   behind swirling water spraying from them!

Water comes in from them coming to us: foaming, spraying, and roaring, out on the sea.[11]

The whale is, because of its shape, associated very closely
with the sacred *ngainmara* mat, which is itself an emblem of
the womb. The triple identification aims at showing that life
at sea comes into existence in the same way as on land,
and that this, as the mention of the mat shows, is itself a
sacred matter. Once this point is established, the song proceeds to describe the movement of the water, and this too is
symbolical, as water in these songs always is. None the less
it behaves as water does and should, and the details of its
movements and appearance are happily described with perceptive insight so that its living nature may be clear and that
all may see in what diverse ways it works. This is essentially
a poetical task, and these songs, which are indeed far removed from our own methods of thinking, are an attempt to
present a mystery not only in visible forms but in its wide
influence and enthralling multiplicity. Such songs are of
course in no sense pure art. They serve a practical purpose,
which is always present, explicitly as well as implicitly, and
this makes them perhaps less attractive and less immediate
than other songs in which the aim is kept more in the background and intrudes less into the words. Yet if we knew
these rites from the inside, as their singers and audiences do,
we should feel less discord between the delightful details and
the somewhat repetitive rites to which they belong. The symbols of any religious belief are bound to look alien and
even unattractive to those who do not know it from inside,
but to the men who take part in the Djanggawul ritual what
feels a little chilly to us may well have the appeal of an absorbing mystery.

Not all ritual songs about ancestors keep so closely to their
main matter as those of the Djanggawul cycle, and in certain
others we can see how the desire to make a mythical ancestor
live for his descendants leads the song-maker into expanding
or elaborating his theme beyond the strictly necessary limits.
This may well add to the attractiveness of his song and bring
its subject into a more familiar orbit than if it were presented simply for its inherent oddity. Ancestors are seen to
resemble men, and the more they resemble them, the more
the song-maker can do with them as material for his art. An
illuminating case of this expansive technique is the Aranda
song of the honey-ant men, of which we have already seen
a section. In it they leave their old home at Ljaba and go
on a long journey to another territory. After passing a curve
in the range of hills, they know that henceforward Ljaba will

be hidden from their sight; so they halt and look back towards it. Tears fall from their eyes, and they sing.

> Enfolded by plains lies Ljaba;
> Beyond the far horizon lies Ljaba.
>
> Enfolded by plains lies Ljaba,
> Dimmed by the enveloping mists.[12]

Then they move on. The point is not strictly relevant to the
myth, but it has a human pathos and appeal and is introduced for that reason. When the rite is performed, the singers
are deeply moved by these lines, which embody their own
feeling for home and their understanding of what it costs to
leave it.

A somewhat similar art is displayed in the Aranda song of
the Ulamba ancestor, who after violent struggles on earth is
changed into stone. He is sick to death, but must return home
for his final sleep. The song presents the strong emotions of a
hero who, worn out by his efforts, turns his thoughts to home:

> High in the heavens shines the afternoon sun;
> His heart is filled with yearning to go home.

He sets out on his journey and sees his home in the distance:

> "My own home, my dear home,
> O Ulamba, rugged chasm-cleft!"

He hears the birds twittering:

> The birds are twittering with many voices,
> At Ulamba, chasm-cleft Ulamba.

He sees the place where he used to sleep and notices that in
his absence it has been spoiled by the birds:

> "My own home, my dear home,
> Whose feet have disfigured it?
>
> "The mulga parrots have disfigured it;
> Their feet have scratched the deserted hollow." [13]

Then he sinks down and passes into his last, unbroken sleep.
This is a dramatic and effective close to the hero's career,
but we might feel that in his fine handling of the theme of
home the song-maker has strayed a little from his main
subject. Yet he has justification for it. The hero goes to sleep
in his own place, and that is why his presence is bound to
it forever, and the song indicates that in his love of it he
is in return worthy of honour and affection. The symbols

of his career, still visible in the stones which mark his final collapse, bear witness to his love for the land which bore him and which, in his state of dreaming, he still protects.

It would not be far wrong to claim that in this poetry which deals with the enigma of being alive almost every element is more or less symbolical in that it contributes to the general task of elucidating universal mysteries. Yet it is this overpowering sense of mystery which sharpens the perceptions of the song-makers and inspires them to so keen an interest in the physical scene. Just because it contains so many hidden forces, they apply their daily knowledge of it to giving colour and charm to their songs. In Arnhem Land some aborigines have a cycle of songs on the Moon-bone, behind which lies the myth that the moon dies and is born again. Before he dies, he goes to the sea, where his bones become the shell of the nautilus, and before he is born again he casts away this relic of bone. This simple myth of death and rebirth enables the song-man to introduce a variety of well-observed, picturesque details about life in the water, and this he is fully entitled to do since water is closely connected with the process by which the Moon revives. One song in the cycle illustrates its possibilities:

> The prawn is there, at the place of the Dugong, digging
>   mud with its claws . . .
> The hard-shelled prawn, living there in the water, mak-
>   ing soft little noises.
> It burrows into the mud and casts it aside among the
>   lilies . . .
> Throwing aside the mud with soft little noises . . .
> Digging out mud with its claws at the place of the
>   Dugong, the place of the Dugong's bed,
> Calling the bone *bukelili,* the catfish . . . the frog . . .
>   the sacred tree,
> The prawn is burrowing, coming up, throwing aside the
>   mud, and digging,
> Climbing up to the lotus plants and up to their pools.[14]

In the rebirth of the Moon the prawn plays a special part. When it calls the Moon by the name *bukelili,* its uses a "power-name," which works as a supernatural agency, and to get it into action is the task of the prawn both in the myth and the ritual. It has an important place in the whole scheme, but the song-man feels that he must explain how this happens, and his account of it as it comes out of the mud and climbs upward is not only in close accord with observed fact but has a strong symbolical influence in relation to the new rising of the moon. He stands in so intimate a relation with his myth that he cannot but make everything as actual as possible, but in doing this he strengthens the symbolical associations of the song. The magical procedure for which he sings looks entirely reasonable, and at the same time he infuses it with the wonder and awe that he feels before it.

The primitive use of symbols differs from that in civilized poetry. First, though these lucent, concrete images may be said to symbolize something beyond themselves, such as the processes of fertility, they are not wholly separate from it but partake of its essential nature. In most modern symbolism a symbol may indeed embody much that is important to what it symbolises, but it is separate from it, as the Cross embodies many Christian associations but is not the same as Christianity. But primitive symbolism asserts a real identity. The whale and the womb, the roots of a tree and the male member, are treated, if not as exactly identical, at least as different examples of a single thing, which is both natural and supernatural and perfectly at home in the familiar world. Secondly, primitive song draws symbols from every day to bring the remote and the uncomprehended into a more approachable orbit. The parrots and the prawn help to make the mysteries of perpetual sleep and of rebirth less obscure. But modern poetry usually works in a different way. It uses an image to give a new significance or to cast a new light on what has been dulled by familiarity or devitalized by abstraction. Its aim is less to reduce a mystery than to enhance or revive one, or to reveal it where its presence has not been suspected, and this is natural enough in a world where much is understood and explained through general notions, which indeed provide an approach to most experience but in the process discourage wonder and awe. Primitive man has these so abundantly that he feels no need to stimulate them by artificial means but wishes rather to keep them in control and to subject them to some kind of system. Thirdly, in modern poetry symbols are on the whole dispensable. They are not rare, but much poetry thrives without them. But in primitive song they are necessary for almost any subject beyond what is immediately seen by the physical vision, and even then they may be needed to explain its significance in a world where everything is explained by associations and similitudes. This is true not only of the Australian songs, which are rare in their elaboration, but of the simpler songs of the Gabon Pygmies and the Semang. In these societies songs are so often concerned with the unknown that symbols come naturally to them and are practically indispensable for any full effect.

This is the primitive method of peering through the curtain of appearances to the powers that work behind it and of making these powers understandable by giving a vivid impression of their character and their methods.

Yet both primitive and modern types of symbolism are in fact applications of what is ultimately a single mode of thought. The purpose of a symbol is to express as forcibly and rightly as possible the essential nature of something which is otherwise beyond the reach of ordinary descriptive words because they cannot convey its unique individuality. This may indeed be elusive or intangible, but none the less it imposes its character on us and calls for adequate presentation in speech. This trouble arises because words are unable to deal with such impressions through their usual methods. Just as primitive language fails before many physical and metaphysical processes because its vocabulary is not competent to handle them, so modern language often fails because it is too analytical and lacks ready means to convey the many associations, emotional or imaginative, which cluster round a subject and give to it a distinctive, personal character. In both cases symbols are needed to remedy the deficiencies of conventional speech, which has for the most part been developed for quite different functions. In their use of symbols primitive song and modern poetry differ not in kind but in degree. They resemble one another in feeling a real need for symbols and in using them to make their impact more subtle and more inclusive and more impressive.

CHAPTER 10 Some Conclusions

THE SONGS of primitive peoples are purposeful attempts to put into coherent words thoughts and feelings which may in their raw state be far from coherent, and this alone indicates that songs belong to a later stage of development than the dances and rites which they so often accompany. The priority of dance over song is clear from the large number of dances which have no words and are entirely self-sufficient and self-explanatory without them. The dance is one of man's earliest attempts to move in an imaginary world of his own creation, which none the less stands in a close relation to the actual world and fulfils some function in it, whether magical or religious or ceremonial or merely diverting. For all our peoples the dance has a proud place in the round of communal activities, and there is every reason to think that its ancestry goes back to Late Paleolithic times. Even in historical times the evidence for it is, by our standards, remarkably ancient. In the twenty-fourth century B.C. the young Pharaoh Pepi II wrote to his general Herikuf in words of some excitement about a dwarf (Deneg), whom the general has captured and is bringing to Egypt.[1] Pepi insists that the greatest care must be taken with this rare prize and that he must not be allowed to fall overboard and that every night he must be visited ten times by the watch to see that he is safe. The vital point about the dwarf, for us as for Pepi, is that he is said to dance "the dances of the gods," and this ability is counted very highly to his credit in a country where the gods are never very far from the royal mind. The dwarf is of course a Pygmy, who comes from the Land of Yam, which is south of the Sudan on the way to where Pygmies still survive in Ruanda. Nor is he the first of his kind mentioned in Egyptian records, since the same inscription speaks of an earlier Deneg, who in the time of Izozi was brought from the Land of Punt, which corresponds roughly with Somaliland. In remote antiquity Pygmies were prized in Egypt for their powers of dancing, which was believed to have a religious use in pleasing the gods, and it may be from some faint echoes of such dances that Homer speaks of Pygmies warring against cranes.[2] A dance dramatising battles against birds may have been regarded as an imitation of fact, and from this grew a rich and fruitful legend. Nor is it at all unlikely that such dances reflected actual practice, and had some magical purpose. The Bushmen, who are remote kinsmen of the Pygmies, still sing about the blue crane and pursue it eagerly with charms, and it is possible that for its successful pursuit they held dances depicting fights against it. Through dances primitive peoples express their emotions with all the force that dancing allows, and work an enchantment on some prey or show their identity with their totems or illustrate some myth or hold intercourse with their gods. All these things their songs also do, but without the dance the song would hardly exist. It is derived from the dance and historically posterior to it, and that is why dances without words are commoner than dances with them. Words are introduced when the act of dancing is for some reason thought to be not enough and to need the support of words, and then their first duty is not to exist for their own sake, but to provide a supplementary aid. They have indeed large possibilities before them, but at the start these are neither intended nor foreseen.

In Late Palaeolithic times dances were often magical rites connected with man's desire to exert his will over animals and thereby to kill them, and such in some places they still are. Just as dancers of the Magdalenian age are depicted with antlers, horses' tails and the like, so some Australians put on tails to resemble dogs or kangaroos, and in both cases the intention must be the same. When at Chancelade men conduct a dance-like rite around a dead bison, they celebrate its death very much as modern Pygmies celebrate the death of an elephant.[3] So too a common form of primitive dance is for one or more dancers to take the part of animals and for others to pursue them. In Later Palaeolithic times such dancers appear as chamois bucks at Teyjat, as musk-oxen at La Madeleine, and as deer at Lourdes, and this corresponds very closely with the imitations of hunted animals by the Bushmen and the Pygmies. The functions and even the fashions of the dance have remained constant for thousands of years, and though some totemistic dances, such as the Bushmen perform at puberty ceremonies or some Australians for mythical ancestors, may imply relatively complex ideas and assumptions, these need not necessarily be more advanced than the idea behind the dancer beside an ibex at Veija in Spain who looks as if he were exerting some influence over the dead animal and might even stand in a totemistic relation to it. We cannot doubt the magical purpose of such prehistoric dances, and it must have been so obvious to those who took part in them that it called for no commentary in words. Of this kind are most of the dances still practised by primitive peoples. When Pygmies act the parts of baboons or wild boars,[4] or the Andamanese of turtles,[5] or the Tasmanians of kangaroos or emus or fish,[6] or the Yamana of sea-lions,[7] the meaning is perfectly clear from the action and no words are needed to explain it. It follows that song is a later invention than the dance, to which it is in its beginnings secondary and certainly not indispensable. This may well mean that in Late Palaeolithic times words were not yet used to give a fuller force to rites, or to explain what the dance in itself made clear enough. At least we have no reason to think that they were or that they were felt to be necessary to add a new dimension to the dance.

The adaptation of words to song must have been a very slow process and may have taken thousands of years. The development of intelligible speech from the earliest emotive cries is itself so wrapped in mystery and so hard to unravel that it is almost impossible even to guess at what period of their development men were sufficient masters of words to put them to so fine and so exacting a purpose as the composition of songs. Even when speech had grown from undifferentiated cries to specialized functions such as exclamation, question, and statement, it was still very far from the abundance which is characteristic of primitive languages. No doubt the artists of Lascaux were able to speak to one another with some exactness in performing their skilled and difficult tasks, but that does not mean that they possessed vocabularies anything like as rich as the Eskimos or the Yamana or the Australians of Arnhem Land. Just as the scope of primitive languages implies an enormous growth in vocabulary as words are made to describe, with an ever growing discrimination, sensations and feelings and impressions, so the growth of intelligible song from spoken words must have taken an

incalculable period of time. It is likely that even the most
primitive songs now known to us, including the senseless
lines of the Yamana and the most elementary charms, are a
far more advanced art than later Palaeolithic man was capable
of, and it is wise to leave him at this point. But in his time
the dance existed, and since song arose from it, our primitive peoples are in this respect his lineal heirs and carry on
his activities at the point where he left them.

Song, starting almost from nothing, takes more elaborate
forms and flowers into a conscious art, composed with a
special concentration and admired for the force which it
puts into its words. In this process the first steps count for
a great deal, and the first of all was the application of meaningless sounds, like those of the Yamana and the Selk'nam,
to music. To us this may seem so easy that we hardly notice it, but it was a truly momentous change to accompany
dance not with spontaneous ejaculations, varying from
singer to singer, but with standardized, formulaic sequences
of sounds. Behind this lies the assumption, in itself highly
important, that the dance, being a special ceremony, calls
for a special discipline in vocal sounds. On this point the
development of speech in children provides no analogy. Before a child begins to use words, he makes noises, but they
are not standardized for special purposes, nor are they artic-
ulated into fully formed sounds. Even when song had been
established, there was still a long way to go before meaningless sounds were replaced by meaningful words drawn from
actual speech. This implies not only a considerable exercise
of verbal skill in languages totally untrained to such duties
but a conviction that words were after all necessary. The
dance, which had hitherto been a self-contained and self-
sufficient art, was thought to need sometimes this extraneous
aid. For this there must have been strong reasons, and we
may surmise what some of them were. A rite which had
been practised for so long that its actual meaning was ob-
scured called for explanation in words to bring home its
intention and relevance; in approaching gods or spirits for
any special or defined purpose it might be inadvisable to assume that they would know what it was unless it was
explained or at least adumbrated to them; in celebrating human occasions like birth or marriage or death words might
be necessary to display the less obvious meaning of what
happens and to relate it more closely to other human experience. Whatever the reason may have been, the result
was epoch-making and called for a powerful and sustained
effort of the intelligence. The right words must be found
for the special purpose and fitted into a tune. Such songs

were by our standards extremely simple, but they were the beginning of a true art of poetry, in which words were turned to new purposes outside their ordinary functions and chosen with a discriminating care for the demands of their new task. Their choice called for a rigorous and perceptive judgment since, whatever their purpose might be, it was important and unusual and delicate. In this, much was gained from the highly sensitive and expressive nature of primitive language and even from its lack of general or abstract words. Poetry thrives on particulars, and the more precisely words catch the finer shades of emotion or sensibility or perception the more suitably they fall into song. To choose the right, acceptable, powerful words when so many alternatives are available implies a firm notion of what song must be if it is to do duty as a worthy accompaniment of the dance.

No doubt in different places this happened at different times, and in Tierra del Fuego it hardly got beyond the first stage of unintelligible sounds, but once the process started it was carried on by its own momentum and must have followed similar lines everywhere. For this reason the study of primitive song is an evolutionary study, legitimately conducted by comparative methods. It begins at the very beginning, when words replace mere noises, and shows how the most elementary forms turn into others more elaborate and more heavily loaded with meaning, until a form reaches its limits and seldom passes beyond them. Despite its internal richness and variety primitive song is confined in its scope, and in this it reflects the human circumstances in which it is born. Modern primitives live the life of their Palaeolithic ancestors and have added almost nothing to it. Their songs are indeed songs of the Stone Age before it takes to agriculture and the domestication of animals. The scope of song is firmly determined by the habits of its singers, and these are in their turn shaped by the needs of hunting and the outlook which they create. The main thoughts of our primitives cannot be very different from what men in their position have always thought, and the emotions which govern them are certainly basic to human nature when it has to struggle daily for existence. They reflect a special class of experience, which is indeed not small but quite different from anything in more advanced societies. It includes the fundamental emotions and instincts of man, but it restricts them to a limited sphere and imposes a dominating character on them. Just because primitive song is held within such boundaries, it has a marked character of its own, which none the less lies behind much of later song, from which it looks so different on the surface, and it shows in what ways song starts its career and what efforts it makes in its first stages to understand man's predicament in the world.

In primitive songs everything is concerned with particular points, and there is no attempt to generalize beyond them. What counts is the rite performed on the occasion celebrated, and to this the song adheres closely without trying to advance beyond it into more abstract or more theoretical fields. But this does not mean that a song is sung only once. On the contrary, so much in primitive life is repetitive that even a highly detailed song may be appropriate on many occasions which closely resemble each other both in their main character and their particular points. In most of these songs, even when they are highly personal, there is an element of ceremony, and ceremony calls for doing something in an established and expected way. Even the Andamanese repeat their hunting-songs when the opportunity arises, and in most songs of the Dama there is a strong conventional element which helps to put the theme in its right perspective and relate it to the rest of life. Just because songs are repeated they give a sense of continuity and coherence to much more than high religious festivals, where of course standard songs are to be expected as part of the rite. The song-man aims both at describing what is most significant on a single occasion and what it has in common with other occasions like it, and this means that he chooses his themes with care and concentrates on what he thinks to be essential. Through this he finds his own kind of depth, which is displayed through hints of what really matters and must not be omitted. He naturally omits a good deal, especially what may seem to him not of central importance. What he selects has its own overriding significance for him and sums up what counts for most in the situation as he feels and sees it. For instance, when the Veddas summon the spirit of an ancestor to help in some undertaking, they fix an arrow upright in the ground and dance slowly round it with an invocation:

> My departed one, my departed one, my God!
> Where art thou wandering?[8]

Nothing is said of the purpose for which the spirit's help is needed, nor indeed is the notion of help mentioned. The words are a summons couched in affection, need and anxiety; that is all that matters, and it enables them to be used on many different kinds of occasion. The spirit may be trusted to understand the situation and to perform what is asked of it. The prayer aims at establishing a relation and employs the briefest possible means. The occasion is distilled to its essence, and though the result is very short and simple, it has, none the less, reserves of power in its very restraint.

Such a technique is not well suited to anything that borders on narrative, and we have seen how the mythical songs of the Aranda consist of a series of individual, simplified themes, each of which is more or less complete in itself. Yet sometimes primitive song-men tell of actual events for their own sake and do so with a characteristic economy. Such songs not only presuppose a knowledge of the main events which they recall but even from these select some very special point. For instance, among the Veddas two men once went out to gather honey, but strangers cut the ropes by which they had climbed, and killed them. When the Veddas' wives made enquiries about their husbands, the strangers said that they were bathing in a stream. The wives, suspecting foul play, went out, found the bodies at the foot of a precipice, and killed themselves. A song says very little about all this and selects for its theme the moment when the wives still believe that their husbands are alive but are anxious because they are so late in returning:

> Elder sister, elder sister, come to go.
> Our husbands have not yet returned:
> Come, younger sister, let us go to look for them.
> Younger sister, younger sister, the husbands of us both
>   come running.
> Younger sister, younger sister, come to look.
> Elder sister, elder sister, I am afraid, I cannot, I cannot.
> Younger sister, younger sister, come, come.
> The husbands of us two come running from
>   Wellikandiya.
> Come and see.[9]

The episode is chosen with care. It tells of the crisis when the two wives are already apprehensive about the prolonged absence of their husbands and see two figures, who are actually the murderers, but whom the elder sister thinks to be the husbands, while the younger has anxious doubts. It is a moment of uncertainty, suspense, and even fear, and as such falls into a song which combines these feelings in the simple dialogue of the two wives and leaves out as superfluous any introduction or explanation. This may not be the only part of the story which has passed into song, and it is quite possible that other parts were treated differently, but so far as this part is concerned, the song-man shows insight and originality in his approach and puts into it his imaginative understanding of the conflict in the women's minds.

This art of selection passes very easily into the concentration of as much as possible meaning into a very few words, and such words must be chosen aptly and put together impressively. With their rich vocabularies primitive languages permit a very high degree of concentration in a short space. For instance in the western part of South Australia children sing about a falling star. Such a star is thought to be a "devil-devil," an evil spirit feared because it forebodes trouble. The song consists of four words:

kandanga daruarungu manangga gilbanga[10]

which may be literally translated: "star—falling—at night-time—you (star) go away." It is a charm against the evil which the star portends, and it is constructed with an unobtrusive art. The internal rhymes in *-anga* help to make it complete in itself and give it an interior balance; its complete lack of any reference either to the fear which the star inspires or to the reason for this fear is part of its technique, of its desire to fix on the main point and nothing else; its extreme brevity has the commanding force of an order or a prayer, and it is both of these. In its small compass it does all that is asked of it and satisfies its purpose with an accomplished assurance. In the same way a complaint of a Yamana to his god about the weather is reduced to its indispensable, entirely relevant minimum. The situation is that he has put out to sea and been caught by a sudden change of weather to the west, which is dark and stormy. He says simply:

watauineiwa haia kumekaleni,[11]

which means "the Old One—to me—weather from the west." It is a bald statement of fact, but it is none the less infused with emotion, with anxiety and implied complaint. Each word does its utmost by hinting beyond what it actually says, and nothing could be more compressed. But it is certainly a work of art, an exhibition of words set to action through passion by restraint. It catches what matters most in the mood of the man who has been caught by the unexpected change in the weather and with an impressive economy conveys his feelings about his god. The rigid moderation of what is actually said emphasizes the driving passion of the central mood, of the seafarer's complaint against the supernatural power who sends vicious weather. So in the cycle of songs about Kunapipi from Arnhem Land one short piece deals with the coming of the rainy season, which is the time of fertilization and has a primary significance in the whole ritual. It says concisely:

wadada murunda ngarandjel badi:nja[12]

"raining—filling swamps—white clouds—coming down," that is, the rain falls down from white clouds and fills the swamps. It could not be shorter or simpler, and yet inside its narrow frame it conjures up a vivid scene and asserts its claim on our attention.

This highly selective technique, whether of themes or of words, is closely related to the part played by the emotions in primitive songs. They do not often convey much information, and their main strength lies in their emotional impact, in the overriding and obsessing mood which they create in those who hear them, in their ability to dominate men's thoughts through their emotions. If we list their subjects in abstract categories, they are limited enough, but each song has an individuality through the quality of the emotions which infuse it and not only keep it firmly to its point but mark it off from other songs on similar subjects. Just because the songman feels so deeply about his theme and is thereby absorbed in it, he marks what is most important in it and through this gives distinction and character to it. This does not exclude quite complex or even conflicting emotions, as we can see from the Pygmy woman who has lost her child, the Eskimo who has broken his sledge, or the Bushman girl who has the gripes. Just because primitive man responds with his whole, undivided nature to whatever strikes him, so at times, without any conscious art, he presents with an effortlessly natural ease a tangled complex of emotions which are at work simultaneously in him. This immediate understanding of the emotions means that situations which excite a number of different responses are fused into a single song which makes a single impact. For instance, a Dama song of farewell is sung to a woman:

Tomorrow I shall go away.
Shall I come to my land?
I am a bird at the parting of the waters.
The women who went down to the water have left me.
Say it to me, you, the unadorned!
Say it to me, you with the broad face!
O you the unadorned,
Shall I come to the far land?
Shall I come to Okawango?
That is what my harp has to say![13]

The man is going on a journey, and his first thoughts are of this and the chances of arrival, but he combines them first with an expression of his loneliness now that most of his womenfolk have left him and then with words to one woman, who shows by her lack of ornaments that she is going with him. The little poem contains a mixture of anxiety and affection, of fear at going into the unknown and consolation that the traveller is not going alone but has a companion to share his fortunes. We may analyse his feelings into constituent elements, but the final effect is single and complete.

These impelling, dominating emotions are by no means confined to personal songs but may often be seen at work in songs and prayers to supernatural powers, as indeed we should expect among peoples who regard gods and spirits as beings very like themselves and hope to establish personal relations with them. Though the Hottentots, in their present degraded status, have lost their old hunting and gathering habits, they keep some of their old songs, which show how intimate their approach to the gods is. When Valentijn touched at the Cape in 1705, he noticed that they had "a supreme ruler ... who dwells on high, and to whom they showed respect, especially during great storms of thunder and lightning ... saying, if it thunders, 'The Great Chief is angry with us.'" So even now, if a thunderstorm is approaching, they assemble for a religious dance and sing a song:

> Son of the Thundercloud!
> Thou brave, loud-speaking Guru!
> Talk softly, please,
> For I have no guilt:
> Let me alone! Forgive me!
> For I have become quite weak.
> Thou, O Guru!
> Son of the Thundercloud![14]

This echoes a familiar mood, in which people feel that their god is angry with them because they have done something wrong, and yet they know that they have not. In the same breath the Hottentots protest their innocence and ask to be forgiven, and on both points they speak with honest conviction and impelling urgency. The unity of their mood transcends the contradictions in it, and the song rises straight from their anxiety.

This reliance on emotion as the source of song brings more than one advantage. First, it means that though thought is never lacking and has a considerable range and relevance, it is always infused with emotion and not presented dryly or abstractly. It is part of the living experience of a full man and cannot be separated from his feelings. Emotion sets it going and gives to it the concentration which a man finds when he is forced by the very strength of his feelings to think hard about some matter which touches and troubles him. It is his emotions which in the last resort enable him to extract what is really essential from a complicated theme and to give full attention to it. That is why in primitive song we feel no discord between the actual thought and the emotion which infuses it. Each supports and reinforces the other, but the emotion comes first and sets the thought in action and by its very strength shapes it and tidies it up. What might otherwise be an assortment of different thoughts connected by tenuous ties and certainly not ordered in any artistic form gains order and harmony from the strength of the originating, driving emotion. For instance, when a Pygmy mother gives birth to a child, she sings a song, which is indeed traditional but was plainly composed by someone who knew what the joy of motherhood is and reduced it to a shapely unity:

> My heart is all happy,
> My heart takes wing in singing,
> Under the trees of the forest,
> The forest our dwelling and our mother.
> On my thread I have taken,
> A little, a very little bird.
> My heart is caught on the thread,
> On the thread with the bird.[15]

The uniting theme is simply joy, and this is expressed in a very apt and illuminating image. Much else might be said, but since the mother's dominating mood is joy, the song concentrates on this and presents it in its essential purity. This happens in most of these songs and in each case it is the strength of emotion which secures this result.

Secondly, the emotional impulse behind a song is largely responsible for the character of primitive imagery. In languages which lack abstractions, imagery takes their place, and when a man's mind is set busily to work, he falls naturally into it as he tries to express clearly what he feels and to bring out its real temper. By parallels and similitudes he says much more than he would in plain statement, and says it much more effectively, especially since his images are drawn from the natural world about him and make an immediate impact on his audience, who know what he means and pick up at once his allusions. For instance the Dama celebrate the coming of rain:

> You little earth-vole, rich in sounds,
> Ant-eater killed by the Ku-Bushmen,

You cloud with your trailing track,
You, from whose chasm I drink the wonder-water of my
    friend,
Has a suitor appeared that men chatter?
Has a bridegroom appeared?
Do they trail game around?
You, who lighten and rain and chew the flesh of men,
You, who own water like the sea-bird!
O you who rejoice, you who rejoice!
You who are sated, sated!
You who give birds,
You mother of us all,
You with the big belly![16]

A series of images is used to express joy and relief and
security, and each image, aptly and strikingly chosen, shows
from a new angle what the coming of rain means. The rain-
cloud is first called an earth-vole because, when the first drops
fall, the ground looks as if thousands of these little creatures
performed a dance on it, and this is the first sign that the
rain has come. It is rich in sounds because it is preceded
by thunder, and this too is a welcome portent. Next it is
called an ant-eater, since this is renowned for its rich flesh,
and the rain gives a similar sense of well-being, of a satiety
welcomed and prized. In the third line the cloud is mentioned
for the first time in its own character and praised for the
other clouds which follow it, and in the fourth the song refers
to the holes in the earth where water is stored under the pro-
tecting spirit of a dead friend. The occasion is one of such
bustle and excitement that it recalls the arrival of a suitor or
a bridegroom, as animals emerge to drink and to be caught
at the water-holes. Yet the cloud has a formidable side, when
its lightning strikes men and is thought to devour them, and
this must not be neglected, because by contrast it emphasizes
the relief which comes with the rain. The cloud is then compared with a sea-bird, presumably because it drips with water, and the conclusion comes when the cloud is seen as
resembling men in its happiness and satiety and honoured for
giving sustenance, almost as if it were a pregnant mother.
The song moves through a series of distinct and separate steps
and uses images to convey different aspects of a single situation, but the whole effect is of delight because the dry season is over and men can find food with ease. The images
convey affection, excitement, awe, and pleasure, but they all
arise from a single, driving mood and help to give this a
concrete shape.

Yet in primitive song, as in most poetry, there comes a
point when emotions are not the only driving force and must

be tempered and reduced because some complex message or instruction has to be delivered. It is true that this affects only a minority of songs, such as those in the Djang-gawul cycle, but when it happens, it weakens the instinctive impulse to creation. Such songs illustrate and explain a sequence of ritual events, each of which is separate but among which many resemble one another in structure and in details. They differ from other primitive songs in their extended didactic purpose; their business is to explain what happens in the long rites to which they are attached. Since the rites certainly call for explanation and must be explained fully and correctly, the songs perform a useful function and develop many incidental virtues, notably in their sensitive feeling for physical things and for the living powers at work in them. But they lack the direct, immediate onslaught of emotion which we find elsewhere, and illustrate how even at this stage of its career poetry begins to sacrifice some of its essential strength when it puts thinking before emotion and is not quite able to fuse the two and make them work together. Of course the thinking in these songs is different from our own; it moves more by association of symbols than by development of ideas, and its method of explanation involves a vivid use of images and instances. None the less this remains an intellectual more than an emotional process, and for this reason the songs fall into a special category. To some degree they make up for this deficiency in emotional strength by being infused with a secondary, derivative excitement at seeing things, as it were, for the first time and feeling wonder and awe at the springs of life and growth. Yet this is less compelling than the primary emotions to which we are accustomed and inspires the songs less than it is itself inspired by the rites. The thinking comes first and shapes the rite, and then the emotions follow in its wake with less than usual force. It is an exceptional art, which in its manner and method lies rather outside the common scope of primitive song and lacks its more obvious and more generous appeal. Only here do we feel that a mental process comes between the song-maker and the raw material of his theme, and that he is hampered by having to conform to something which does not necessarily inspire him. He has to accommodate himself to accepted beliefs, and his art, despite its energy and its invention, lacks the direct appeal which is one of his chief gifts. When he moves beyond his normal manner of composition, he is faced by difficulties which are familiar to all poets whose first aim is to explain and instruct. He has begun to explore territories in which he is not fully at ease, and his old technique is strained beyond its resources. Primitive song depends for its strength on being the immediate expression of a man's whole being, and when he sacrifices one part of it for another, he divides his forces and weakens his impact.

Primitive song is the basic form of poetry, and though other forms which have grown from it bear little resemblance to it, it sets the start for them and provides the elements of their technique. With the passage of time and the development of new classes of poetry, these original elements tend to become less important, but they undeniably belong to its first appearances and account for much in it that most strikes the attention. First, song is in its beginnings intimately welded with music; it is actually sung, and we recognize this by our own use of metaphors from music when we speak of poetry. Primitive song is meant to be sung, and the tune, which gains greatly from its association with words, has entered into its being. If it is taken by itself, it still exists in its own right but largely because through its association with music it has its own rhythmical movement, which may not indeed be musical in any true sense but is certainly quite different from anything to be found in common speech. Moreover because the words have to be rhythmical, they call for other distinctions which do not necessarily belong to rhythm, notably in the choice and balance of sounds by their tonal qualities. Once words have begun to be accommodated to music, they display qualities which might not be expected of them in their ordinary duties, and have not only lilt and balance, but tone and quality. The comparison between them and musical tunes is justified by the similarity of the effect which both make on us. The melody of words exerts an attraction like that of a musical melody, and both match something in ourselves. What it lacks in actual music it makes up in meaning and association, and to this degree appeals more to the intelligence than to the ear, but it still appeals to the ear and through this enforces what it has to say. Primitive song is aware of this, and though it has tunes which complete and amplify its words, the words also are carefully fashioned for their own rhythm and self-contained, satisfying harmonies. They are more carefully chosen than other words and have the compelling power which comes when words are loaded with evocative meaning and enabled to make the most of this by their own distinction. The prime discovery of primitive song is that words are able to do this and in doing it to add a new dimension to their use. This is abundantly visible in these songs and does much to explain why, once composed, they are remembered and held in honour, as if it would be difficult to create other songs with the same quality and attraction. But for this discovery we may doubt whether poetry would ever have come into existence. Once this was understood and practised, poetry began its career as an art in which words pass beyond mere statement and create undivided, exhilarated states of mind.

Secondly, when, through their sound and rhythm and sense, words exert so strong a hold on us that we can think of nothing else, we still speak of their enchantment, and though this is no more than a metaphor, it was not always so and is indeed a relic of what song once was. In primitive song it still has a powerful place and is accepted both by singers and audiences as entirely natural and proper. The primitive song-man feels within himself an eruptive, domineering force which he must release upon others. He wishes to exert an influence, to impose a special vision, to create in others a state of mind which is more than understanding or sympathy and implies some degree of subordination to his will. He wishes to extend his control as a means to expressing himself, and if he does not do this, he feels that he has failed in his task. Even when he sings of a secular theme, he wishes to dominate his hearers mentally and emotionally and to force them to identify themselves with him and his subject. He sees song as an instrument by which some special force in himself is directed at others and works his will on them. What is true to this degree of secular song is true in a far larger degree of religious song, which aims at influencing supernatural powers. It may do this indirectly through charms or directly through hymns and prayers, but in either case it seeks a practical result. Primitive song is certainly not a case of art for art's sake. It may sometimes be composed simply to relieve the feelings, but more commonly it pursues something positive and purposeful, and just for this reason it has to polish its art and keep it to a high level, since otherwise it might fail in its ambition. Because it is so often magical, it has a concentration of energy which comes from its desire to control things physical or metaphysical through words, and in such a task words must be charged with a very unusual power. Even if their first duty is to influence gods and spirits, they cannot but have an effect on the men who sing or hear them and respond to their more than natural strength. Modern poets, writing with different aims, have indeed their own reserves of strength but they lack this impelling compulsion which makes song-makers exert themselves to the utmost in a sphere which calls for all the greater attention because it lies largely outside their understanding and has to be approached by the most effective means that can be devised. If all poetry has a practical end in so far as it seeks to capture and hold the consciousness, primitive song normally aims at something more precise in that it wishes to bring about a change not merely in men but in the supernatural powers around them.

In this respect primitive song is close to prayer, and this is to be expected, since its technique of words certainly owes something to prayers, invocations, and the like, which are not sung but spoken and provide models on which the words of a song can be built. The element of prayer enters into song in the intensity with which a request is made and the eagerness of the hope that it will be answered. Such prayers may be quite straightforward appeals to spirits or gods who are named or easily identified, as the Bushmen pray to the moon or Eskimos summon their guardian spirits; they may equally have a vaguer intention, especially when they are charms or incantations which exert their control on a world of spirits without specifying to whom in particular they are addressed. But in either case, though the song-man knows that he is dependent on the supernatural world for everything that keeps him alive, the thought of its existence and of his own relation with it gives him confidence and awakes his energy and desire for action. This is what some Eskimo magic words do in a very direct way. They are thought to bring vitality, and that is why they are used. But they say nothing of this explicitly:

> The gull, it is said,
> The gull, who cleaves the air with his wings,
> Who is usually above you.
> You gull, up there,
> Steer down towards me,
> Come to me.
> Your wings
> Are red,
> Up there in the coolness.[17]

The implicit comparison is between the lively movements of the gull and a like vitality which the man wishes for himself. He sees it clearly and finds a living image for it. Though on the surface he speaks to the gull, he in fact addresses unknown, unnamed powers behind and beyond it. That is why his song has a special intensity and concentration. It has a driving purpose which can be attained only through the help of spirits, but even while he sings it, the singer has already begun to find what he seeks. The mere thought that such a thing is possible makes the magic work. So in much primitive song the sense of dependence on supernatural beings sustains men in their daily tasks and, even when they feel that they are harshly treated, gives them enough courage to complain frankly about it. Just because the supernatural provides a centre for primitive thought, so primitive songs gain much of their strength from their intimate contact with it. The consciousness of it is nearly always present and means that almost every song is permeated with a sense of the mystery of things and with man's desire to know a little more about it.

The mystery which provokes song into being and enthrals us through it is present both in the visible and in the invisible world, in the life of living things and in the powers which lie within and without them. This, primitive man takes for granted and hardly distinguishes the one kind from the other. For him the physical fact of death is no more and no less mysterious than what may happen to the soul after it, and the ubiquitous presence of spirits is no more and no less remarkable than that of men and animals and trees. This gives a singular unity of outlook. Any theme may suggest an unknown background and indeed usually does so sooner or later, as the song-man puzzles over it in his mind and asks what it means. It may be enough merely to hint at this or to imply it, but it cannot be entirely shirked and even the most commonplace human actions may have an inexplicable side which points to unknown distances. Not everything can be stated clearly, and often it is enough to convey a sense of strangeness, which everyone will recognize and which yet has no place in common thought. For instance, an Andamanese song says:

> From the country of the Yerewas the moon rose;
> It came near; it was very cold,
> I sat down, Oh, I sat down,
> *I sat down, Oh, I sat down.*[18]

The singer feels something uncanny in the drop in the temperature at moonrise, and his action in sitting down indicates his perplexity at it. His words convey his apprehension of something supernatural which he cannot relate to his other beliefs and must therefore describe just as it strikes him. Yet all things belong to a homogeneous universe in which gods and spirits intermingle and behave in much the same way. If they are often inscrutable, so also is man, and that is why he is convinced that he can form relations with the unseen and try to understand it, at least as far as his own interests are concerned, and to fashion means of getting the best out of it. In dealing with gods and spirits primitive song may well pierce beyond the ordinary limits of feeling when it feels awe and fear before the unknown. What touches everyone is the mystery of power at work in the world, and this informs many sacred songs and is never far away when the singer contemplates natural things or wishes to secure some hold on them. Such power as he can get comes from the gods, and in his struggle to win his own ends he knows that he can do little without help from divine sources which remain a mystery to him and arouse his passionate attention and searching curiosity.

A similar sense of mystery pervades secular songs, for the good reason that, though they tell of perfectly customary matters, they touch on much that is unexplained. To primitive man any event may contain a startling element of surprise, which strikes him with all the more force because of his narrow experience. It calls for a considerable mastery of his ignorance, his fears, his wayward impulses, but just because he is fascinated by its ultimately unintelligible character, he finds a vent for his feelings in song. In his normal state, when he is not suffering from some unexpected blow or his own infirmities, he has a philosophy in which bodily action and imaginative thought combine to make him stick to his task and in the end to enjoy it. Because after all he has considerable experience in his own kind of action and knows what it means to him, he is able to master his doubts and his self-depreciation and to exert himself once again. So the Eskimo Ikinilik sings of trout-fishing in a song which is also his philosophy of life:

Thus I often return
To this song.
To this song,
To my fishing-hole above it I often return.
I, who otherwise am not good at going back
To the trout with the hook.
Up stream
The trout are few down there.
Without giving myself time to stand waiting for them,
I get into the way of saying they are too few.
Those that I usually eat I do not wait for long enough,
Because I give it up all too quickly ...
And yet it is glorious
On the ice surface
To walk as long as one can.
I am no longer one who can go on an errand from my
     hut,
Because I now sink to my knees.

Otherwise it is lovely,
A song I cannot think of,
For a song such as a bird sings is not my lot,
Although I often try to repeat it,
I, who am otherwise not good at returning to the trout.
Those I want, yes, all of them.[19]

Ikinilik is getting old and knows that he is no longer the man he once was, but he recalls his fishing days and compares them with the singing of songs for the delight and sense of well-being which they give. His love of life is still strong, and he interprets it through this apt comparison, in which the mysterious workings of nature and man becomes less formidable. He records what he sees and feels, but behind it there is much that he does not understand, and that is why his song has a peculiar charm. In the presence of the unknown he is drawn on by a keen curiosity and makes his own attempt to solve its riddles.

This is why song has so prominent a place in primitive life. While it makes sense of daily pursuits and relaxations and enhances interest in them, it is even more useful in dealing with problems which trouble man and call for a solution acceptable to his ways of thought. When he tries to grasp his place in the scheme of things, he is impelled by a curiosity mingled with fear or excitement or hope, and song is his means for expressing his conclusions. In it the images and emotions which are busy in his consciousness take a more solid and more coherent shape, and his ability to sing of them makes him feel less uneasy in his precarious predicaments. Because he is able to put his thoughts, no matter how perplexed or excited or troubling, into order, he is not quite lost in his world. If emotion sets him to work, it does so by inflaming his thoughts and uniting his nature, and from this his songs are born. They reflect his being when he is most consciously and most eagerly himself and feels driven to put into words something that obsesses him. That is why he uses song alike for his many secular interests and for his religious occasions. Both force him to fix his faculties on a single point, and it does not matter to what order of being this belongs. Song enables him in the first place to clear his mind, to come to decisions which affect his whole outlook, to secure for himself a position where he feels at home. He would not resort to it if he were not impelled by some inner necessity and desire to find through the right words an assurance for his whirling thoughts, and it is certainly his best instrument for setting them in order. In the second place song enables him to master the emotions which give birth to it, and in mastering them to give a finer and truer expression to them in the thoughts which they inspire. The control and the discipline which he exerts bring their reward in helping him to understand more clearly his condition and his nature. Just because he can put even the most tumultuous emotions into song, he is no longer their helpless victim, but sees them with some degree of objectivity and knows what they mean. Of course not all songs bring consolation or comfort, nor are they expected to do so, but most do something to abate the strain of troubling thoughts and obsessing anxieties, even physical pain. Even when they spring from delight, they make this less overwhelming and bring it into the sphere of more usual experience. The pressure of emotions which might otherwise be too violent loses some of its anarchic power, as the singer regains mastery of himself and faces his decisions with a new firmness.

Primitive man needs song because it provides him with protection in the extreme uncertainties and hazards of his existence. In making him drill his emotions and compose his thoughts it gives him a defence of which he is truly in need. In comparison with civilized man he is at a great disadvantage through his ignorance of the world and his lack of means to understand it. His practical knowledge of nature is no substitute for scientific explanation and leaves him in the lurch as soon as he is faced by phenomena which he cannot grasp or control. His theology is not of a kind to give him faith that he is looked after from above in this world or likely to be rewarded in the next. However much he may respect or praise or appease his gods, however well he may think that he knows them, he also knows that they cannot be trusted for unqualified support and may well follow their inscrutable whims into doing him harm. He has not the settled confidence which comes from living off the land and knowing that with proper care it will yield its fruits in due season; every day he starts out afresh in search for food, conscious that he may not find it or be able to secure it. He has nothing that can really be called a home, since his flimsy dwellings are extremely temporary and mean nothing to him. Nor has he the security which comes from belonging to an ordered society, in which many members depend on one another and means are easily organized to meet want or crisis. In the last resort he must rely upon himself and a very few companions, and the slightest loss among them may spell ruin for all. He alone is responsible for his wife and children, and he knows that, if anything happens to him, they will inevitably suffer. In all these chilling uncertainties he has to maintain his fight for life, and in this his best protection is his capacity for living in the moment and getting the most out of it. Yet though he does this, and song both reflects and supports him in it, it is but a flimsy defence against the misgivings and fears and doubts which assail him. At the best he surmounts these by his resolute determination not to be defeated, even when he knows that circumstances are conspiring against him. The strength of his appetite to live is the measure of his capacity to do so, and there are times when, though he feels himself enfeebled or defeated, he yet refuses to surrender and summons up his will to win. So the Eskimo Ikinilik composed a song which, he claimed, made him rise from his bed when he was sick:

> I, who no longer move about indoors
> And no longer get out
> To the great open air, since last winter,
> As I do nothing but faint away,
> I who no longer move about outside—
> Pastime in the open air usually gives meat,
> Usually it is right!
> I who no more get very far
> On the great ice since last winter,
> Because I do nothing but faint away,
> My implement for hunting I have not used,
> My fish-hook, since last winter.
> And yet my stomach desires,
> It longs for meat—poor me,
> Who usually make a hole in the ice at the wrong
>   place.[20]

This song is an incantation which Ikinilik sings over himself. By reminding him of the call of an active life, it enables him to assert himself and throw aside his sickness. This is primitive man at his best and most resolute, and this is the mood which enables him to survive the many perils and discouragements of his existence.

Yet he is not always like this. The melancholy of primitive peoples certainly owes much to the abominable way in which "superior" races have harassed them, or to the barren or brutal regions to which they are confined, but it lies deeper than this and seems to be inevitable, sooner or later, to their way of life. Primitive man has many moments when neither the lure of action nor the pleasure of relaxation meets his needs, and he sees himself as the disinherited outcast of a savage world, homeless and unprotected and unwanted. At such times he feels that his gods have deserted or betrayed him and that he is indeed lost, cut off from his

human roots and left with nothing to guide or guard him.
The despair which sounds in some of these songs is all the
more poignant because it reflects some vaster catastrophe
in which primitive men believe themselves to be doomed to
extinction. When the lure of action or the anodyne of dance
ceases to hold them, they fall easily into dark forebodings
about their place in a trackless world and their failure to
appease their gods. So the Gabon Pygmies have a song in
which they unburden their doubt and their desolation:

> The light becomes dark,
> The night, and again the night,
> The day with hunger tomorrow;
> The Maker is angry with us.
> The Old Ones have passed away,
> Their bones are far off, below.
> Their spirits are wandering—
> Where are their spirits wandering?
> Perhaps the passing wind knows.
> Their bones are far off, below.
> Are they below, the spirits? Are they here?
> Do they see the offerings set out?
> Tomorrow is empty and naked;
> For the Maker is no more there,
> Is no more the host seated at the hearth.[21]

Such is the dark background against which primitive life is
passed. For much of the time it is forgotten in the thrills of
action and the warmth of human ties. There are many heart-
ening moments of exultation in achievement, of hope beck-
oning onwards, of heads and hands busy with absorbing
skills and practised accomplishments. Yet behind these dis-
tractions and solaces lie uncertainty and fear, and primitive
man has to use all his resources to prevent himself from
yielding to a naked and brutal reality. When he loses hope,
he loses everything, even the desire to live, and it is from
this, quite as much as from slaughter and disease, that
primitive peoples have perished so disastrously in our time.
Yet even in their menaced and derided existence they still
find redeeming compensations when they can be themselves
as they would wish to be, and then too they turn to song,
which reflects and increases their desire to live and to maintain their own place in the world.

Primitive song is indispensable to those who practise it.
In the restriction of their arts and crafts, the narrow range
of their needs, their inability to look for long beyond the
passing moment, they cannot do without song, which both
formulates and answers their nagging questions, enables them

to pursue action with zest and confidence, brings them into touch with gods and spirits, and makes them feel less strange in the natural world. Because it is so urgently needed, because it gives order and harmony to their sudden, overmastering emotions and their tumbling, jostling thoughts, because it is so inextricably part of their lives, it gives to them a solid centre in what otherwise would be almost chaos, and a continuity in their being, which would too easily dissolve before the calls of the implacable present. Through it they rise to face the struggle for life and keep their minds and their energies awake at full stretch. Above all it is an art and does what art always does for those who practise it with passion and devotion. It enables them to absorb experience with their whole natures and thereby to fulfil a want which is fully satisfied neither by action nor by thought. In the end, like all true art, it enhances the desire and strengthens the capacity to live. It has, after all, a justifiable claim to be called a form of enchantment, since through its words men, who might otherwise give in to the malice of circumstances, find their old powers revived or new powers stirring in them, and through these life itself is sustained and renewed and fulfilled.

NOTES

Abbreviations

C. H. Berndt *a*	C. H. Berndt, 'Expression of Grief among Aboriginal Women', *Oceania* XX 286-322
C. H. Berndt *b*	C. H. Berndt, 'A Drama of North-eastern Arnhem Land', *Oceania* XXII 216-44, 275-89
R. M. Berndt *a*	R. M. Berndt, *Djanggawul*, London, 1952
R. M. Berndt *b*	R. M. Berndt, *Kunapipi*, Melbourne, 1951
R. M. Berndt *c*	R. M. Berndt, 'Song Cycle of the Moon Bone', *Oceania* XIX 16-50
R. M. and C. H. Berndt	R. M. and C. H. Berndt, *The First Australians*, Sydney, 1952
Bleek *a*	Dorothea F. Bleek, *The Mantis and His Friends; Bushman Folklore*, Cape Town, 1923
Bleek *b*	Dorothea F. Bleek, *The Naron, a Bushman Tribe of the Central Kalahari*, Cambridge, 1928
Bleek *c*	Dorothea F. Bleek, 'Bushman Folklore', *Africa* II 302-13
Bleek-Lloyd	W. H. I. Bleek and L. C. Lloyd, *Specimens of Bushman Folklore*, London, 1911
C.A.E. XIV	*Report of the Canadian Arctic Expedition 1913-18*, Vol. XIV, Ottawa, 1925
Eberle	O. Eberle, *Cenalora*, Freiburg im Breisgau, 1955, A. P. Elkin, *The Primitive Australians*, 2nd ed, Sydney, 1943
Elkin	
Evans	I. H. N. Evans, *The Negritos of Malaya*, Cambridge, 1937
Grosse	E. Grosse, *Die Anfänge der Kunst*, Freiburg, 1894
Gusinde	M. Gusinde, *Die Feuerland Indianer*, 2 vols, Vienna, 1931-37
H. T.	*A History of Technology*, edited by C. Singer, E. J. Holmyard and A. R. Hall, 5 vols, Oxford, 1954-58
Hahn	T. Hahn, *Tsuni-Goam*, London, 1881
Harney-Elkin	W. E. Harney and A. P. Elkin, *Songs of the Songmen*, Melbourne, 1949

Howitt	W. A. Howitt, *The Native Tribes of South-east Australia,* London, 1904
Kloss	C. B. Kloss, *In the Andamans and Nicobars,* London, 1903
Kunhenn	P. Kunhenn, *Pygmäen and andere Primitiv-Völker,* Stüttgart, 1952
Kurtz	B. P. Kurtz, 'Twelve Andamanese Songs', *University of California Publications on Modern Philology,* XI (1922) 79-128
Man	E. H. Man, *The Andaman Islanders,* 2nd ed, London, 1932
Maringer	J. Maringer, *The Gods of Prehistoric Man,* London, 1960
Nettl	B. Nettl, *Music in Primitive Culture,* Harvard, 1956
Parker	K. Langloh Parker, *The Euahlayi Tribe,* London, 1905
Pritchard	J. B. Pritchard, *Ancient Near Eastern Texts,* Princeton, 1955
Rasmussen	K. Rasmussen, *The Netsilik Eskimos,* Copenhagen, 1931
Roth	H. Ling Roth, *The Aborigines of Tasmania,* 2nd ed, Halifax, 1899
Schapera	I. Schapera, *The Khoisan Peoples of South Africa,* London, 1930
Schebesta *a*	P. Schebesta, *Die Negrito Asiens,* 2 vols, Vienna, 1957
Schebesta *b*	P. Schebesta, *Die Bambuti-Pygmäen vom Ituri,* 3 vols, Brussels, 1941-50
Schebesta *c*	P. Schebesta, *Among Congo Pygmies,* London, 1933
Schmidt	W. Schmidt, *Die Tasmanischen Sprachen,* Utrecht-Antwerp, 1952
Seligmann	C. G. and B. Z. Seligmann, *The Veddas,* Cambridge, 1911
Skeat-Blagden	W. W. Skeat and C. O. Blagden, *Pagan Races of the Malay Peninsula,* 2 vols, London, 1906
C. Strehlow	Carl Strehlow, *Die Aranda- und Boritja-Stämme in Zentral-Australien,* 7 vols, Frankfurt-am-Main, 1907-20
T. G. H. Strehlow *a*	T. G. H. Strehlow, *An Australian Viewpoint,* 1950
T. G. H. Strehlow *b*	T. G. H. Strehlow, *Aranda Traditions,* Melbourne, 1947
T. G. H. Strehlow *c*	T. G. H. Strehlow, 'Ankotarinja, an Aranda Myth', *Oceania* IV, 187-200
T. G. H. Strehlow *d*	T. G. H. Strehlow, 'Australian Aboriginal Song', *Journal of the International Folk Music Council,* VII 37-40
Trebitsch	R. Trebitsch, *Bei den Eskimos in Westgrönland,* Berlin 1915

Trilles *a*   R. P. Trilles, *Les Pygmées de la Forêt Equatoriale,* Paris, 1931

Trilles *b*   R. P. Trilles, *L'Ame du Pygmée d'Afrique,* Paris, 1945

Vedder   H. Vedder, *Die Bergdama,* 2 vols, Hamburg, 1923

NOTES TO THE CHAPTERS

CHAPTER 1

Primitive Man, Ancient and Modern

1 Pritchard 228
2 L. Dindorf, *Historici Graeci Minores* I 476
3 H. T. I 300, fig 191
4 Gusinde II 270 ff
5 Elkin 10
6 Schmidt 43-61
7 Schebesta *a* II, 2,292
8 Herodotus II 32-33
9 Gusinde II 276
10 T. G. H. Strehlow *b* xxi
11 Gusinde I 158-159
12 Roth 172

CHAPTER 2

Composition and Performance

1 Gusinde II 1057
2 *Ibid* 1059
3 *Ibid* 1063
4 Schebesta *b* III 69
5 *Ibid* III 69
6 *Ibid* III 67
7 Gusinde II 1071
8 Schebesta *b* I 255
9 Howitt 423
10 Schebesta *c* 103
11 *C.A.E.* XIV 418
12 Rasmussen 321
13 *Ibid* 518
14 *Ibid* 517
15 *Ibid* 517
16 Gusinde I 754
17 Kurtz 109
18 *C.A.E.* XIV 459
19 Trilles *a* 334-335
20 Roth li
21 Vedder II 63
22 *Ibid* 81-82
23 Skeat-Blagden II 233
24 Schebesta *a* II 2.144-145
25 Bleek *a* 183-184
26 Trilles *a* 276-278

CHAPTER 3

Technique

1 Gusinde II 115
2 *Ibid* II 771
3 *Ibid* II 770
4 *Ibid* I 1040
5 *Ibid* I 1039
6 Seligmann 366
7 Nettl 23
8 Howitt 388
9 *Ibid* 397
10 Bleek-Lloyd 227
11 *C.A.E.* XIV 464
12 *Ibid* 492
13 Vedder II 95
14 Bleek *a* 186
15 Bleek-Lloyd 235
16 *C.A.E.* XIV 494
17 *Ibid* 486
18 Bleek *a* 238
19 Gusinde II 1070
20 Trilles *b* 191
21 Vedder II 65
22 Rasmussen 287
23 Skeat-Blagden II 129
24 Seligman 369
25 R. M. Berndt *a* 65
26 Rasmussen 338
27 *C.A.E.* XIV 497
28 Vedder II 91
29 *Ibid* II 83-84
30 Trilles *b* 157
31 C. Strehlow iv. 3.94
32 *C.A.E.* XIV 480
33 *Ibid* 480
34 Bleek *a* 231-232
35 Seligmann 368
36 Schapera 176
37 Skeat-Blagden II 128
38 Schebesta *a* II 2.229-230
39 Schapera 173
40 T. G. H. Strehlow *b* 22-23
41 Vedder II 97
42 Grosse 282
43 Seligmann 370
44 Pritchard 228
45 C. Strehlow iii. 21
46 R. M. Berndt *b* 194
47 Gusinde II 769
49 Harney-Elkin 8
50 Schebesta *a* II 2.228
51 Parker 54
52 Roth xlviii
53 Trilles *a* 27
54 E. Schwyzer, *Dialectorum Graecarum Exempla Epigraphica Potiora* 403

CHAPTER 4

Manner and Method

1 Kloss 189
2 *Ibid* 189
3 Hahn 29
4 Trilles *b* 56
5 Schebesta *a* II 2.169
6 Bleek *c* 206
7 Trilles *a* 110
8 C. H. Berndt *a* 316
9 Vedder II 78
10 Bleek-Lloyd 23
11 Trilles *a* 149
12 Bleek-Lloyd 415
13 Vedder II 62
14 R. M. Berndt *b* 189
15 *Ibid* 111
16 Trilles *a* 189

17 Man 168
18 Kloss 189
19 Trilles *a* 460-470
20 *C.A.E.* XIV 412
21 Trilles *a* 237

22 C. H. Berndt *a* 316
23 Trilles *a* 79
24 Vedder II 101
25 Gusinde I 754
26 *C.A.E.* XIV 435-6

CHAPTER 5

Songs of Action

1 Rasmussen 283
2 Seligmann 204
3 Bleek *d* 307
4 Rasmussen 280
5 *Ibid* 288
6 Trebitsch 43
7 *Ibid* 43
8 Vedder II 62
9 *Ibid* II 106
10 Rasmussen 278
11 Kurtz 107
12 *C.A.E.* XIV 425
13 Kurtz 116
14 Rasmussen 325
15 Kurtz 127
16 *C.A.E.* XIV 437
17 Trilles *a* 494
18 *Ibid* 358

19 *Ibid* 460-461
20 Kurtz 102
21 *Ibid* 105
22 *C.A.E.* XIV 446
23 Trilles *a* 492
24 Vedder II 63
25 Schebesta *c* 225
26 Vedder II 63
27 Hahn 72
28 *Ibid* 73
29 Rasmussen 328
30 Trilles *a* 238
31 Rasmussen 515
32 Vedder II 63
33 *Ibid* II 63
34 *Ibid* II 101
35 Trilles *a* 503
36 Vedder II 66

CHAPTER 6

The Natural Scene

1 Skeat-Blagden II 129
2 *Ibid* II 130
3 C. H. Berndt *b* 285
4 R. M. and C. H. Berndt 136
5 Schebesta *a* II 2.227-228
6 Skeat-Blagden II 128
7 Rasmussen 279
8 Seligmann 202
9 *Ibid* 202

10 Hahn 29
11 Eberle 127-128; cf. Schebesta *a* II 2.228-229
12 Bleek-Lloyd 221-223
13 *Ibid* 221
14 Bleek *b* 45
15 *Ibid* 60
16 *Ibid* 65
17 Rasmussen 353

18 *Ibid* 372
19 *Ibid* 336-337
20 C. Strehlow iv. 3. 17-18
21 *Ibid* iv. 3. 29-30
22 T. G. H. Strehlow *a* 25
23 Eberle 132; cf. Schebesta *a*
   II 2.143
24 R. M. Berndt *b* 96

25 *Ibid* 96
26 *Ibid* 101
27 R. M. Berndt *a* 79
28 *Ibid* 64
29 *Ibid* 69
30 *Ibid* 73
31 *Ibid* 97
32 *Ibid* 194

CHAPTER 7

The Human Cycle

1 Trilles *a* 368
2 *Ibid* 372
3 *Ibid* 379
4 Parker 54
5 *Ibid* 54
6 Trilles *a* 343
7 C. H. Berndt *b* 310
8 Rasmussen 338
9 *Ibid* 339
10 *Ibid* 335
11 Trebitsch 87
12 *Ibid* 57
13 Vedder II 103
14 R. M. and C. H. Berndt 66
15 Trilles *a* 413
16 *Ibid* 269 ff

17 *Ibid* 273 ff
18 Rasmussen 335
19 Gusinde I 760
20 Trilles *a* 163
21 Rasmussen 324
22 Vedder II 63
23 *Ibid* II 64
24 *Ibid* II 72
25 *Ibid* II 80
26 C. H. Berndt *b* 316
27 Gusinde II 1070
28 *Ibid* II 1068
29 *Ibid* II 1067
30 C. H. Berndt *b* 324
31 Trilles *a* 424

CHAPTER 8

Primitive Imagination

1 *C.A.E.* XIV 488
2 *Ibid* 490
3 Trilles *a* 127
4 Howitt 369
5 Shapera 180
6 Trilles *a* 140
7 *Ibid* 141
8 *Ibid* 141

9 *Ibid* 142
10 Parker 74
11 Howitt 422
12 Shebesta *a* II 2.158
13 Parker 57
14 C. H. Berndt *a* 294
15 *Ibid* 300
16 *Ibid* 296

17 *Ibid* 297
18 *Ibid* 298
19 *Ibid* 293
20 *Ibid* 303
21 *Ibid* 304
22 Trilles *a* 429-430
23 Schebesta *a* II 2.142

24 *Ibid* II 2.142
25 Eberle 141
26 Schebesta *a* II 2.143
27 *Ibid* II 2.143
28 T. G. H. Strehlow *a* 21-22
29 *Ibid* 24-25
30 *Ibid* 25

CHAPTER 9

Myth and Symbol

1 Trilles *a* 105
2 *Ibid* 105
3 Schebesta *a* II 2.230
4 *Ibid* II 2.230
5 *Ibid* II 2.231
6 T. G. H. Strehlow *d* 40
7 T. G. H. Strehlow a 20-21

8 T. G. H. Strehlow *c* 190-192
9 R. M. and C. H. Berndt 15
10 R. M. Berndt *a* 188
11 *Ibid* 66
12 T. G. H. Strehlow *b* 32
13 *Ibid* 32-33
14 R. M. Berndt *c* 39

CHAPTER 10

Some Conclusions

1 Alan Gardiner, *Egypt of the Pharaohs* (Oxford, 1961), 58-59
2 *Iliad* III 5-6
3 Trilles *a* 460
4 *Ibid* 358
5 Eberle 138
6 *Ibid* 321
7 *Ibid* 179
8 Seligmann 161
9 *Ibid* 322-333, 370
10 Harney-Elkin 15

11 Gusinde II 1073
12 R. M. Berndt *b* 199
13 Vedder II 103
14 Schapera 381
15 Trilles *b* 228
16 Vedder II 99-100
17 Rasmussen 284
18 Kloss 189
19 Rasmussen 515
20 *Ibid* 514
21 Trilles *b* 96

INDEX

Aborigines, 16, 29; courtship-songs, 174-76; future of, 34-35; inability to advance, 22-23; languages of, 27-28, 31-33; ritual songs of, 56-58; and sickness, 181-82

Action, developing, 71; reduced to moment, 103; rhythmical, 38-39, 41 (*see also* Dance)

Action, songs of: hunting, 51-52, 53, 80-83, 105, 114-28, 132-33, 139-40; war, 129-32

Aëta people: and agriculture, 31; funeral-song of, 29-30; love-songs, 174

Africa, totem belief, 25

After-life: belief in, 184, 200-207; husband and wife in, 202-206

Agriculture: depressing effect of, 25; distaste for, 31; Neolithic establishment of, 24

Alawa people, 100

Albacete rock-paintings, 18

Albocacer, Cueva de los Caballos at, 18

Alliteration, 85, 87

Allusiveness, 99-102

Altamira, 14

Alternatives of theme, and elaboration, 103-105

Ancestors, as source of song, 47

Ancestors, mythical, 222-26; Aranda, 226-31; duties of, 226-29; images of, 211-15, 218; ritual songs about, 56-57, 61, 72-73, 234, 236-37

Andamanese people, 16, 21, 24, 59; after-life doubted by, 200; agriculture, 25; composing of songs, 44; dances, 243; diety, belief in, 27; extinction of, 33; fishing, 18; hunting-songs, 120, 121-22, 123, 127-28, 246

Andamanese songs: communication of, 49; refrain in, 50-51, 77; spontaneity, 91, 102

Animals: character and personality, 146-47, 151-55, 156-57; dance-like rites over, 242-43; dogs the only domesticated, 20; fables about, 155-56; hunting of, *see* Hunting; nature-songs about, 144-45, 146 *et seq.*; Neolithic, 24; relation to man, 125-27, 145 *et seq.*;

MENTOR Books of Special Interest

Literature and the Arts

Eight Great Tragedies *edited by Sylvan Barnet, Morton Berman, and William Burto.* The great dramatic literature of the ages, and essays on the tragic form.　(#MQ461—95¢)

Eight Great Comedies *edited by Sylvan Barnet, Morton Berman, and William Burto.* A companion volume to *Eight Great Tragedies,* containing plays and essays.
(#MQ343—95¢)

The Golden Treasury of F. T. Palgrave, *enlarged and updated by Oscar Williams.* Great lyric poems of the English language from 1526 to the present.　(#MQ305—95¢)

The Silver Treasury of Light Verse *edited by Oscar Williams.* Over 600 sparkling poems from Chaucer to Ogden Nash and Gertrude Stein.　(#MT372—75¢)

The Notebooks of Leonardo Da Vinci *ed. by Pamela Taylor.* This famous work mirrors Leonardo's genius as painter, sculptor, architect, engineer, and inventor. Illustrated.
(#MT312—75¢)

Good Listening (revised, up-dated) *by R. D. Darrell.* Expert advice to help increase your musical enjoyment, including list of best LP recordings.　(#MD122—50¢)

Enjoying Modern Art *by Sarah Newmeyer.* The unconventional lives of the great modern painters, from early French rebels to today. Illustrated.　(#MP389—60¢)

American Folk Tales and Songs *compiled by Richard Chase.* Tales, ballads, games, dances, and customs that form an important part of the American heritage. Drawings and music.
(#KT376—75¢)

The Painter's Eye *by Maurice Grosser.* A brilliant analysis of techniques of painting from the Renaissance to the present, illustrated. (#MT371—75¢)

The Creative Process *edited, with introduction, by Brewster Ghiselin.* Some of the greatest minds reveal how they begin and complete creative work in art, literature, etc. (#MP383—60¢)

Company Manners *by Louis Kronenberger.* A penetrating appraisal of American culture with emphasis on art, theatre and television as well as individual manners. (#MD156—50¢)

The Liveliest Art *by Arthur Knight.* The exciting history of motion pictures, its stars, writers, directors, producers, flops and hits. Thirty-one photographs. (#MD263—50¢)

The Negro in American Culture *by Margaret Just Butcher.* The impressive accomplishments of the American Negro in many cultural fields. Based on material left by Dr. Alain L. Locke. (#MT206—75¢)

Books That Changed the World *by Robert B. Downs.* The fascinating histories of sixteen great books—from Machiavelli's *The Prince* to Einstein's *Theories of Relativity*—that have changed the course of history. (#MP400—60¢)

The Wonderful World of Books *edited by Alfred Stefferud.* A book that shows how to benefit from the world's treasuries of wisdom and knowledge, to explore fascinating realms of adventure and entertainment, to find greater success and happiness, through the magic of reading. (#MT157—75¢)

**Addressed to YOU
as a book reader
by Edward R. Murrow**
Director, United States Information Agency

Hardly a day passes that someone somewhere in the world does not make inquiry about these United States. If it be true that in only some places are we the object of affection, it is equally true that in every place we are the object of curiosity.

In this ever-changing world in which many peoples in one generation seek to accomplish the changes of centuries, this country has a great role to fill. We are, if we choose, to carry on a great dialogue between man and that better part of himself known as knowledge. The world is hungry to know and to learn. We must satisfy that hunger. Our Information Agency seeks to satisfy it through Voice of America broadcasts, libraries, film and television showings, exhibits and lectures in more than 100 countries overseas.

The desire for knowledge remains great. Books are knowledge. They are the tools of truth and freedom. A book is the heart of a child and the hope of a man.

But millions of people around our globe—both children and men—have no books. Students in many countries undertake their lessons—but without books to read. Theirs is the legacy of the uninformed. The task is the challenge of the unavailable.

It is to meet this unavailability that, with the New American Library of World Literature, our Agency has joined in this campaign. A packet of representative BOOKS USA will go abroad to service the burning desire to know that is so much of this modern world. We urge your support.

Director, U.S. Information Agency

The world wants to know more about the U.S.
HERE'S HOW YOU CAN HELP

You can bring the knowledge and enlightenment of fine literature to thousands of individuals in a country of your choice. Outstanding books, sent in your name to areas where the need is greatest, will be read, re-read, absorbed and discussed by persons who want to know more about the United States. Here's how the BOOKS USA plan operates:

The New American Library of World Literature is providing on a non-profit basis a library packet of eight representative American books which sell retail for $5.15. To send them, you pay only $3.00 plus $1.00 to cover the delivery to the country you specify, a total of $4.00. The packet will be distributed by the U.S. Information Agency to a library, school, or other center where thousands will read these outstanding books.

Join this drive to spread knowledge through fine literature. Your gift will be acknowledged directly to you by the recipient overseas. The readers of your books will, in turn, inspire others to new goals of enlightenment, freedom, and decency among men.

ART AND DRAMA

THE HISTORY OF WESTERN ART by Erwin O. Christensen	MQ357
MUSIC AND IMAGINATION by Aaron Copland	MD261
SUNRISE AT CAMPOBELLO by Dore Schary	D1868
MY FAIR LADY by Alan Jay Lerner	D2251
ACT ONE by Moss Hart	T1849
THE STORY OF JAZZ by Marshall Stearns	MT478
THE PAINTER'S EYE by Maurice Grosser	MT371
AMERICAN SKYLINE by Christopher Tunnard and Hope Reed	MD175

Simply fill out this coupon and mail with your check or money order.

To: New American Library, P.O. Box 2310
    Grand Central Station, New York 17, New York

Send (one or more) BOOKS USA library packets containing the 8 books listed above, in my name, to the country (or countries) checked below. Here's my check (or M.O.) for $............. (for........packets at $4.00 each).

☐ ARGENTINA ☐ GHANA ☐ KENYA ☐ NIGERIA ☐ TANGANYIKA
☐ BRAZIL ☐ INDIA ☐ KOREA ☐ PAKISTAN ☐ THAILAND
☐ CEYLON ☐ INDONESIA ☐ LIBERIA ☐ PHILIPPINES ☐ TRINIDAD &
☐ CHILE ☐ JAPAN ☐ MALAYA ☐ RHODESIA   WEST INDIES
☐ FINLAND ☐ JORDAN ☐ MEXICO ☐ SUDAN ☐ UGANDA

NAME ....

STREET .... CITY............... STATE..........
Since this coupon goes to us for order fulfillment and the books must be freighted abroad by the U. S. Information Agency to the country of your choice, allow at least four months for acknowledgment. This offer is good until Sept. 30, 1963.